# SOCRATES FOUNDING POLITICAL PHILOSOPHY IN XENOPHON'S *ECONOMIST, SYMPOSIUM,* AND *APOLOGY*

# SOCRATES FOUNDING POLITICAL PHILOSOPHY IN XENOPHON'S *ECONOMIST*, *SYMPOSIUM*, AND *APOLOGY*

THOMAS L. PANGLE

THE UNIVERSITY OF CHICAGO PRESS
CHICAGO AND LONDON

The University of Chicago Press, Chicago 60637
The University of Chicago Press, Ltd., London

Published 2020
Printed in the United States of America

29 28 27 26 25 24 23 22 21 20     1 2 3 4 5

ISBN-13: 978-0-226-64247-5 (cloth)
ISBN-13: 978-0-226-64250-5 (e-book)
DOI: https://doi.org/10.7208/chicago/9780226642505.001.0001

Library of Congress Cataloging-in-Publication Data

Names: Pangle, Thomas L., author
Title: Socrates founding political philosophy in Xenophon's Economist, Symposium, and Apology / Thomas L. Pangle.
Description: Chicago : University of Chicago Press, 2020. | Includes bibliographical references and index.
Identifiers: LCCN 2019037138 | ISBN 9780226642475 (cloth) | ISBN 9780226642505 (e-book)
Subjects: LCSH: Socrates—Political and social views. | Xenophon. Oeconomicus. | Xenophon. Symposium. | Xenophon. Apology.
Classification: LCC B317.P334 2020 | DDC 183/.2—dc23
LC record available at https://lccn.loc.gov/2019037138

♾ This paper meets the requirements of ANSI/NISO Z39.48-1992 (Permanence of Paper).

# CONTENTS

# INTRODUCTION

Cicero informs us that prior to Socrates, philosophic science "dealt with number and motion, and that from which all things originate and into which they return; and studied the size, distance between, and course of stars and of all celestial things." But as regards civic life, the pre-Socratic philosophers tended to look down upon it, as dominated by deluded religious beliefs and moral conventions lacking foundation in nature (see esp. Plato, *Laws* 888e–890b). Rational study of politics was largely appropriated by so-called "sophists," who employed the critical and constructive tools of philosophic science to discover and to teach, for pay, the power of exploitative-manipulative public rhetoric. "Opposed to the sophists was Socrates" (writes Cicero) "who with subtle argumentation made it his practice to refute their teachings." Socrates "was the first to call philosophy down from heaven and to set it in cities and to introduce it into the household and to compel it to inquire into life and mores and good and bad things." Out of the "wealth of his discourses there emerged most learned men; and it was then, it is said, that there was discovered the philosophy that was not the natural philosophy that had been earlier, but the philosophy in which there is disputation over good and bad things and the life and mores of men."[1]

In these characterizations, Cicero follows above all the eyewitness presentation of Socrates by Xenophon. Cicero may have had primarily in mind a famous passage in Xenophon's *Memorabilia* (1.1.11–16).[2] But Cicero chose to devote his labors to executing and publishing a translation into Latin of Xenophon's shorter but more dramatic as well as more didactic Socratic writing, the *Economist* (*Oikonomikos* = "Skilled Household Manager").[3] My aim in the present book (a sequel to T. Pangle 2018) is to show how the account of Socrates in the *Memorabilia* is decisively deepened as well as complemented by the three shorter writings that Xenophon devoted to portraying Socrates in action. Xenophon's *Economist*, *Symposium*, and *Apology of Socrates to the Jury* are evidently intended to be read, at least in part, as sequels to the *Memorabilia*. Some scholars have gone so far as to suggest that Xenophon's four writings on Socrates originally comprised a single work, whose chapters were subsequently split up.[4] Yet this utterly fails to do justice to the extraordinary contrasts among the four works, in terms of both style and substance. In fact, study of Xenophon's shorter Socratic writings reveals that the *Memorabilia* is in major respects radically incomplete—that it is intended by Xenophon to be not only supplemented, but even in some measure corrected, by the three oft-designated "lesser" Socratic writings.

The most obvious limitation of, or constraint upon, the *Memorabilia* is that the work is overwhelmingly defensive—in purpose, message, and tone. The opening sections are devoted to refuting the charges, of impiety and of corrupting the young, upon which Socrates was convicted and executed; then this refutation is made the foundation for the erection, in the bulk of the work, of a monument to the active justice of Socrates, demonstrating that he was not merely innocent of wrongdoing toward his fellow men, but that he "was, in every affair, and in every way, beneficial; so that it is manifest, to anyone who investigates and perceives with measure, that there was nothing more beneficial than being together and spending one's time with Socrates" (*Memorabilia* 4.1.1; see also 1.3.1). In almost the last statement that the *Memorabilia* quotes from Socrates he is reported declaring that his life as a whole has been "the noblest preparation for a defense speech," inasmuch as he has spent it "doing no other thing except thoroughly investigating the just things and the unjust, and doing the just things and refraining from the unjust" (ibid. 4.8.4). And Xenophon presents Socrates as repeatedly proclaiming that by "the just" he means above all the legal, or obedience to the laws, unwritten as well as written (ibid. 4.4 and 4.6.5–6). To demonstrate that Socrates lived in accordance with unwritten as well as written lawful custom (*nomos*), Xenophon highlights throughout the *Memorabilia* all the ways in which Socrates through his virtues—not only of justice, but of piety and self-control and moderation and prudence—resembled conventionally respectable "gentlemen" (*kaloi k'agathoi*: literally, "the noble-and-good").[5]

In contrast, the three shorter Socratic writings of Xenophon, led by the *Economist*, make more vivid how Socrates, in his virtues, or in his peculiar version of "gentlemanliness," and in his conception of scientific household management or "economics," diverges from normal gentlemen: from their virtues, from their "nobility-and-goodness," and from their ideas of sound household management and governmental rule over fellow human beings.

In the shorter Socratic writings, both Xenophon and his Socrates are somewhat less guarded, less reticent, more forthcoming than in the *Memorabilia*. The *Economist* makes us part of the privileged audience for an amazing autobiographical report by Socrates; the *Symposium* lets us be "flies on the wall" at a private drinking party in which gradual inebriation loosens the tongues of all present, including Socrates; the *Apology of Socrates to the Jury* gives us access to the inner deliberation by which Socrates arrived at his decision to give the astonishingly arrogant defense speech that he offered at his trial.

Put another way: the *Memorabilia*, for its part, is the most perfect document we possess articulating that central thesis of classical political philosophy that was best formulated in modern times by Shaftesbury, the great early-modern student of Xenophon:

> 'Tis not Wit merely, but a Temper which must form the Well-bred Man. In the same manner, 'tis not a Head merely, but a Heart and Resolution which must compleat the real Philosopher. Both Characters aim at what is excellent, aspire to a just Taste, and carry in view the Model of what is beautiful and becoming. Accordingly, the respective Conduct and distinct Manners of each Party are regulated; The one according to the perfectest Ease, and good Entertainment of Company; the other according to the strictest Interest of Mankind and Society: The one according to a Man's Rank and Quality in his private Nation; the other according to his Rank and Dignity in Nature.
>
> Whether each of these Offices, or social Parts, are in themselves as convenient as becoming, is the great Question which must some-way be decided. (Shaftesbury 2001, "Miscellany" 3, chap. 1 end)

This last, pregnant comment adumbrates "the great Question" that becomes unmistakably the theme in Xenophon's three Socratic writings other than the *Memorabilia*. That question is: Which of the two profoundly alternative and deeply distinct ways of life and human character types—that of the Socratic political philosopher with his philosophic virtues, or that of the gentleman with his familial, civic, and moral virtues—is superior, standing as most truly the normative standard for all human existence and politics and "economics"? And above all, what are the grounds, the foundations, for this ranking?

It is in his *Economist* that Xenophon makes most dramatically evident the gulf—and how the gulf is tenuously bridged—between the traditionally respectable gentleman household-manager exemplified by the figure

Ischomachus (who embodies the moral virtues later elaborated and refined in Aristotle's *Nicomachean Ethics* and in Cicero's *Offices*), and the political-*philosophic* virtues of the very different, though in some sense kindred, moral character exemplified by Socrates and his philosophic science of economics.[6]

Above all, the *Economist* exposes and focuses upon something scandalous about Socrates that one would never guess from reading the *Memorabilia*: well into his maturity, the philosopher by his own confession neither practiced nor understood "virtue" (*aretē*). Xenophon presents Socrates telling of the great day on which he underwent a radical transformation—when he became the moral and political citizen-philosopher famous to posterity, from having previously been a pre-Socratic thinker lost in the clouds, "reputed to engage in idle chatter and to measure the air," who confessed to having no clue as to the meaning of the "noble/beautiful" (*kalon*), or as to what "gentlemen"—the "noble-and-good"—are and do (6.13–17 and 11.1–6).[7]

Socrates reports that the perfect gentleman Ischomachus, after having heard this extraordinary confession of moral ignorance—culminating in Socrates having implored him, "relate completely your works so that, having learned whatever I can by listening, I will try, starting tomorrow, to imitate you; for that is a good day to begin virtue!"—at first replied: "you're joking, Socrates." The gentleman recognized Socratic irony. Nevertheless, Ischomachus then agreed, with his characteristic gentlemanly gravity, to provide the requested didactic account of his virtuous way of life—beginning of course (he stressed) with his lawfully pious attentiveness to divinity (11.6–8).

The counterpoint between the ironic levity of the philosopher[8] and the weighty seriousness[9] of the perfect gentleman is a subtle but all the more pervasive leitmotif of the *Economist*—which thus proves to be a work that is even more deliciously-delicately droll than was the *Memorabilia*.

In his *Symposium* Xenophon makes most manifest the gulf—and how that gulf is tenuously bridged—between the erotic playfulness of conventionally respectable gentlemen (led by the famous, wealthy, and "upper-crust" Callias) and the philosophically erotic playfulness of Socrates. By its title, Xenophon's *Symposium* naturally invites orienting comparison with Plato's more famous and familiar work of the same name.[10] Plato's *Symposium* is an acme of that author's project of forging a shining new cultural hero (Lutz 1994). Socrates appears as the prized guest and the eventually victorious rival of the greatest living poets. His battlefield courage is memorialized, and he is portrayed as possessing a "superhuman" continence (Huss 1999, 402). These qualities form, so to speak, the rostrum upon which he stands to give the oration in which he presents to the world a new philosophic-religious doctrine centered on love as the "ladder" to the transpolitical, eternalizing forms of the good and the beautiful.

Xenophon, in contrast, recalls a banquet of conventional gentlemen (*kaloi kagathoi*) to which Socrates was a last-minute, reluctant invitee—together with a rather mixed train of his followers, including somehow Xenophon himself. A memorable feature of the party is a beauty contest in which a ludicrously boastful Socrates preposterously complains about being decisively defeated by the handsome young Critobulus. The drama enters its culminating stage when Socrates has to stoop to advise, so as to defuse the pesky hostility of, a hired foreign impresario; in this way Socrates contrives to win the floor long enough to deliver without interruption an oration exhorting his host to a love life purified by becoming more centered on the beauty of civic virtue. But it is less Socrates's speech than it is the impresario's subsequent, sensual show that shapes most of the company's spirits at the conclusion. In the course of the evening, Socrates discloses his susceptibility to the inebriating effects of wine, as well as to youthful beauty; he admits to some concern about his paunch; and he confesses to failure in his project of managing, through education, other humans—first and foremost his wife. More noteworthy still are some challenges with which he has to deal, even from his own followers.

Xenophon's *Symposium* thus comes to sight as a gentle Socratic self-satire. In it, the character of Socrates, and of his not altogether harmonious circle, find expression through their being portrayed as partaking in the playful posturing of conventional gentlemen in their cups. Xenophon creates a safe medium for providing some far-reaching indications concerning the way of life, and the way of understanding life, that he learned to share with Socrates. He helps us descry the endpoints of some of the major avenues of inquiry we see opened up by the Platonic Socrates: in this work Xenophon leaves behind, and only gestures, in a passing reference, to the most distinctively characteristic Socratic activity—puzzling over the meaning of justice and gentlemanliness (*Symposium* 4.1; 8.3); Xenophon dedicates this work to helping us discern what this activity led to, or resulted in, as a way of living—what the existential conclusions were that Socrates was able to draw from his puzzling over justice and gentlemanliness.

The heart of the matter is the Socratic understanding of the capacity of the beautiful/noble (*to kalon*), in both its spiritual and physical dimensions, to evoke loving ("erotic") devotion—to individuals, to the community or to public service, to virtue, and to divinity. Through this drama, Xenophon brings to thought-provoking life the distinct ways in which a variety of fundamental human types are oriented by and toward the power of *eros*. The interaction between Socrates and the rest is crafted so as to reveal how he differs from them all on this central aspect of existence, and how the others range themselves in degrees of proximity to, and distance from, the political philosopher's enlightenment in this regard. Xenophon portrays the variety of attractions to and suspicions of Socrates that arise as a consequence of his interrogations; and how these friendships and hostilities are dealt with, through political philosophy's varied contribution to the moral education of the community, on a number of different levels gauged to the fundamental diversity among the citizenry.

Last but not least, it is in his *Apology of Socrates to the Jurors* that Xenophon spotlights the "greatness of soul" (*megalopsychia*), or self-consciousness of superiority, and hence of worthiness of being honored, that distinguishes Socrates the philosopher—in comparison and contrast with the greatness of soul of the conventionally recognized gentleman: who is now exemplified, however, by a peculiarly unorthodox outlier among conventional gentlemen, one Hermogenes. Xenophon brings to light Socrates's distinctively philosophic self-esteem through an account, reported by and through this Hermogenes, first of a crucial conversation prior to the trial, about Socrates's intentions in his planned defense, and then of selections, as recalled by this Hermogenes, from Socrates's defiantly offensive courtroom speech, in which he provocatively proclaimed the excellences that made him superior to his fellow men. Unlike the defense or apology on behalf of Socrates that Xenophon presents in his own name in the first part of his *Memorabilia*, the courtroom appearance and speech of Socrates, as reported by Xenophon's character Hermogenes, goes on the offensive—to a degree rarely if ever equaled in recorded forensic history.

CHAPTER ONE

# The Socratic Science of Economics

Xenophon begins his *Economist* abruptly: "And I heard *Him*[1] once also engage in dialogue about household management, in some such words as follow: 'Tell me,' he said, 'Critobulus,' . . ." (1.1). This opening, following upon the laconic, one-word title,[2] evinces a presumption that the reader will recognize the initiation of yet more of the author's "recollections of Socrates." Xenophon "creates the impression" that we have here "simply a continuation of the *Memorabilia*."[3]

Accordingly, Xenophon does not at the outset indicate—as he emphatically does in starting his *Symposium* and his *Apology*—any distinguishing purpose or intention of his *Economist*. Since the *Memorabilia* consists mainly of numerous short dialogues depicting Socrates's practice of beneficent and educative justice, Xenophon initially allows the reader to assume that the *Economist* will be devoted to showing still more of such short conversations, focused in some way on skilled household management.

But the *Economist* turns out to be a single, very lengthy conversation, the larger part of which consists in Socrates unfolding to a young interlocutor the tale of the dialogic encounter through which Socrates received his own education in economics, and indeed in morality as part of economics—from a perfect gentleman named Ischomachus. "The abrupt beginning" of the *Economist* "conceals the profound difference between" this work and the *Memorabilia* (XSD 90).

## THE INTERLOCUTOR CRITOBULUS

The comedic nature[4] of the *Economist* is signaled at the outset when Xenophon has Socrates address by name, and thus identify, the singular character who will be the framing dialogue's (sole) interlocutor. For Critobulus is the most amiably unserious, the most lightheartedly erotic, of all the members of the Socratic circle portrayed by Xenophon.[5] In the *Memorabilia*, we meet Critobulus as "the son of Crito" whom Socrates in mock horror advises to go into exile for a year, while describing him to the onlooker Xenophon as "a great hothead and one who will stop at nothing"—all on account of Critobulus's having dared to kiss a beautiful, beloved boy. When Xenophon replies with the avowal that he himself might share in such foolhardiness, Socrates extends his mock aghast, chastising denunciation to our author (*Memorabilia* 1.3.8–15: Xenophon presents himself as tinged with a streak of the waywardly erotic Critobulus). In a later, extended dialogue with Socrates on friendship (ibid. 2.6, containing a high concentration of profane expletives), Critobulus's gaily festive, wide-ranging, erotic proclivities continue to be evident—and Socrates's disapproval appears much less severe. We learn from the *Symposium* (3.7, 4.9–29, 5.1–6.1) that Socrates found the handsome scamp to be an attractive and amusing companion. We learn from the *Economist* (3.7) that Socrates was drawn into long, early morning treks to attend rural comic dramas with the young man (we can assume that the expenses for good seats were paid by the wealthy[6] Critobulus). We even learn, again from the *Symposium* (4.22), that Socrates allowed himself to be "dragged around" by Critobulus to wherever the latter would be able to contemplate his beloved beauty, Kleinias. As for Critobulus's attitude toward Socrates, "we are free to suspect" that "he admired Socrates more, much more than his own father," a possible reason why Crito's "influence on his son" might "have been altogether insufficient" (XSD 101). In the *Symposium* (4.24) Socrates reports that because of Critobulus's intoxication with his boyfriend Kleinias,[7] "his father handed him over to me, so I might be able to help in some way." In the *Economist*, again, we will soon find Socrates telling Critobulus to his face that he "pities" him because the young man, thinking himself affluent, is "neglectful in devising means of making money, and devotes his thought to affairs of boyfriends." It was doubtless in large part on account of Socrates's friendship with his lifelong comrade Crito, and in response to the latter's anxious concern about his son's erotic frivolities and escapades, that the philosopher undertook to educate Critobulus in his responsibilities and requirements as a wealthy household head.

This is the dramatic context of the framing dialogue of the *Economist*—a context which, we soon learn, is not without some comical risk to Socrates, of becoming entangled in a care for Critobulus's household that goes way beyond what the philosopher is willing to undertake (2.9–18). We may conclude that Socrates's intimacy with the devil-may-care Critobulus mixed the fulfillment of friendly educative duty with affectionate pleasure: Critobulus was a rather good-looking, generously rich, and amiably jocund young ne'er-do-well with whom Socrates had fun, while trying to help the young fellow, not least for the sake of the young man's father, Socrates's old friend Crito. Xenophon has made it abundantly clear (see esp. *Memorabilia* 4.1.1–2) that Socratic fun is always leavened with provocation to deep and serious thought for onlookers. And by his very first word in the *Economist*, as well as subsequently, our author Xenophon indicates that he is (fictively) portraying himself, in his younger days, in the role of an eyewitness to the dialogue—which Xenophon indicates he is reporting only selectively, and not word for word (*toiade*; see also the *pōs* at the start of chap. 2). Xenophon invites us to join him, vicariously, as the appreciative audience of what was a deeply illuminating and singularly beneficial comic performance: a drama that Socrates put on for the profound instruction, above all, of his beloved young friend Xenophon.[8] This, I am inclined to judge, is the most important sense in which the *Economist* embodies and conveys "*the* Socratic Discourse written by Xenophon" (XSD 86, 130, 165) and even "*the* Socratic dialogue" (XSD 129): what we see portrayed here is nothing less than a version of the discourse that was a or the crucial part of the education that Socrates gave to young Xenophon (and maybe also to Plato?).[9]

## THE HIGH STATUS OF THE THEME OF "HOUSEHOLD MANAGEMENT"

But, lest the previous observations strengthen or confirm a blinding bias from which readers may initially suffer—a prejudicial doubt as to the comparative lack of seriousness of the theme of "the economist" or "skilled household management," in contrast with such apparently loftier themes as "statesmanship," or "political and military leadership," or "kingship, royal rule," or even "divine providence" and "God's rule over the cosmos"—let us preface our interpretation of the framing dialogue between Socrates and Critobulus with a look at the closing homily that Socrates reports his teacher Ischomachus having delivered to him (21.2–12).

The perfect gentleman proclaimed that at the heart of skilled household management, in which farm management bulks large, is an intellectual capacity together with a divine spiritual endowment that is at the heart of skilled rule universally: namely, the ability to inspire the ruled with "ardor, and with competitive love of victory in regard to one another, and with love of excelling in honor." One who manifests this capacity Ischomachus "would declare to have something of the character of a king," and

Ischomachus further asseverated that "one who is going to be capable of these things needs even education in the full sense (*paideia*), and, to be possessed of a good nature" and—"what is the greatest matter"—"to become divine!" For "it seems to me that this—ruling over the willing—is not altogether a human good, but rather, divine." For the gods "clearly reserve it for those who are truly initiated into the sacred mysteries of moderation" (*tois alēthinōs sōphrosunē tetelesmenois*). The perfect gentleman thus gave testimony to Socrates of a profound, personal,[10] religious experience—of mysteriously sacred spiritual participation in, and elevation to, divinity. Such religious experience constituted the core of the gentleman's own lifetime experience of the ruling vocation. "In contrast," he solemnly affirmed, "the gods give tyrannizing over the unwilling, it seems to me, to those whom they hold to deserve to live out their lives as Tantalus is said to in Hades: spending all time fearing lest he will a second time die." The gentleman conceives the tyrant's life as a divinely allotted Hell of an immortal afterlife of endless mortal fear.

This divine rank that Ischomachus thus assigned to expertise in rule over the household—as on a par with statesmanship and kingship, differing only in the number of those led or ruled—was to be later ratified by his philosopher-student,[11] if in the latter's own distinctly philosophic way. Socrates was to designate as "household managing" (*oikonomōn*) God's "ordering together and holding together the whole cosmos, in which all things are noble-and-good (gentlemanly), things which He always provides, unworn, and healthy, and ageless, (thus) serving the users, quicker than thought, and unerringly."[12] In learning the gentleman's understanding of his vocation as ruler over the household, Socrates would seem to have been simultaneously learning the gentleman's conception of divine rule over the universe, which, according to Ischomachus, his gentlemanly household rule not only reflects but mysteriously instantiates on the human plane.

## ECONOMICS AS A UNIVERSAL SCIENCE

Xenophon recalls Socrates having opened the dialogue by asking Critobulus if "household management" (*oikonomia*) is "a name for some science" (*epistēmē*), as are the words "skilled doctoring," and "skilled bronze working," and "skilled wood working." Conceiving household management in this unconventional way,[13] as a science or craft, conduces to thinking of it as something one needs to learn from an expert teacher or teachers. Socrates would seem to have been taking the first step on a path that would bring Critobulus to realize his need for such an education. But Xenophon immediately lets us see that Critobulus had not grasped the radical implication of this uncommon perspective on household management. For when Socrates next characterized, more conventionally, as "arts" (*technōn*) the other three forms of expertise that he had adduced, and asked if, even as "we" could "say what the work or function of each of these arts" is, so "we" would "also be able to say, in the case of household management, similarly what the work or function of it is," Critobulus fell back on common opinion: "it is opined, at any rate (said Critobulus)[14] that it belongs to a good household manager [*oikonomou agathou*] to manage well *his own* household" (1.2). A gentleman is conventionally supposed to mind his own business (Aristotle, *N. Ethics* 1142a1–2); his concern as household manager is supposed to be primarily and chiefly the well being of his own household—to which concern he is presumed to be motivated by deep love of his own. (In *Memorabilia* 2.9.1 Socrates quotes Crito, the father of Critobulus, describing himself as one those men who "wished to mind his own business.")

Challenging this conventional gentlemanly opinion on the basis of the nature of science, Socrates asked if it is not the case that "he who is a scientific knower (*epistamenos*) of skilled carpentry" would be able to do the relevant work for another, even as for himself; and "in the same way, wouldn't the skilled household manager (*oikonomikos*—economist)"[15] be able, "if he should wish," to "manage well the household of another, even as his own, if someone turned it over to him"? In assenting, Critobulus once again showed that he was aware of departing from common opinion—and this time he addressed Socrates by name, thus indicating the distinctively "Socratic" character of this unusual perspective on the matter (1.3).

We see that Socrates as political philosopher has an understanding of skilled household management in which the component of scientific knowledge (of how to achieve what is good, or well done, for any and every given household) eclipses the love of one's own (XSD 93), thus reversing the normal gentlemanly perspective. The scientific art as such aims only incidentally at the benefit of the expert's own household. And the love of one's own household contributes little or nothing to the expert's scientific knowledge of how to manage well even his own household.[16]

But Socrates was not naively or abstractly ignoring the love of one's own as essential human *motivation* to the *practical implementation* of the universal scientific knowledge. This became clear when the philosopher proceeded to ask a concluding question: Therefore, is it not possible, for "one who has scientific knowledge of this art (*tēn technēn tautēn epistamenōi*), if he himself happens not to have riches (*chrēmata*), to manage the household of another"—and "*get paid*"? (1.4). Socrates seemed to presume that an expert's putting into practice his knowledge of the scientific art would not be disinterested, and, moreover, that the gratification that derives intrinsically from the skilled practice, and in addition from repute and gratitude for such skilled practice, would not be sufficient motivation. Socrates spoke as if the knower of the science of household management seeks, from the practical implementation of his knowledge, an extrinsic reward that contributes to the needed financial resources of his own household. So Socrates by no means entirely jettisoned Critobulus's conventional characterization of a "good household manager."

## THE TRUE, SCIENTIFIC MEANING OF RICHES

Socrates's suggestion of a skilled household manager-for-hire struck a vibrant chord in Critobulus: "By Zeus! And it is big pay (said Critobulus) that he would gain, if he were able, in taking over a household, to disburse the needed expenditures and, by making a surplus, increase the household!" (1.4; and see also 1.6 end). Did not Critobulus glimpse a solution to his troubled household budget—and to his own problematic disinclination to spend the requisite time and energy on managing his household (see 2.9–12)? Was not a hope stirred or reawakened in him that his indigent but wise friend Socrates might contribute to that solution—even if only by helping him to find and to hire someone else who would be a surplus-producing, skilled household manager (consider *Memorabilia* 2.8 and 2.10)?

Socrates did not respond or give any encouragement to such hopes. On the other hand, he did not challenge the assumption of Critobulus that the goal of a skilled household manager is "increasing" the household. Socrates did, however, ask his young interlocutor to reflect on what exactly is encompassed, "for us," in "whatever things of the household (*oikos*) one has acquired (*kektētai*) outside the habitation (*oikia*)." Critobulus at once proclaimed his own expansive (some might say all-too-Athenian-imperialist) view: "by me, at least (declared Critobulus) it is opined that all things, even if not in the same city, belong to the household, as many as one acquires" (1.5).

When questioned further, however, our young householder quickly and emphatically conceded that this needs correction, to avoid what he regarded as the "laughable" error of including in the valuable household the increase of the "many enemies" that—"By Zeus!"—some "acquire." He declared that what he means by "acquisitions/possessions" (*ktēmata*) are what is *good* (*agathon*), "by Zeus!"—i.e., "beneficial" (*ōphelima*). Critobulus certainly does not mean—"by Zeus!"—what is bad (*kakon*), i.e., "harmful" (*blaptonta*).[17] When Socrates concluded that Critobulus seemed to be "calling the things that are beneficial, for each, 'possessions,'" his young interlocutor emphatically agreed, and added: "and the harmful things, I, for my part, believe to be loss (*zēmian*) rather than *riches* (*chrēmata*)!"[18]

Socrates asked if this doesn't entail that a horse that someone might buy, *not knowing how* to use,[19] with the result that purchaser hurt himself by falling off, would *not* be his "riches." Critobulus assented, though with a note of surprise: "No—if indeed riches, at any rate, are good."

But when Socrates submitted that "therefore the earth is not riches for a human being" who suffers loss in cultivating it (Socrates did not say the loss is a result of lack of knowledge), Critobulus for the first time dug in his heels a bit. He agreed only that "the earth is indeed not riches, if instead of providing nourishment it provides famine (*peinēn*)." Presumably Critobulus had enough worldly wisdom to have noted a persisting benefit of land to its owner, even if the (Zeus-sent[20]) weather puts a farm temporarily "in the red"—so long as starvation is not in the offing (1.8; cf. 5.18–20).

Socrates blithely moved on, bypassing this demurral, and ignoring the gesture toward grave (theological) limitations on the decisive value of human expertise: "therefore isn't it *the same* with herd animals?—If someone through *not knowing how* to use herd animals suffers loss, the herd animals wouldn't be riches for him?" When Critobulus assented, Socrates drew the seemingly rather otiose conclusion that "you then, it looks like, hold the beneficial things to be riches, and the harmful not." The young man naturally assented (1.9). Only after having thus built a certain momentum with his student did Socrates propose a conclusion that is much more general, and radical (and controversial or even dubious, since it does not follow from, and indeed is drawn into question by, their dialogue concerning the earth and what that dialogue gestured toward): "then the same belongings/beings (*onta*) are riches for the one who knows how to use each of them, but for the one not knowing, not riches"—and Socrates adduced the example of "flutes,"[21] which he claimed are "no more than worthless stones for the one not knowing" how to use them.

Critobulus reasonably objected:[22] "Unless he found a buyer (*apodidoito*) for them!"

Socrates treated as a friendly amendment this pregnant introduction of what Adam Smith and his great successors, building from Aristotle's *Politics* 1257a6ff., were to call "exchange value." Socrates asked, "is this then evident to us: that for those finding a buyer, the flutes are riches, but not if they don't find a buyer, and keep them as possessions—that is, for those who do not know how to use them?" Critobulus's sense of paradox was evident in his slightly qualified assent. However, Critobulus then felt a need to reformulate their conclusion: "now if they are not offered for sale (*pōloumenoi*),[23] the 'flutes' are not riches—for they are of no use; but offered for sale, riches" (1.11). Critobulus appeared to think of "riches" as including an exchange value, distinct from use value, that is aimed at an accumulation of buying power (money). Certainly Critobulus sensed that markets are more resilient, the exchange value of commodities more durable (as unsold "inventory"), than Socrates seemed to be allowing in what we see is his insistent argument for the decisive importance of human knowledge of *use* value.[24]

Xenophon's authorial intervention at this point (1.12) signals the momentousness of what Socrates says next, in massive qualification of Critobulus's reformulation: "if, that is, one has (scientific) *knowledge* of offering for sale" (*ēn epistētai ge pōlein*), and Socrates then explained the paradoxical sort of "knowledge" he had in mind. For he turned out to mean (pace XSD 95) not "salesmanship," or knowledge of how to work the market shrewdly to maximize exchange value and hence buying power, but instead knowledge of use value (again): "if one were to offer to sell in return for what one would not know how to use, then, not even in being offered for sale are they riches"—"according to *your* argument," the dialectical Socrates rather puckishly added.

One might suppose that Socrates was thinking of barter, but Critobulus knew better, and his reply expressed his provoked astonishment: "You seem to be saying, Socrates, that not even the cash (*to argurion*) is riches, if someone doesn't have knowledge of how to use it!"

Socrates retorted: "but *you* also seem to me to agree with this—that things from which one is able to benefit are riches!" (1.13). Socrates proceeded to give compelling illustrative evidence for his paradoxical scientific-economic thesis that cash as such, or accumulated buying power, is not riches: he adduced the case of a man harmed—physically, spiritually,[25] and financially—by using (a large sum of) cash to purchase a courtesan (*hetaira*).[26] We may suspect that this was calculated to hit home especially with the erotically wayward Critobulus; certainly his assent was not only emphatic but idiosyncratic, equating such a mistress with a poisonous hallucinogenic[27] (wisdom gained from bitter experience?). And at this point Socrates evidently felt in a position to issue a major, paradoxical imperative of the science of economics or household management as he conceives it. Addressing Critobulus by name for the first time since the opening, Socrates said: "so let the cash, if one does not know how to use it, be thrust far away, Critobulus, given that[28] it is not riches!" (1.14). Exchange value must ultimately be measured by, subordinated to, use value and the knowledge thereof.[29]

Here we see very clearly the two levels, theoretical and practical, on which Xenophon is having his Socrates proceed in this dialogic performance before a cadre of students, including above all young Xenophon: Socrates is elaborating the universal principles of the science of household management as he contends he can show must be conceded by every honest interlocutor, while making the elaboration beneficially provocative and admonitory for the particular case of the problematic young householder Critobulus.

To what extent did Critobulus pay heed? Socrates relieved the wealthy youth of the embarrassment of responding to the fraught scientific admonition regarding cash accumulation, or even retention. Socrates instead switched immediately to asking about a very different, warmer kind of possession—with regard to which the philosopher elicited another unconventional implication of economic science: "but as for friends/loved ones (*philoi*[30]), if one knows how to use them so as to benefit from them, what shall we declare them to be?" Critobulus replied with enthusiasm: "Riches, by Zeus!"—"and much, indeed, more than cattle (*bous*), at least if they are more beneficial than cattle."[31] Socrates did not elaborate with his interlocutor the implications of the Socratic science in regard to those *philoi* whom one does not how to use so as to get much benefit from them.[32] Xenophon has Socrates proceed instead to draw a related, and again radically unconventional, scientific conclusion, which contradicted what Critobulus began by thinking was absurdly obvious (1.15): "and then even the enemies, according to your argument, *are* riches, for one who is capable of being benefited from enemies."[33] Showing how far he had advanced in economic science, Critobulus replied: "to me at least, it therefore seems so." Socrates drove home the radicalism of Critobulus's revision of his own outlook: "so then, to a household manager who is good (*agathos*), it belongs also to have knowledge of how to use the enemies so as to be benefited from the enemies?"—"In the strongest terms!" (*ischurotata ge*), answered Critobulus, in effect conceding that he had been refuted in his earlier very confident and strongly asserted opinion.

But Socrates went further: "for also you see (he said), Critobulus, how many households indeed there are of private persons that have increased from war, and how many from tyrannizings."[34] The art of war is thus evidently a part of the Socratic science of household management. Is there not also a scientific art of tyrannizing that is part of the Socratic science of household management? For the full answer to this troubling question, we would have to study Xenophon's *Hiero, or One Skilled in Tyranny*—the work that is the antistrophe to the *Economist*. But in *Hiero*, the role of the wise man is taken by the morally somewhat dubious poet Simonides.[35] How could this question still be open for the political philosopher Socrates, when the very possibility of beneficial tyranny would seem to have been utterly denied by his gentleman teacher Ischomachus, in the closing words of the latter's concluding homily—which we have previously quoted? In a few moments, however, we will hear Socrates declaring that "when enemies in war who are gentlemen enslave some, they compel many to be better by chastening them, and make them lead the rest of their life more easily."[36] What is more, we cannot avoid observing that while we will hear Ischomachus also teaching Socrates that "it is the part of a sensible man and wife to make it so that their properties" will "accumulate to the greatest extent possible, by *noble and just* means" (7.15; see similarly Cyrus, in *Education of Cyrus* 8.2.20-23), that qualification is missing from the Socratic science of economics as here presented. "To say the least, Socrates and Critobulus are silent here on justice or legality";[37] they are equally silent on the noble. Yet how could Socrates as mature political philosopher have forgotten, or why would he playfully omit, such a crucially restraining dimension of what he was taught by his gentleman teacher about legitimate acquisition of riches? Xenophon has Socrates here make the science of household management appear so single-mindedly fixated on the good (the beneficial) that competing and traditionally limiting moral considerations, of lawfulness, justice, and nobility, are eclipsed. Xenophon provokes us to wonder: What are the Socratic grounds for such a primacy of the idea of the good—and how did those grounds become discovered or confirmed from Socrates's report of his experience of being taught virtue by Ischomachus?[38]

These grave questions are muted or veiled by the reaction Xenophon reports from the morally insouciant young Critobulus, who said that he found what had been said "*nobly* spoken, in my opinion at least, Socrates!" (This is the sole mention of the noble in the Socratic account of the economic science, or indeed in the first three chapters.)

## VIRTUE IS KNOWLEDGE

The introduction of strenuously risky wars and tyrannizings as eligible modes of scientific increase of the household evidently provoked our leisure-loving young householder Critobulus to raise another sort of critical question, one that is revelatory of additional deep implications of the outlook of Socratic economic science (1.16).

How, Critobulus asked, are we to understand people who possess the requisite knowledge, and also have the resources available "from which they have the power, by working, to increase the households," yet are "*unwilling* to do so" (*mē thelontas poiein*)—rendering (Critobulus thinks) "their knowledge of no benefit to them"? Doesn't it necessarily follow, on the basis of the Socratic thesis, at least as Critobulus understands it, that "neither their knowledge nor their possessions are riches"? These questions express with some cleverness a commonsense doubt about the emerging Socratic contention or presumption that knowledge of the good has sovereign psychological power to govern one's choices—that such knowledge is virtue, or that virtue is such knowledge.

In addition, the wealthy but nonetheless financially pressed Critobulus would seem to have been raising a thinly veiled, critical, personal question about his impecunious teacher—and pointing again to the possibility, and now to the seeming Socratic logic, of the two of them entering into an economic partnership. In doing so, Critobulus ignored (and thereby prompts us to note) the possibility—which was incarnate in the Socrates standing before him—that the true knowledge or science of household management dictates that the knower minimize, as much as possible, his involvement in the work of monetarily or materially increasing anyone's household, starting with his own, and that he instead devote his energies to increasing the riches of knowledge for its own sake and acquiring friends who contribute to such increase (Ambler 1996, 108–9).

Socrates did not respond to Critobulus's implicit personal challenge. He did not give a defense of his own financially unenterprising economizing. But he afforded a veiled glimpse of the understanding of spiritual freedom that is at the core of his life, and of that life's unqualifiedly scientific economics.

Socrates began his response by asking a question that seems at first to exhibit misunderstanding of the import of Critobulus's questions: "is it about slaves (said Socrates) that you are trying, Critobulus, to involve me in dialogue?" (1.17). "By Zeus, no!"—Critobulus remonstrated—"I am not!" Then, evidently seeking to overcome what he thought was Socrates's obtuseness, Critobulus adduced "some who are reputed to be of the best fathers" (*eupatridōn*[39]), whom he saw have knowledge of either the warlike or the peaceful arts of acquisition, but are "not willing" (*ouk ethelontas*) to do the *work* of implementing this knowledge—precisely because they are *not* slaves, or do not have masters (who might compel in them a willingness to work)! Critobulus's observations (not least, perhaps, of his own character) had made him sure that knowledge of the good is insufficient without the addition of will, or willingness, to labor at achieving the known good.

But Socrates rejected the very possibility of such a human condition (1.18): "And how (said Socrates) could they *not* have Masters (*despotas*), since, praying to be happy and wishing to do that from which they would have good things, they are prevented from doing these things by rulers?!"

The bemused Critobulus naturally asked, "And who indeed are these, who, being unevident, rule over them?!"

Swearing by Zeus for the first time, Socrates exclaimed that "they are not unevident, but entirely evident!" They are the Beings whose "wickedness" Critobulus himself "believes in" (asserted Socrates): "Idleness, and Softness of Soul, and Carelessness," along with "other deceptive Mistresses (*despoinai*) purporting to be pleasures—Dice Playing" and other "human associations that are without benefit" (1.19). A few moments later Socrates added, as additional "harsh Masters," Gluttonies, and Sexual Lusts, and Drinking Bouts, and Ambitions that are foolish as well as expensive (1.22).[40] These Masters "rule so harshly over humans whom they dominate, that, so long as they see the humans in their prime and able to work, the masters compel them" to "bring the fruits of their labors as tributes"[41] to the desires for these Masters; while the "Mistresses never cease tormenting the bodies of humans and their souls and their homes, so long as they rule over them" (1.22). It is necessary—"Oh Critobulus!—to keep fighting for freedom against these, no less than against those who try to enslave with weapons!" (1.23; see similarly *Memorabilia* 4.5.5). The philosopher playfully personified, as evilly despotic demons or divinities, the psychological forces that make humans who "pray to be happy," and *wish* to do what they think they know will make them happy, do in fact the opposite. He thus gently invited Critobulus to contemplate and to react against his own self-enslavement of this kind. More profoundly, Xenophon helps us to descry the true, serious meaning of the famous Socratic thesis, "virtue is knowledge":[42] opinion about the good is only "knowledge" (in the Socratic sense) when that opinion is held by a consciousness in which practical reason has achieved domination over the passions, and especially the desires for pleasure; otherwise, the passions enslave the practically rational mind by beclouding or bedazzling it, thus producing the *practical-psychological incapacity of the mind to grasp the good, in a nonabstract way, for what the good truly is*—and this mental incapacity, this being mentally blinded, is commonly (and mistakenly) conceived as willful evildoing or as clear-sighted lack of self-restraint. Moreover, Xenophon has Socrates draw attention to one momentous form that the beclouding or bedazzling by passion takes: the imagination's creation of the apparent experience of being infatuated or bewitched and thus blinded by external, superhuman Masters and Mistresses (see also *Education of Cyrus* 6.1.41).

Critobulus apparently did not want to ponder this insinuation that he might be subject to a profound sort of inner, mental slavery. Perhaps spurred by the amazing proliferation of Socratically invented, superhuman Masters and Mistresses, Critobulus moved to another objection (no longer as a question, but assertively), an objection on a very different footing from the previous one. He pointed out that there is another class of people who are not at all impeded by the sorts of "Masters and Mistresses" Socrates had conjured up—that is, not at all troubled by lack of self-control over their passions: people who work hard, and who devise sound methods of income, and who nevertheless wear out their households and wind up without resources (1.21). In other words, reminding us of his answer to Socrates's question about the earth, Critobulus pointed again, and more emphatically, to the enormous limitation imposed on any practical rationalism by human reason's helplessness in the face of the truly external, superhuman powers of fortune or destiny.

Socrates's response (1.22–23) perversely ignored this powerful objection—despite his immediately preceding reference to "*praying* to be happy" (*euchomenoi eudaimonein*: 1.18). With apparent obtuseness, Socrates elaborated further his jocuse creation of evil divine or demonic Masters and Mistresses against whom Critobulus must keep fighting. Xenophon provokes us to wonder: What is the scientific ground for Socrates's ignoring of Fortuna, and/or the divinities to whom humans pray, and for his unabashed introduction of new, hostile divinities (*daimonia*)?[43]

## THE WEALTHY PHILOSOPHER AND THE IMPOVERISHED YOUNG MAGNATE

Critobulus persisted in shrugging off Socrates's inventively jocular call to the struggle for inner liberation: "in my opinion I've heard quite sufficiently from you about such, and" (the young man fatuously added) "examining myself, I think I have found myself reasonably self-controlled in such matters."[44] What Critobulus said he needed from Socrates was advice on how to *increase* his household—"or," he asked, with a hint of the tone of one of the upperclass condescending to a plebian, "do you pass judgment (*kategnōkas*) on us, Socrates, as being sufficiently wealthy, and do we seem to you not to need more riches?" (2.1).

Socrates responded tongue in cheek,[45] as if Critobulus had invited an assessment of the comparative sufficiency of his own and Critobulus's wealth. He earnestly declared himself to be "sufficiently wealthy." But "you, oh Critobulus, seem to me to be very impoverished, and—by Zeus!—there are times when I very much pity you!"

Critobulus reacted by laughing in Socrates's face, and asking: "And how much—before the gods!—do you think, Socrates (he said), your possessions would fetch if put up for sale, and how much would mine?!"

With a straight face, Socrates replied (2.3) that if he "chanced on a good buyer," his entire household and contents would "easily" get five *minas* (= 500 drachmas)[46]—which, he said, he knows is less than one percent of the price that Critobulus would get for his.

Critobulus drove home the comic preposterousness of Socrates's assessment: "and *you don't* need more riches, but pity *me* as impoverished!?" (2.4).

Socrates stubbornly contended that he had resources adequate to procure what is sufficient for him but soon added (2.8) the following crucial and not conventionally gentleman-like supplement to his initial evaluation of his resources: "if I should need something in addition, I know that you too are aware that there are those who would assist, so that, by providing very little, they would *deluge* my life with abundance." (We recall that "friends are riches, by Zeus!"—1.14; see XSD 102–5).

But as regards the "pitifully poor" Critobulus, Socrates declared that, in striking contrast to himself, the young magnate is so engaged in practicing, and becoming reputed for, magnificence (*megaloprepeia*)—the moral virtue of grand generosity that Aristotle (*N. Ethics* 1122a18-b33) ranks close to the peak of the adequately "equipped," morally serious life—that even if the young man's wealth were four times as great as it is, it still would not seem adequate. It thus transpires that the heart and root of Critobulus's financial difficulties is not his illusory estimation of himself as wealthy, nor his careless failure to devise ways to make more money, nor even his thinking that he can devote all his attention to affairs with boyfriends; all these deplorable deficiencies do not by themselves render Crito's son "pitiably" at risk of "suffering incurable evil and winding up in great want" (2.7). What threatens him with ruin is his moral virtue of magnificence in action, both in deeds of great private generosity (such as sacrificing to the gods and hosting strangers as well as fellow citizens) and, above all, in public deeds obeying the city's demands upon him for much more massive civic generosities, in peacetime and in war (consider also *Education of Cyrus* 8.2.20–23).

Obviously, the philosopher Socrates does not even attempt to join in these private and civic activities of the moral virtue of magnificence: as Aristotle declares (*N. Ethics* 1122b28), "a poor man would not be magnificent"—and "one who tries is foolish." But Aristotle also concedes that the activities of the moral virtue of magnificence can be undertaken if one has sufficient resources not of one's own but through one's "connections" (ibid. 1122b32); could not Socrates gain access to the requisite resources for the practice of this moral virtue by way of his connections with Crito and his family—even by becoming the authoritative advisor to Critobulus in the latter's household management as a whole, including his philanthropy? Yet Socrates speaks of Critobulus's practices of magnificence as involving burdensome "compulsion" (*anangkē*), under the "imposition" of "commands," accompanied by threats of being made "bereft of allies," and of no longer being "tolerated," and of becoming "severely punished" by the city of Athens. Socrates does not speak of the activities of grand generosity as being either "nobly" sacrificial or as "nobly" and "pleasantly" fulfilling—in contrast to what he will report he heard from, and replied to, Ischomachus (11.9–10). Even more striking is the contrast with Aristotle, who characterizes such expenditures as being "similar to votive offerings," as "for the sake of the noble," as "not for oneself but for the common," and yet "also pleasant while lavish," looking to "what is honorable" and "what is most beautiful/noble" and, as such, objects of "admiring contemplation—and the magnificent is admirable" (*N. Ethics* 1122b7-a5). Someone might suggest that the major reason for the dim view Socrates takes of the active engagement in magnificence by Critobulus is that the young magnate has to practice the virtue in Athens (as Socrates underlines here), which is governed by a democratic regime that is constitutionally incapable of properly appreciating the public virtue of magnificence and that inevitably distorts the practice of the virtue by using it to try deliberately to impoverish the wealthy practitioners.[47] But in that case one might expect Socrates to give some indication—along the lines of Aristotle in his *Nicomachean Ethics*—of aspiration to, or admiration of, magnificent expenditure when practiced in a virtuous regime. Socrates does not do so.[48] Nor does he give to Critobulus any recommendation to follow the prudent and somewhat defensive public generosity that the Athenian gentleman Ischomachus taught Socrates that he engaged in with (mixed) pleasure (11.21–22). Xenophon compels us to wonder: What did Socrates learn from listening to Ischomachus, or from observing the reactions of young men to whom he has told the story of his education by Ischomachus, that led him not to recommend imitation of this peak activity of the morally serious gentleman? (With a view to Plato, we may submit that insofar as there is a Socratic philosopher's magnificence, it is a virtue of an altogether different order, on an altogether different footing.[49])

## SOCRATES EVADES RESPONSIBILITY

The philosopher's effort to awaken the young man to his dire financial situation seemed to have succeeded all too well. "The time has come, Socrates,"

Critobulus declared, "for you to take charge of me, so that I will not in reality become pitiable!" (2.9; our young bon vivant of course did not agree that he was already pitiable—that suggestion, he probably assumed, was merely a Socratic joke).

After a moment's resourceful reflection (*akousas oun*), the master responded by launching into a fabulously fibbing account of the previous conversation (2.9). Socrates asserted that Critobulus had not only laughed at the philosopher's claim to be wealthy, as showing that Socrates is ignorant of the very meaning of "wealth," but had forced the philosopher "through refutation" to admit that he possesses not even a hundredth of the possessions of Critobulus: had forced Socrates to admit, in other words, that he is financially impoverished, rather than wealthy as he claims—and, by implication, had forced Socrates to realize that he is thus the last person in the world who should be asked to take charge of anyone's estate.

Critobulus is phlegmatic enough (or familiar enough with Socrates's penchant for playful prevarication) not to dispute this falsification of their immediately previous conversation. Instead, the young magnate insisted on facts that he regarded as simply unfalsifiable: Socrates knows one crucial work of becoming wealthy—making a surplus; and if he can achieve that from a little, it is not unreasonable to "hope" that he can achieve it from a lot (2.10).

In response, Socrates continued his fibbing. He asked whether Critobulus didn't recall how, in the preceding dialogue, the young man insisted—without allowing poor old Socrates even to grunt[50] in demurral!—that for one who lacks knowledge of how to employ horses, or land, or herd animals, or cash, or any other resource, these all cease to be riches: "and how do you suppose that *I* would know how to use any of these, when absolutely none of these have ever belonged to me?" (2.11). Suddenly, in his drive to escape responsibility for Critobulus's affairs, Socrates introduced the importance of knowledge based in practical experience—from which he had previously abstracted.

Critobulus stubbornly reminded Socrates that (2.12) "it seemed to us that even if one did not happen to have riches, all the same, there is a certain *science* of household management; so, what prevents you too from knowing it?"

"By Zeus!"—Socrates expostulated—"the very same thing that would prevent" anyone from knowing how to play a musical instrument if he himself never possessed an instrument, and no one else ever allowed him to learn on theirs!—"And that holds for me as regards household management!" (2.12–13). Socrates spoke as if he were homeless, and thus totally ignorant of what it means to manage or to grow a household or to balance its expenses against its resources.[51]

Critobulus "was not buying it": he rejoined by reproaching Socrates for "trying so intensely to escape giving help to me, in any way, so as to more easily bear the burden of my necessitated affairs!" (2.14).

"By Zeus, no!"—Socrates exclaimed—"I am not! I shall eagerly guide you in any ways that I can"; and Socrates proceeded to secure the young man's agreement that he could not blame Socrates (for, Critobulus declared, that would "not be at all just"[52]) if the philosopher, being himself ignorant of the needed knowledge, should show to the beleagured young householder others who are much cleverer in these matters, and who will even (Socrates seemed to promise) be grateful if Critobulus were to become their student. Socrates further declared that if Critobulus were willing to become their student, Socrates thinks that the young man would become a "terrific money maker"—"if," that is, "the god should not oppose you" (2.15–18).

The basis Socrates gave for his promise to Critobulus was a rather bizarre account of the philosopher's activity in the city (2.16–18)—an account that is odd both in its formulation and in its substance.[53] Socrates "confesses" (*homologō*) that he "has been attentive to whoever among those in the city are the most expertly knowledgeable (*epistēmonestatoi*) about each of the things." He was motivated to this because "there came a time" (*pote*) when he "learned" that "from the *same* works" (*apo tōn autōn ergōn*) "some are very much without resources, and some very wealthy"—and about this dramatic disparity he "very much wondered."[54] His "investigating" (*episkopōn*) led to his "discovery" of a cause that he characterizes as "altogether intrinsic" (*panu oikeiōs*) to the matters : "those who practice these affairs without method (*eikē*) suffer penalty, but I came to the judgment (*kategnōn*) that those who apply themselves with an intent judgment (*gnōmē suntetamenē*) proceed in the affairs more quickly and easily and profitably." Strangely, however, immediately after this account of his discovery of an "altogether intrinsic" cause for humans either progressing or failing in business, Socrates indicated to Critobulus that the young man's success as a money maker would depend decisively also on a cause or power that is not intrinsic to business practice based on sound judgment: divine providence—"if the god should not oppose you" (2.18).[55] As we will soon hear, Socrates learned from the perfect gentleman Ischomachus that the latter "believed that he had learned that the gods" grant "happiness" only to "some of those who are prudent and diligent, and to others of these not," and hence prudence and diligence must be supplemented by pious devotion (11.8–9). Is this not a clue to what made Socrates "very much wonder" about what might be going on to cause some humans to be without resources, and some to be wealthy, from the *same* works? Does this not call into question Socrates's previous apparent insistence or contention that success or failure in business is due simply to human knowledge and self-control (recall 1.16–22)? Looking again at the passage before us in 2.16–18, we see that Socrates does not in fact say that he learned that business guided by intent judgment leads to success *simply*, but only that it leads to proceeding "*more*" quickly and more easily and more profitably than lack of method, which he "saw" leads to "suffering *penalty*" (*zēmioumenous*—from whom; the gods? Is Socrates hinting that he discovered that the true divinity favors intelligent human diligence and frowns on the lack thereof?).

Socrates makes it sound as if, in the time prior to his life-changing learning and then wondering and then investigating and discovery, he had lived in an extraordinary "economic" aloofness (compare Plato's *Theaetetus* 173c–175b)—and as if his investigations, while leading him back down to earth, and to discovering an "altogether intrinsic" cause for human progress or failure "from the same works," did not at all move him to join his fellow humans in their preoccupation with money-making business, or with gentlemanly household management.

This is the first testimony that Xenophon or his Socrates has given to a major turn in the latter's philosophic life and activity (cf. Plato's *Apology* 20e–23a and *Phaedo* 96): there is no reference to any such turn in the *Memorabilia*, or in Xenophon's *Apology*.

After a moment's pause to take all this in (*akousas tauta*), Critobulus declared that he would not let Socrates off the hook before the latter kept his "promises made in front of these friends here" (3.1): this is the first we have heard of the audience of friends (but see the reading of the best mss. at 2.15, "from *us*," not "from *me*"). However great is the divergence—appearing wider and wider—between the way of life of Socrates and the way of life for which Critobulus needs help, the two lives do nonetheless share some of the same friends, above all Xenophon.

Socrates responded to Critobulus's injunction by proposing to keep his promises—but in a manner quite unexpected. For previously it sounded as if Socrates was promising to introduce Critobulus to teachers from among those in the city who are much more clever than Socrates at increasing a household. But now, instead, Socrates asked if he would seem to be "displaying" to Critobulus one of the "*works* of skilled[56] household managers" (*tōn oikonomikōn ergōn*) if he showed him two contrasting sets of house *builders*: one of whom builds useless houses that cost much cash and the other of whom builds houses having everything needed and costing much less (3.1;

Socrates seems to think the skilled household manager needs to design his own home; consider *Memorabilia* 3.8.8–10—could he have in mind builders of highly unconventional "Socratic" houses?). When Critobulus emphatically assented, Socrates asked similarly about what he said follows closely (3.2): What if he displayed to Critobulus the following two contrasting sets (Socrates does not call these sets of house builders, or household managers): one of which has a lot of implements (*epipla*) of all sorts but, when the implements are needed, neither has them at hand nor even knows if they are safe and sound—thereby causing much grief to themselves *and to the servants*; and the other of which has fewer implements, that are ready to hand when needed (no servants mentioned)?

Critobulus evinced his starting to think and to learn by asking his own question in reaction to that of Socrates (3.3): "what else is the cause of this, other than that for the one group, the implements are thrown down wherever each one might chance to wind up, while for the other group, each is set in order" (*hekasta tetagmena*)?

Swearing by Zeus, Socrates agreed—but then added, with a touch of impetuosity, a major supplement: "and not in a chance place, indeed, but where it is fitting, there they are each thoroughly arranged!" (*entha prosēkei, hekasta diatetaktai*). Critobulus replied by declaring his opinion that Socrates was speaking also in this case about something that belongs to "skilled household managers" (3.3). Socrates neither agreed nor disagreed. Had he not, in his own eyes, taken a step transcending household management?

Socrates next asked if he would seem to Critobulus to be also showing "a work of household management" (Socrates did not say of "skilled" household management) worthy of being observed if he showed two sets of household slaves (*oiketas*): one where pretty much all are in bonds, though they still often try to escape, and one where they are unbound and willing to work and to remain (3.4). By dropping the qualifier "skilled," could Socrates have been hinting that there is a kind of *skilled* household management that does *without* household slaves—because his own (impecunious) household does without slaves?[57] But Critobulus for his part expressed strong satisfaction—swearing by Zeus—at the thought of contemplating this contrast concerning household slaves: perhaps his household troubles include restive slaves. (Recall our discussion of the concluding oration of Ischomachus, on the sublime challenge of slave rule.)

The fourth of Socrates's proposed "displays" was to be two differing sets of farmers running very similar farms—one set of farmers complaining that they are being destroyed by farming and who are without resources, the other set having "in abundant and noble/beautiful fashion all the things that they need from the farm" (3.5—again Socrates did not call the latter *skilled* household managers; Socrates's own household management of course does not in the least include engaging in farming). Critobulus again emphatically welcomed this proposed display (swearing by Zeus)—and, as an attentive student, he contributed the suggestion that the contrast is "perhaps" because the former's expenditures extend beyond what is needed, to what is even harmful to oneself and to the household (3.5). But Socrates rejoined that while there are "probably such," they are not those to whom he was referring. He had in mind, rather, persons "professing to farm," yet not having the wherewithal to spend even on the things that are necessary. When Critobulus in his surprise asked what would be the cause of this, Socrates refused to say but promised to take Critobulus to such "farmers," so that he would learn by observing them (3.6). Why this teasing mystery? Who are these farmers who lack even the necessary wherewithal, to whom Socrates will take Critobulus? Could the answer be that Socrates was jesting about how he and his sort—by the end of this work he will *claim* to know the art of farming—come to sight as "farmers" (XSD 108–9)?

Critobulus is accustomed enough to Socrates's teasing, and is catching on enough, so that he expressed emphatic doubt, swearing by Zeus, as to whether he has the "*capacity*" to learn by observation the cause of the strange condition of such farmers lacking wherewithal. To this, Socrates insisted that Critobulus "ought to test himself" as to whether he will know by observation—but then Socrates abruptly lamented the fact that, while Critobulus wakes the two of them up early in the mornings in order to go on long treks to look at comedies,[58] he has never once invited Socrates to the spectacle now proposed. (Critobulus has never seriously tried to understand what causes the Socratic way of life to be so unconventional.) In reply, Critobulus expressed good-naturedly his awareness that to Socrates he appears laughable; swearing by Zeus Socrates assured the young man that he in fact appears even more laughable to himself (3.7–8). Critobulus was dimly aware that he was being made a figure in a kind of comedy.

Socrates in his urbanity did not bear down upon the young man's consciousness of his own risible shallowness. Socrates proceeded to propose a fifth object of educative display, one especially relevant to Critobulus's experiences: two sets of practitioners of the (upperclass, expensive[59]) art of horsemanship—one set whose members have, from their practice of the art, fallen into lack of resources even for the required things,[60] the other set having become very well off, and indeed preening themselves on the profit they've made from the practice (3.8). Now from what are we to suppose that this substantial profit would come? Would it be from gentlemanly victory prizes in, and gambling on, horse races? Or, was Socrates not referring above all to more commercial enterprise: horse raising, horse trading, and horse selling? Is such moneymaking a major component of the not-so-gentlemanly "Socratic" art of equitation? Xenophon is the author of an authoritative and purportedly comprehensive treatise on skilled equitation, which in gentlemanly fashion makes no reference whatsoever to gaining a profit in any manner as a part of the art—though the treatise provides extensive lessons in what to look for in *buying* a horse, as the very cornerstone of the art of equitation, and although Xenophon remarks that good practice of the art of horsemanship "makes horses worth more than when they were received" (*On Skilled Horsemanship* 11.13).

Critobulus replied with the lament that while he is sure that he already observes and knows both these sets of horsemen (he is very familiar with horsemanship), he nevertheless doesn't become one of the profit makers (3.8). Critobulus was apparently losing money on horses.

Socrates laid blame on Critobulus (3.9), by oddly assimilating the young man's failure as an observer of horsemanship to his failure as an observer of tragic as well as comic drama: you do not watch the plays "so that you may become a poet" but merely "so that you may take pleasure in seeing or hearing something." Of course, Socrates added, Critobulus does not wish to become a poet—and so "maybe" his superficiality in watching dramas as mere entertainment is, for him, "correct" (3.9). We are rather obviously being prodded by the author to reflect that in the *Economist* Xenophon creates a comic drama, in which the main event becomes Socrates creating, for the benefit of his students, a comic-dramatic portrait of his own experience of being supposedly educated by Ischomachus; Socrates and his student are comic poets of a kind, having learned from watching attentively many comic dramas with an eye to their authors' intentions.[61]

But as regards horsemanship, Socrates continued (3.9): "since you are compelled[62] to make use of skilled equitation, don't you think that you are a moron if you do not inquire into how you will not be an amateur in this work?—especially since the same belongings/beings[63] are good for use, *and are profitable belongings/beings if offered for sale*?" At this, our young aristocrat was ruffled, not to say mildly shocked: "are you bidding *me* to break colts, Socrates?!"[64]—"*No*, by Zeus!" (Socrates thus retreated and proceeded to reassure his high-minded young horseman-interlocutor): "no more than I would bid you to form farmhands by purchasing them as children." (Is this such a bad suggestion, in long run economic terms, if Critobulus were to take up farming for profit?) But, Socrates opined, as regards *buying* horses, as well as humans, there is an optimal purchase age with a view to owning horses who can be expected to undergo "progress" or improvement.

Socrates thus made it clear that he could—but that the young aristocrat will not deign to permit it—direct Critobulus to the acquisition of the highly profitable version of skilled horsemanship, even as he will eventually teach the young man the art of profitable farming (minus, however—sad to say—animal husbandry and therefore profitable horse raising[65]). If Socrates were ever to be approached by a father and son who were enmeshed in the sort of financial trouble, due to horses, that Aristophanes portrays Strepsiades and Pheidippides enmeshed in, Socrates (after his life-changing turn) could have acted as a go-between, taking them to experts in profitable horsemanship who might have helped to reverse the family's fortunes—unless the father and son were too proud to be helped.

Without a pause, Socrates sailed on: "And I can display also, as regards women whom they marry, some who use the women so that they have them as fellow workers in increasing the households, and some for whom the households are thus to the greatest extent ruined" (3.10). When Critobulus asked whether the man or the woman is to be held responsible in such cases, Socrates drew a parallel between the relation of husband to wife and the relation of a herder to a sheep and to a horse. The philosopher (educated by the gentleman Ischomachus) glided with disconcerting rapidity from artful use and training of animals and slaves to artful use and training of one's wife. But the philosopher perhaps redeemed himself from sounding condescending toward wives when he asked if the husband oughtn't "justly be held responsible" if he fails to teach his wife to become "a knower of the gentlemanly/noble-and-good things"—and then Socrates asserted that the wife "perhaps ought justly to be held responsible if, having been taught by the husband the good things, she does bad" (3.11).

Homing in on the case of Critobulus, Socrates got the young husband to confess in private ("for we who are present here are friends") that he had been woefully neglectful of conversing in any way with his "especially young child bride,"[66] despite his enormous reliance on her supervision of "the serious matters" of the household. What's more, it seems never to have occurred to Critobulus that any and every gentlemanly Greek husband needs to "educate" the young wife to whom he conventionally hands over the domestic management of the household, and especially its domestic expenditures: for Critobulus wonderingly asked, "those whom you say have good wives, Socrates, did they themselves educate them?" That this is not a surprising or unusually naive question from an Athenian husband, given

Greek marital culture,[67] is made evident by Socrates's noncommittal answer, followed by his promise to introduce Critobulus to Aspasia, "who, as more knowledgeable than me, will show you all these things."[68] It would appear that there is no husband whom Socrates knows, in all of Athens, who is as eligible to teach about the education of young wives as is this unmarried foreign woman who is the most notorious of all Greek courtesans.[69]

CHAPTER TWO

# The Case for Farming

Socrates abruptly returned from his startling offer to take Critobulus to Aspasia to a version of his previous promises: "And I think that I can display (*epideixai*) to you those working in a manner worthy of account at each of the other sciences as well, if you believe that you are in need of something more" (3.16). Socrates no longer limited himself to experts working *within the city* (contrast 2.16), and he now did not suggest that he would actually bring Critobulus to meet them: Critobulus might need to learn by observing them only through the Socratic "display." The reason for these changes soon becomes obvious, after we hear how Critobulus reacted—with predictable upper-class snobbishness.

For the young aristocrat announced his disdain for learning about arts and sciences other than the ones held to be "most noble" and "especially fitting for me to attend to."[1]

Socrates congratulated his fastidious interlocutor on "speaking nobly" and then elaborated (4.2–3) the prejudicial reasons why the "banausic" (artisanal, handicraft, or mechanical) arts are "decried" (*epirrētoi*) and held in disrepute "in the eyes of the cities" (*pros tōn poleōn*)—especially "those cities opined to be good at war," which actually forbid by law their citizens from engaging in such occupations (that would be especially Sparta, of course)—with a view to fostering civic warriors who are Homeric-like[2] "defenders of the fatherlands" (*tais patrisin alexētēres*).

"So," asked Critobulus in response (4.4), "which arts do you advise *us*" (that is, us high-class young Greek aristocrats), "Socrates, to employ?"

Now as we soon learn, Socrates's plan was to try to persuade Critobulus to become *seriously* engaged in *farming* as a solution to his financial troubles and personal irresponsibility. This project encounters a major obstacle inasmuch as among young Athenian aristocrats, many or most of whom admired

Sparta, it was not unambiguously clear that farming escaped the prejudice against banausic arts: Sparta, the most powerful and most renowned regime in Greece—"the only one that practiced gentlemanliness as a matter of public policy" (*Regime of the Lacedaemonians* 10.4)—forbade its citizens to engage in farming (that was left to the Helots).[3] So, apparently in order to dispel the young aristocrat's likely contempt for such a prosaic and laborious undertaking, Socrates unfurled a dazzling rhetoric. He suddenly proposed that they think big and bold: "shall we be unashamed to imitate the king of the Persians?"[4] (that is, the wealthiest and most powerful and most prestigious ruler on earth). "For they say," declared Socrates, "that since he holds farming as well as the art of war to be among the most noble and most necessary concerns, he is strongly concerned with both."

That Socrates and Critobulus might well be ashamed of taking as a model the Persian emperor[5] would derive from the fact that, in addition to being the age-old, inveterate, and most threatening enemy of all Greeks, the Persian emperor presides as despot over "slave" subjects,[6] in a political system that is held to be the antithesis of Greek civic republicanism.

But Critobulus, so far from expressing shock or repulsion, showed himself to be intrigued (if somewhat incredulous): "And *this* (he said) do you believe, Socrates—that the king of the Persians partakes of concern for something pertaining to *farming*?!" (4.5).

## THE MOST RESPLENDENT FARMING

Socrates replied by submitting the following for Critobulus's consideration. First, "we agree" on how sedulously the Persian emperor looks after military matters—and Socrates then detailed (4.5–7) how thoroughly the Persian empire is organized and supervised as a sort of police state, in which the "acropolises" are totally dominated by "mercenaries" and other imperial troops, whose officers are made dependent on the emperor by honors and "great gifts" of wealth along with "harsh punishments" and threats of being replaced—and constantly surveiled by an elaborate network of secret spies.[7] Then Socrates detailed (4.8–11) how, in parallel fashion, the empire's *farmlands* are thoroughly organized and supervised, as a sort of single, vast plantation administered by appointed imperial "rulers" distinct from the military officer corps; these civilian "rulers" are given lesser "gifts" and honors, and punishments that are not so harsh (cf. 4.7 with 4.8 and 4.15), and they have some countervailing power to bring accusations against derelict military commanders in their respective regions—except "where a satrap is set up, who supervises both" spheres.

This picture convinced Critobulus that if the king does this, he "cares no less for the deeds of skilled farming than of skilled war" (4.12; Critobulus is evidently either not very familiar with, or was not thinking about, the actual deeds of the skilled farming done by a Greek citizen-farmer; Socrates had not himself mentioned "skilled" farming and would not do so in his own name throughout his presentation of the Persian emperor as model farmer).

Oddly, however, Socrates was not satisfied with his success. He escalated. He ascended to the "noble" and even the "gentlemanly" dimensions of the Persian emperor's *personal* dedication to "farming" (Socrates had been silent on the "noble" or *kalon* in his previous depiction of the Persian military and agricultural administrations). Socrates told of the emperor's care for "the garden-parks called '*paradises*'" (*kēpoi hoi paradeisoi kaloumenoi*)[8] that are full of "everything gentlemanly/noble-and-good" that the earth brings forth; it is in these luxurious parks that the emperor spends most of his time, so long as the weather permits (4.13). Curiously, Socrates did not speak of any pleasure taken in these parks.

Critobulus was most favorably impressed with this picture of the emperor's concern for "*paradises* equipped as nobly as possible"—"By Zeus!"—with "trees and all the other noble/beautiful things the earth brings forth" (4.14).

But Socrates was still not satisfied. He waxed yet more eloquent in his depiction of the Persian emperor as *the supreme* model farmer (4.15–16). "They say," Socrates said, that in the speech that accompanies his distribution of gifts, the emperor honors equally his agricultural and his military servants. What's much more, "it is said" that the most famous emperor—the great Cyrus, whose conquests founded the Persian empire—once told those who were summoned to receive his gifts that it was "he himself who would justly receive the gifts," since (he declared) "he was the best at cultivating the land and defending the cultivators."

"If Cyrus did say these things," Critobulus replied (4.17), "well then, he preened himself no less on making the lands productive, and cultivating them, than on being skilled in war!"

Still not satisfied, and now himself swearing by Zeus, Socrates added that if only Cyrus had lived (to become emperor) it seems that he would have become the best ruler. For "it is said" that when Cyrus campaigned fighting against his brother (the king) over the kingship (in a fratricidal rebellion), none of Cyrus's followers deserted to the king, while "many tens of thousands" of the followers of the king deserted to Cyrus;[9] "and I hold this to be a great testimony to the virtue of a ruler, that they voluntarily obey him and willingly stick by him in terrible circumstances." Moreover (Socrates went on to say), "all the friends of Cyrus fought on his side while he lived, and died fighting around his corpse when he was killed" (4.18–19)—except of course (Socrates had to concede) for Cyrus's close friend, and leading officer, the notorious Ariaios.[10] The sudden emergence of "the virtue of a ruler" in the midst of Socrates's display of the highest splendor of farming foreshadows (along with 5.14–16) the extraordinary claim that we have seen is going to be made by the perfect gentleman Ischomachus in the conclusion of the *Economist*: that the skilled management of a farming household manifests the divinely highest art of ruling. Here, conversely, Socrates declared that the most powerful ruler on earth is seriously dedicated to farming. Both speeches (which are not without comic aspects) indicate that to deny this peak rank to farming leadership is to leave military leadership unrivalled in civic status, and is thus to fail to provide a basis for ranking peaceful civic affairs and rule as higher than military affairs and rule. That this is a timeless problem for human civilization is obvious from every known civic culture's monuments—which do not memorialize farmers or farming or "economists."

Socrates then added an amazing piece of anti-Hellenic gossip (4.20–25). "It is said of this Cyrus" that the Spartan admiral Lysander (victor over the Athenian empire's navy in the decisive battle of the Peloponnesian War, and thus "the greatest contemporary Greek authority"[11]) confided or boasted to a host in Megara (i.e., in private, and not to a fellow Spartan, and certainly not in Sparta) that when as emissary for the Greeks he visited Cyrus, the latter showed him "the paradise-garden" in Sardis; and Lysander said that he found himself so admiring of the garden's ordered beauties (*kala*) that he declared to the barbarian despot his much greater admiration for the designer and orderer—only to be informed by the gratified Cyrus that the latter had himself designed and ordered everything, and even planted some of it. The Spartan hero then related that, as he gazed at Cyrus and took in appreciatively all the "noble beauties" of the oriental clothing and luxurious jewels and perfumes with which the Persian despot was adorned, he expressed his wonder that Cyrus could have thus dirtied his hands; the oriental despot replied, swearing by Mithra[12] (the only god mentioned in this tale): "when I am in health, I never dine before breaking a sweat in something either of the skilled deeds of war, or of farming, or always expressing ambitious love of honor in some one thing." Lysander, a supposed paragon[13] of Spartan and thus Greek republican leadership and civic virtue, testified that he reacted to this by taking Cyrus's hand in adoring friendship, and earnestly addressing to him the opinion that the despot was then "justly happy," for he was "happy as a good man."[14] (Lysander obviously did not at that moment think it necessary for Cyrus to worship and to honor Zeus or other Greek gods in order to be justly happy, as a good man.)

Socrates did not give Critobulus any opportunity to reply to this astounding disclosure of the privately Medizing, religiously trans-Hellenic, pro-farming outlook of the greatest living hero of Sparta and hence of Greece. Socrates launched without a pause (5.1) into a long, ornately rhetorical oration[15] in praise of farming life on an altogether different basis—as it is carried on by the independent, private property–owning, Greek republican farmers. Xenophon has his Socrates segue from holding up the Persian despot as model farmer to celebrating the bucolic life of the free Greeks with the following words (5.1): "these things, O Critobulus, I am going through (said Socrates) because from farming not even the very blessed [pl.] are able to abstain. For the concern with it is likely to be at the same time a certain pleasant experience and an increase of the household and a discipline of bodies for the capacity to do whatever is fitting for a real man (*aner*) who is free." Xenophon has Socrates save until the end of this ambiguous statement his leap from despotism to freedom. We are thus provoked to wonder: *Which* are "the very blessed"—the Persian emperor, or the real men who are free? Or both? And is it so clear that Cyrus the Great is *not* a real man who is free? Why in this sentence are these two radically different exemplars of blessed manly freedom—the Persian despot and the Greek yeoman—being thus momentarily run together by Socrates?

We are also prodded to wonder why, if "not even the very blessed are able to abstain from farming," Socrates himself abstained. If we ask our author Xenophon himself, "who do you hold to be most truly 'blessed?' "—we find that the only person our author ever characterizes in his Socratic writings as blessed is Socrates, inasmuch as he led reading groups on great old books: *Memorabilia* 1.6.13.

We are obviously aroused to wonder what in the world Xenophon has his Socrates up to here, in this preposterous eulogy of the Persian despot as the model farmer for young Greeks like Critobulus and as the one who, in the eyes of the greatest living Greek republican leader, is the paragon of what it means to be justly happy as a good man. With a view to persuading Critobulus to consider taking up farming in Athens, this eulogy is plainly "over the top."[16] But how might this outlandish Socratic performance be the appropriate comedy with a view to provoking educative reflections in the minds of young Xenophon and the other friends who make up the audience?

Socrates, we submit (cf. XSD 113–20), is slyly suggesting that underneath the by no means superficial Hellenic-republican abhorrence of oriental despotism there is at work a half-conscious vector—of ambition for magnificent rule, and of admiration of prestigious grandeur—that points toward emulation of the Persian king (above all, the great Cyrus: consider again

*Education of Cyrus* 8.2.20–23) in his apparently splendid supremacy (consider Plato *Republic* 619b-c). This vector reveals itself in conventional gentlemanly disdain and in conventional gentlemanly magnificence[17]—and even in each conventional gentleman's household management, inasmuch as this ruling aims at ceaseless noble increase in material wealth and its attendant honor, including rule over ever more slaves. What's more, this vector is manifest even in the greatest Spartan, despite his being bred in a communal republican regime in which—at the opposite extreme from the Persian emperor—he is legally forbidden, even or especially when ruling, from increasing his household wealth in any way, especially by farming.[18]

In Xenophon's *Education of Cyrus*, and to some extent in his *Anabasis of Cyrus*, this vector is fully elaborated and subtly explored. It is not far-fetched to speculate that here in the *Economist* we may have a depiction of the sort of speech in which his teacher Socrates provoked or inspired Xenophon to undertake that at once imaginative and rigorous exploration.

Scholars have for generations been perplexed or shocked by the fact that Xenophon here presents Socrates confusing or blending Cyrus the Great with Cyrus the Younger—treating the two Cyruses as if they were the same—even while relating facts that indicate unmistakably the century and a half of temporal distance that separates the two Cyruses.[19] On the basis of what we have said in the preceding sections, the reason for this Socratic eccentricity is not, we believe, all that difficult to discern (cf. XSD 117–18): Xenophon thus lets us see that, however great the difference is between the two Cyruses when viewed from the perspective, or within the horizon, of political life and political economy, that real difference shrinks into insignificance when viewed from the Olympian heights of the perspective and horizon of the Socratic way of life and its peculiar mode and conception of truly scientific household management or political economy.

## FREE CITIZEN-FARMERS

Socrates now proceeded to exhort Critobulus to the farming life in a manner that paid due tribute to the excellence of the life of the independent Greek farmer or the "free human being" (*eleutheros anthropos*—5.11).[20] Surprisingly, Socrates started (5.2) not from what the Greek farmers do but from what the Earth (*Gē*) does for them: "in the first place, what humans get their living from, this the Earth bears, for those working—and, in addition, what they get pleasure from." In the second place (5.3), the philosopher credited the Earth with providing, along with most pleasant odors and sights, also that with which humans adorn altars and sacred statues,[21] as well as that with which they adorn themselves. No worship of divinities was ever mentioned in Socrates's lengthy display of the "farming" carried on by the Persian emperor.[22] By the same token, the exhortation to the farming life of the free, and its reiteration in 6.6–10, is unsullied by any profane oaths (there have been nineteen such profanities so far, three in the praise of Cyrus as model "farmer"). Xenophon has his Socrates indicate that pious religious worship, including divinization of the Earth, is a leading constituent of the farming life of the free Greeks. The Persian despot, in sharp contrast, absorbs to himself much of his slave-subjects' worship (see L. Pangle 2017). As Xenophon reports that he said to his Greek troops in the *Anabasis* (3.2.13): "the greatest witness to" the superiority of Greeks to Persians is "the freedom of the cities in which you were born and reared, for you prostrate yourselves before no human master but before the gods."

This opening also announces the fact that *pleasure* figures large in Socrates's praise of Greek farming.[23] There was almost no mention of pleasure in the account of Persian "farming" (except at 4.21–22); what was prominent in the latter account was the noble or beautiful or resplendent (*kalon*)—which is now eclipsed (Socrates, in contrast to Critobulus, here mentions the *kalon* only in characterizing a statement made by someone else: 5.17). In this vein, Socrates now spoke, in the third place, of the Earth's growing and raising those delicious morsels (*opsa*) that go with, or on, bread—including not least the meats, produced by "the skilled herdsman's art[24] connected to farming," which are consumed especially at feasts where humans offer sacrifices of domestic animals to propitiate the gods (5.3). Familial rural worship and the pleasures of communal dining (on flesh) go together.

"But while providing the goods without stint," the Earth "does not allow" humans to become soft in taking the goods; She "habituates them to endure the cold of winter and the heat of summer."[25] The Earth is presented as responsible for the regular alternation of the seasons—out of Her tough-loving concern to cultivate human endurance. Moreover, to "those who themselves work, with their hands," She gives "gymnastic exercise" that "adds to their strength," while "those who farm as supervisors" She "makes manly" (*andrizei*) by "getting them up early and compelling them to move around vigorously" (5.4).

With this last, mildly tongue-in-cheek praise of the Earth's habituation of the bosses to manliness, Socrates gently glided into the class distinction that pervades Greek society and that is most vivid in the military (cavalry vs. infantry)—a hierarchy that, with some irony, he treated as a matter of personal choice (and not directly supported by the Earth): "if one should *wish* to defend on horseback the city, then farming [not the Earth] very adequately helps to maintain the horse; if afoot, then it provides one a vigorous body." What the Earth "contributes"[26] is "something to increase love of toil in the hunts, both by providing easy food for the dogs and by helping with the parasitical[27] nourishment of the wild beasts/game" (5.5).

This sudden turn to hunting with dogs is puzzling. Given the context, Socrates seemed to be implying, without being able to bring himself to claim explicitly, that hunting with dogs contributes somehow to civic defense. As we learn from Xenophon's treatise on the subject, hunting with dogs was an activity whose worthiness was conventionally in doubt among non-Spartan Greeks and in need of considerable defense before the non-Spartan Greek public—a defense which Xenophon's treatise tries to provide (see XSD 201–2). Of course (5.6), "the horses and the dogs are benefited from the farming." But Socrates has to stretch to explain ways in which the horses and dogs prove themselves not to be parasitical—by "returning the benefit," if not to farming itself, then at least to "the countryside" (*chōron*). The benefits that Socrates said are provided by the dogs (but to what extent are these *hunting* dogs, and not, rather, sheepdogs and watchdogs?—XSD 202) are more impressive and widespread than the benefits he said are provided by the horses (which the majority of poorer farmers must do without, even as they are not so likely to hunt with dogs). Xenophon provokes us to wonder why he has Socrates impose upon himself the trouble of even mentioning the questionable practice of hunting with dogs. This question is intensified by the fact that the gentleman farmer Ischomachus will not say a word about the subject. The answer appears when we recall that in the *Memorabilia* (3.11.10–14; see also 2.6.9) Socrates understands himself, in comic allegory, to be a hunter with dogs. Is not this the aspect of the Greek farming life that he sees as most akin, at least allegorically, to an aspect of his own idiosyncratic—and publically questionable—way of life? Is Socrates thus obliquely indicating his own peculiar reason for preferring the Greek to the Persian farming: that the former is more conducive to Socratic-philosophic "hunting"?

However that may be, Socrates proceeded to speak more directly of how "the Earth also contributes something to stimulating the farmers to defend the land with weapons": She does this "by nourishing the crops in the open where they can be seized by the strong" (5.7). This somewhat ominous salute to the Earth's "tough love" was followed by a rhetorical question asking which art does a better job than farming at making men competent at running and throwing and jumping (5.8). (Would not the obvious answer be the art of war—at which Cyrus the Great was an indubitable expert teacher? See the *Education of Cyrus*.)

But this "intruding" by Xenophon of "reference to war" does not yet "shatter the idyll" (Pomeroy 255). For this rhetorical question proves to be the first in an anaphoric crescendo of such questions. The stress is (again) on the pleasures and welcome and ease that farming and also the countryside provide, along with the offerings and festivals for the gods—enjoyed not only by the yeomen and peasants, but also by their servants, wives, children, and friends (5.8–11).

Socrates then returned from the praise of human farming to the providence of divine Earth—now as educator. "In addition, the Earth, being a god,[28] teaches, to those who are capable of learning, also justice." The method of Earth's moral instruction is marvelously simple: "to those who serve Her best, She returns the most goods" (5.12). The Earth teaches *commutative-transactional* justice, or quid pro quo. We recall that Socrates had Cyrus the Great speak for, and had Cyrus the Younger viewed by Lysander as exemplifying, *distributive* justice—the more complex, intellectually demanding, and higher justice according to which honors and happiness are allotted in accordance with individual merit (4.16 and 25). Is the latter more at home in monarchic regimes than in republican?

However that may be, at this point Socrates suddenly drew, from Earth's education of Greek farmers to justice, a surprising inference. "Therefore, if (*Ean d'ara*[29]) those engaged in farming are driven off their land by a multitude" of invaders, then, if they are "intensely and courageously educated," being "well prepared in their souls and bodies," they are able to invade the enemy's land and seize what they need as booty—that is, "if a god doesn't prevent it." "And often," Socrates added, "in war it is safer to seek food with weapons than with the tools of skilled farming" (5.13—weapons are not among the tools of skilled farming). Socrates spoke as if the farmers' counterinvasion is derived from and legitimated by Earth's education in commutative justice. But is Earth also the god who might "prevent this"?—If She has not received what She believes is owed to Her? On the other hand, Socrates did not suggest that Earth intervenes in battle to give help to the Greek farmers who serve and learn from Her. Earth evidently expects human farmers to organize and to manage their collective military action all by themselves.

Accordingly, Socrates went on to say that "farming joins also in educating[30] as to how to give mutual aid" (yet another major aspect of justice—Bragues 2007, 17). For "it's necessary to go against enemies in war together with humans [not together with gods], even as laboring on the Earth is done together with humans." Anticipating what he will report that he learned from Ischomachus, and focusing on large plantation farms, Socrates declared that "the one who is going to practice farming well must make the laborers eager in spirit and willing to obey"; and these are "the very same things that the leader against enemies in war must contrive—by giving gifts to those who do what the good need to do, and by punishing the disorderly." Moreover, "the farmer often has to encourage the workers no less than the general does the soldiers." Last but not least, "the slaves need good hopes no less than the free, but even more, so that they'll be willing to stay" (5.14–16). But are the slaves armed and relied upon as warriors, except in emergencies, in the Greek cities? By the incongruity of this last sentence, Xenophon has his Socrates provoke thoughtful listeners to discern the important distinction—which he was playfully eliding—between leadership of slaves on a plantation and leadership of free men in battle. And with this, Xenophon provokes the questions: Is it so clear that managing farmhands, most of whom are slaves, teaches one how to lead free (or, for that matter, slave) troops in battle? Is there not a strong case to be made for the military superiority of the Persian system, separating the professional (slave and free-mercenary) military from the (slave) farmers and their administrators? Does the way of life of farmer-soldiers, spending most of their energies managing their individually owned farms, not incur a grave military price or risk? Is the happy mean to be found in Sparta—or in its improvement, the fictional regime of old Persia depicted at the outset of the *Education of Cyrus*? Or, has not the depiction here of Lysander, and the ease with which Cyrus, in the *Education of Cyrus* (1.5.8–14), was depicted corrupting the citizen-peers of Old Persia, thereby launching them on the path to world conquest, indicated even more vividly what I have called the Persian "vector" that lurks within all classical republicanism? We note that there is no discernible Greek "countervector," toward republicanism, within Cyrus's New Persian system (see the concluding chapter of the *Education of Cyrus*).

Once we recognize that Socrates's oratorical case for farming did not unambiguously establish the superiority of Greek independent farming, we are not so surprised to see that he concluded with an argument that supports and is supported by Persian-despotic farming as well. Socrates quoted and then elaborated someone else's "noble/beautiful" statement that "farming is the mother and nurse of the other arts" (5.17).

The speech that Xenophon has put in the mouth of Socrates has limned the pros and cons of the economic life at the base of each of the two most fundamental, adversarial, political alternatives—"the greatest things, freedom, or empire over others" (Diodotus in Thucydides 3.45.6). Each of the two poles of political life has been presented in its flowering. What is most remarkable and instructive about Socrates's praise of the life of free Greek farmers is his total abstraction from peacetime republican political participation.[31] This abstraction from civic freedom is spotlighted in the immediate sequel, by Socrates's extraordinary fibbing in his claims about what he had said in praise of Greek farming. Contrary to this subsequent claim, Socrates had in fact spoken in such a way as to bring out *not* the *civic* liberty, but what we may call the an-archic vector within the life of the "free human being" (*eleutheros anthropos*, 5.11), in contrast to the "free real man" (*andri eleuthero*, 5.1). Socrates portrayed in the yeoman farmer a vector of liberation from the city and civic life, with its contentious assemblies and courts, toward a rural or extra-urban, private, familial, and rather sensually hedonistic, even while hard working and pious, life. This is the life celebrated by Aristophanes, above all in the *Acharnians*. This is the life that Thucydides (bk. 2 beg.) shows the Athenian people were sorrowfully compelled to abandon under the pressure of Pericles's war defending the empire. Does not Socrates imply, among other things, that it is in the citizenry's republican ruling and being ruled that the ambition to rule, the drive toward imperialism, grows, or can start to pick up steam?

## CRITOBULUS'S TELLING OBJECTION

Critobulus reacted to the Socratic oration with rather perfunctory praise and then immediately expressed a weighty doubt—reminding us of the skeptical objection that Critobulus raised, and Socrates quite failed to dispose of, at the end of the first chapter (1.21). Critobulus pointed out that the happy picture Socrates had painted leaves out the catastrophes of weather, blights, and disease that render "most of what pertains to skilled farming impossible for a human to foresee" (5.18). The excessively blithe oration of Socrates would seem calculated to provoke such a challenge from any listener who is seriously pondering whether or not to take up independent farming.

Certainly Socrates responded (5.19–20) by finally admitting—or, more precisely, by claiming that he had been presuming all along that Critobulus knows—that it is not human rational expertise, but rather "the gods" who "are no less sovereign over the deeds in farming than over those in war." (The soft Critobulus had, characteristically, made no reference to war.) Socrates pointed out that one sees "those engaged in war, prior to their skilled acts of war, try to win over (*exareskeuomenous*) the gods and consult, by means of sacrifices and bird omens, as to what they ought to do and ought not to do." He then asked: "as regards skilled acts of farming, do you think it less necessary to appease (*hilaskesthai*) the gods?"—and concluded by positively affirming (only) that "those who are sensible (moderate) serve (*therapeuousin*) the gods" concerning "moist and dry crops and cattle and horses and sheep and all possessions" (for the reason why skilled warfare, more clearly than farming, requires consultation with the gods through omens, see the *Skilled Cavalry Commander*, esp. 9.8–9).

Critobulus, ignoring the subtle distinction in the Socratic formulation, praised Socrates for "speaking nobly, in urging that one try to begin every action with the gods, on the grounds that the gods are sovereign no less over the actions of peace than those of war"—and then Critobulus applied this supposed Socratic exhortation to the two of them: "so then let us try to do these things thus" (6.1). Critobulus is certainly more conventionally comprehensive in his piety than is Socrates here. He does not attend to Socrates's "intimation of" what he views as the theological (and psychological) "difference between the arts of farming and war on the one hand and all other arts on the other hand" (XSD 124). This exchange between Socrates and Critobulus brings out a major contrast between Socrates as presented here and as presented in the opening of the much more apologetic *Memorabilia* (1.1.6–9; XSD 125). As presented here, it is not clear that Socrates believes that he himself needs to consult, to appease, or to serve the gods—given that he does not ever in Xenophon's writings undertake to engage in either skilled acts of war or skilled acts of farming. We also note that there is no reference in the *Economist* to Socrates's reliance on his famous *daimonion*. Xenophon provokes us to wonder: What might Socrates have learned from listening to Ischomachus, or from observing the reactions of young men to whom he has told the story of his education by Ischomachus, that might have led him to such theological autonomy?[32]

## THE CONVERSION OF CRITOBULUS TO FARMING

After making normative what he takes to be Socrates's strong insistence on the need for pious deference to divinity,[33] Critobulus expressed some dissatisfaction with what had preceded. He asked the master to go back to the point at which he "digressed from household management" (*tēs oikonomias apelipes*) and to "try to complete the matters connected to" those that Socrates was speaking of when he digressed—"because I now seem to myself, after having heard what you've said, to perceive rather better than previously what ought to be done to earn a living" (6.1). Critobulus did not indicate at what specific point he thought Socrates had digressed; did he have in mind only the statement about piety? Or was the young man not somewhat bemused or even bewildered by the entire praise of farming that made the Persian emperor the leading model farmer? Wasn't Critobulus still expecting or hoping that Socrates would "display what he promised" (according to Critobulus—3.1): namely, experts in "what are opined to be the noblest of the sciences" (4.1) from whom Critobulus could "learn to be a terrific money maker" (2.18)? Or, might Critobulus have had the vague impression that Socrates started to digress early on, when he introduced new and strange divinities with his weird teaching on supposed evil "Masters" and "Mistresses"?—For from that point on (1.17ff.), much of what was said had rather invidious or discomfiting implications for the character and conduct of Critobulus and was not tightly focused on the science or art of skilled household management.

Socrates exploited the lack of specificity in Critobulus's request by suggesting that "first we go back over whatever matters we agreed on as went along, so that, if somehow we are able, we try thus to go through the rest in agreement" (6.2). We are not surprised to see that Socrates was aware of some considerable disagreements in the previous conversation. For his part, Critobulus, in assenting to the proposed review, compared what he expected would be their "dialogical" agreement with the "pleasure" that business partners find in agreeing on their monetary accounts: the young man seemed not to have entirely abandoned his hope for some sort of a business partnership with Socrates, or at least with some other expert whom Socrates would recommend.

Socrates gave a retrospective (6.4–10) that was an astoundingly arrant falsification[34]—though it started off in lulling fashion (6.4), by pretty accurately summarizing what was first agreed to about the science of household management (back in 1.1–15). After that, however, Socrates erased the remainder of the conversation prior to chap. 4 (thus removing the various pointers to the severe deficiencies of Critobulus). He lept to their agreement with "the cities" in disdain for artisans (6.5) but then dropped the extravagant and puzzling invocation of the Persian monarch as model farmer, and substituted a brand-new account of military and civic reasons that were supposedly elaborated to explain the conventional Greek disdain for handicraftsmen—now claiming that when enemies attack, farmers are more ready to abandon their lands and to man the defensive walls of the cities (6.6), and to "vote" (in the assembly) for war (6.7). In place of what he had actually said in praise of yeoman Greek farmers, Socrates invented a new praise of farming as most suitable for a leisured, upper-class gentleman. He claimed that he and Critobulus came, after investigation, to the conclusion (*edokimasamen*—see Holden ad loc.) that "for a gentleman, the superior work and science is farming": the reasons being that this seemed to be "easiest to learn,"[35] as well as "most pleasant to work at," while making "the bodies most beautiful and vigorous" and "providing souls with the least lack of leisure in which to join in attending to friends and cities." Finally, coming a bit closer to what he did actually say, Socrates added that "it seemed to us that farming also stimulates the workers to be brave, by growing and tending matters outside the walls." But then Socrates concluded with a stress on the specifically civic dimension of Greek life about which he had in fact been totally silent in his actual previous praise—circumscribing that silence by now proclaiming that "the farming way of life is held in highest repute in the eyes of the cities because it seems to provide *citizens* who are the best, and are best affected toward the *community*."

This radical revision or reinvention of the previous conversation is so congenial to the aristocratic, urbanized, but easy-going Critobulus (XSD 127) that whatever resistance he had had, on account of what was actually said, was dissolved, and he embraced farming as his planned new vocation. (One wonders how long this big plan will last!) If we consider the enormous contrast between this fictive Socratic invention of a conversation that pleases and wins Critobulus over, and the actual dialogue that Socrates had conducted with Critobulus, it becomes still more obvious that the purpose of Xenophon's Socrates in the previous parts of this dialogue had not been mainly the persuasion of Critobulus (Ambler 1996, 104)—who, we fear, had been a bit "used," as a character or butt of a comic drama that the onlooker young Xenophon was doubtless enjoying immensely, even as he was finding it intensely thought-provoking and instructive for himself.

But at this point it transpired that Socrates was not out of danger (doubtless adding to the young onlooker Xenophon's amusement). For Critobulus now indicated that he was so far from hoping or expecting that Socrates would bring him together with *other* experts in farming that he was thinking of Socrates himself as the expert, and, what is more, was thinking of undertaking farming as a *joint* venture *together* with Socrates. Showing that he too was capable of creatively reconstructing what was supposedly said, Critobulus declared: "but because you asserted that you had learned the causes why some farm in such a way that as a result they have from farming what they need in abundance, and why others toil in such a way that as a result farming is not beneficial to them [contrast 3.5–7], these things also I would in my opinion be pleased to hear about from you, in each case—so that the things good, *we* shall do, and the things harmful, *we* shall not do" (6.11).

Socrates once again eluded responsibility (Ambler 1996, 105), this time by ascending to a more dazzling theme and prospect (6.12). "What do you say if I go through, from the beginning, how I once came together with a real man (*andri*), who seemed to me to be in reality (*tō onti*) one of those real men (*andrōn*) to whom is justly applied the title by which a real man (*anēr*) is called 'a gentleman' ['noble-and-good'] (*kalos te k'agathos*)?"[36] Critobulus enthusiastically responded—in his final, somewhat poignant, words: "I would very much wish to listen thus, since I for my part passionately desire (*erō*)[37] to become deserving of this title!" To his credit, Crito's son knows himself well enough to be acutely aware that he fails to deserve this title; and this failure he feels to be so serious that it induces in him *eros* to become thus deserving. But does he truly understand what is the object of his *eros*—what is a gentleman?[38]

CHAPTER THREE

# Teaching Socrates How a Gentleman Educates His Wife

After Critobulus responded with a declaration of his *eros* for becoming himself deserving of the title "gentleman" (6.12), Socrates said that he would tell "how I came to the *investigation* of him/it."[1] The *eros* of Critobulus is replaced by the investigation of Socrates—or is not investigation the expression of Socratic *eros*? The use of the term "investigation" may well lead us to expect the sort of dialogic, refutative questioning or "dialectic" for which Socrates became distinctively famous (*Memorabilia* 4.4.9; Plato, *Apology* 21b–23c); but very little if anything of that kind ensues. In Ambler's (1996, 115) illuminating summary of the character of the conversation that Socrates now proceeds to report: it "shows [Socrates] to have been a patient listener and generally careful not to throw his interlocutor on the defensive"; "Socrates' conversation with Ischomachus is his longest conversation in all of Xenophon's works, but he speaks only slightly more than 25 percent of the lines," many of which "are more or less simple responses to Ischomachus' questions about farming"; and Socrates "never attacks directly the main content of Ischomachus' remarks." In short, "Socrates tactfully draws Ischomachus out in order to understand him better." Ambler pregnantly adds: "the converse is also worth noting: the gentleman makes no effort to learn about the philosopher."

## HOW AND WHY SOCRATES TURNED TO INQUIRY INTO THE NOBLE (*KALON*)

We are given an elliptically jocuse account of the perplexity that animated this "investigation." Socrates presents himself as having become puzzled by the meaning of the noble/beautiful (*kalon*), in its conjunction with the good (*agathon*), in the everyday Greek expression "noble-and-good" = "gentleman" (*kalos k'agathos*). Xenophon does not have his Socrates explain why, or on the basis of what reflections or experiences, this perplexity came to preoccupy him. We recall his earlier account (2.17) of a perplexity that made him turn to an extensive civic investigation (*episkepsis*)—whose successful outcome he immediately, and curiously, put into some question *theologically*. Now, Xenophon has his Socrates once again portray himself as someone who was, at the time of his perplexity-driven turn, radically aloof from and comically naive about ordinary life in the city (see again Plato, *Theaetetus* 173c–75b).

Socrates explains (6.13–14) that it took him only a short time to go around and to see with his own eyes the relation between the "goodness" of craftsmen or artists and what is held to be the "beauty" of their works (he speaks as if in his life previous to this, he had been amazingly ignorant of the arts). But this discovery and learning left him all the more eager to investigate whatever was the work done by those who came to deserve the "august" title "noble-and-good." His soul "very much desired" (*panu epithumei*—he does not speak of *eros*) to come together with such a person. But Socrates presents himself as having been ludicrously ignorant of how even to identify the kind of human in question. Socrates speaks as if he had never yet been together with a gentleman, so far as he knew, and certainly as if he did not think of his own friends and associates as gentlemen.

Socrates relates that his first foray was this (6.15–16): since in the expression "noble-and-good," the term "noble/beautiful" (*kalos*) was joined to the term "good" (*agathos*), and since beauty is strikingly visible, it would be most efficient to go up to anyone whom he *saw* to be a beauty[2] and to try "to learn" if he could "*see*" (*idoimi*) the goodness attached to the beauty. But Socrates says that he learned (he does not say in a short time) that this method would not work: "I seemed to learn that some of those who are beauties in their forms, are very depraved in their souls." Socrates presents himself as having had to learn that the relevant "goodness" is spiritual and therefore invisible. Does he present himself as having been originally a comically extreme materialist or corporealist?

Socrates says that he then made a momentous decision (6.16–17): "It seemed to me therefore that I should, disregarding the *sight* of the beautiful, go to one of those *called* 'noble-and-good' "; and "since therefore I *heard* Ischomachus *called* 'noble-and-good' by everyone—men and women, and foreigners as well as residents of the city—it seemed to me that I should try to come together with this man."

Xenophon has his Socrates present here a caricature of the philosophic turn by which the master founded political philosophy, as the investigation into the meaning of the noble/beautiful (*kalon*)—or what we may call "the moral." As with any expert caricature, much that might be troubling or even offensive, if it were revealed in a serious fashion, can thus be communicated safely, through good-natured lampooning or self-deprecation.

Xenophon allows us to see clearly at least this much: Socrates discovered that the *method of inquiry* into the truth about the nature of things that he had previously relied upon (as someone reputed to be "a *measurer* of the air": 11.3)—that is, reasoning on the basis of visible, material, and mathematically measureable evidence, verified preferably first-hand, and eschewing dependence on mere opinion or speech—was inadequate for inquiry into the truth about the noble/beautiful (*kalon*), for crucial aspects of the latter are accessible *only* through speech, orienting itself primarily by articulate opinion, and even common opinion, shared by "all men and women and foreigners and city residents."

This does not mean that Socrates describes himself as having abandoned learning through observation of deeds. For in telling how he met Ischomachus (7.1), Socrates begins by saying, "*Seeing*[3] him, then, one time sitting in the stoa of Zeus the Deliverer,[4] since he seemed to me to be at leisure . . ."—and then Socrates reports that he asked Ischomachus, addressing him by name, why he was sitting at leisure, since Socrates had previously "*observed*" that it was not characteristic of the gentleman to be thus at leisure and available for a conversational inquiry, rather than busily engaged in action—even or especially when he was in town (which is where, presumably, Socrates had been mainly observing the gentleman, not out on his farm). In other words, Socrates had already drawn from his *observations* (see also 11.20, 11.22) some important conclusions about the gentleman's way of life, in its radical difference from the philosopher's own (XSD 132; Kronenberg 2009, 54). It is also manifest, from the reported reply of Ischomachus, who addressed Socrates by name, that Socrates and Ischomachus had previously become acquainted and were on rather casual terms (consider OT chap. 3a, n. 4 and context), but it took unusual circumstances for Socrates to think that he could even attempt to carry on a dialogue with the gentleman.[5] In his reply, Ischomachus confirmed the conclusion of Socrates about the gentleman's way of life: "nor would you now (said Ischomachus), oh Socrates, see me, if I had not promised certain strangers to await them here" (7.2; see also 11.14–15). Ischomachus "belongs" elsewhere, not idly available in the *agora* for a long conversation with Socrates (consider OT chap. 5, n. 26 and context).

The very first of the noble deeds that Xenophon's Socrates has his audience hear about—from the gentleman himself—is the latter's keeping of his promise, even to strangers, even when doing so is inconvenient or an impediment to his regular gentlemanly activity.[6] Given the length of the conversation with Socrates that ensues, it becomes evident that the strangers "stood Ischomachus up" (XSD 131). But we never sense the urbane gentleman losing his patience, let alone hear him complaining.

Socrates reports that he initiated his dialogical inquiry by calling to witness, for the first time in this work, the gods in general,[7] and by asking Ischomachus how he normally spent his time—explaining that "I very much wish to learn from you whatever it is that you do, to be called 'noble-and-good.' "

Ischomachus responded, Socrates says (7.3), with a pleased laugh (evidently at what he viewed as Socrates's naive and rather flattering lack of decorum[8]), and then by modestly apprising Socrates of the fact that in the civic life of democratic Athens he was not given that honorific title, "noble-and-good," although he was regularly called upon to make enormous financial contributions. Thus the second, and more distinguishing, gentlemanly deed that Xenophon's Socrates has us hear about, from the gentleman himself, is his (unheralded) performance of civic magnificence, or the moral virtue of generosity on a large monetary scale—a peak virtue of Aristotle's *Ethics*, and a moral virtue in which (we have learned—2.5–7) Socrates took no part at all, even or especially after learning all about the virtue from Ischomachus.

## HOW THE SPOTLIGHT FELL ON THE GENTLEMAN'S EDUCATION OF HIS WIFE

Socrates says that he remarked to Ischomachus that he had observed from the condition of the latter's body that the gentleman did not spend his time indoors[9] and that this provoked Ischomachus to declare emphatically that he did "not *at all* spend time indoors," since "as regards matters within the house, the wife is very capable of managing by herself" (7.3: at the time of the conversation between Socrates and Ischomachus, the latter's wife had taken over singlehanded management, or rule, of all that went on inside the house—Pomeroy 19). Socrates says that upon hearing this, he immediately declared (7.4) how "very delighted" he would be to be told about the wife's education (*paideia*)[10] and, in the first place, whether Ischomachus "*himself* had done the educating of the woman" (*potera autos su epaideusas tēn gunaika*), or whether he had received her, from her father and mother, already "expert (*epistamenēn*) in the management of the matters proper to her."

Ischomachus had to inform the astonishingly ignorant philosopher (7.5–6) that of course a young Athenian bride was so far from being "an expert" (*epi-*

*stamenēn*) that she was raised in a way that prevented her from having been taught, or having learned, or even having inquired, *about anything*, except maybe sewing and spinning—though the gentleman did express satisfaction in his bride's having been "very nobly educated" (*panu kalōs pepaideumenē*) by her parents in controlling "matters of the stomach," which Ischomachus declared to be "the most important part of education for man and woman."

Xenophon's Socrates thus portrays himself as having been as unfamiliar with matters pertaining to women, marriage, and family as was the Socrates portrayed by Aristophanes; at the time of the initiation of his inquiry into gentlemanliness, Socrates had obviously not yet begun his association with Aspasia (recall 3.10–15). Still, Socrates had apparently started to move in that direction. For he depicts himself as having become *intently* concerned to hear how a gentleman educated the free young lady who was to be his partner in his noble household's way of life. Did Socrates perhaps have a practical-personal reason for his intense interest in this topic? Was the philosopher considering marriage for himself? Was he considering altering his previously independent or aloof philosophic way of life at least to the extent of embarking on the management or rule of a free female partner? In the *Symposium* (2.10), Socrates declares that he "acquired" his wife Xanthippe because he had come to "wish to make use of and to associate with humans" (there was a time when he had no such wish) and he reckoned that "if I endure her, I will easily get along with all the rest of humanity."[11] Socrates's marriage made his way of life start overlapping (if you will), in one major respect, with the way of life of the conventional gentleman. This gives a sharp new point of focus for the comparison and contrast between the two ways of life.

But did not the philosopher have a more prfound theoretical reason for his intense interest in hearing about the gentleman's education of his wife? For would not this be very revealing of the gentleman's guiding moral principles?[12] What is more, the rule of husband over wife is that part of household management that is most unmistakably the rule of the free over the free, and therefore, as Aristotle stresses,[13] may be taken (somewhat playfully) as *the* paradigm of republican rule. The paradigm works especially if one abstracts from the bearing and raising of children, or if one considers household management and the relation between spouses during the time when the wife has not yet become pregnant or brought forth any children—and that is the case with Xenophon's *Economist*: neither Critobulus nor Ischomachus are presented as having yet impregnated their wives, and the bearing and raising of children is (surprisingly and most thought-provokingly) never thematically discussed as a part of household management.[14]

## THE PRELUDE TO THE GENTLEMAN'S EDUCATION OF HIS WIFE

Socrates presents himself as having immediately discovered that he was even more ignorant than he had supposed he was, as regards a gentleman's rule over and education of his wife—and this as regards *the* most important matters! For when Socrates asked whether Ischomachus had not then educated his wife all by himself, the gentleman expostulated (7.7), "No, by Zeus!—not until I sacrificed, and prayed that I, in teaching, and she, in learning, would obtain the things best for both of us!" Socrates thus learned that the gentleman is keenly convinced that the outcomes of successful teaching of, and learning by, the free partner in his life are by no means intrinsically or necessarily or autonomously beneficial, without providential assistance and support from Zeus and other traditional divinities, in response to ritual sacrifice and prayer for help.[15] This absolutely essential prelude to teaching had not in the least occurred to Socrates.

When Socrates deferentially concluded (7.8), "so then the wife sacrificed with you and prayed the same things?" Ischomachus disclosed that his young bride, apparently without any prompting from him, solemnly promised in many ways, invoking the gods in general as witnesses, that she would become what she ought. The young lady was evidently under the strong impression that the conjugal duties she would be taught would by no means manifest themselves as always intrinsically pleasant or beneficial for her: she realized that her reliable performance of her wifely duties in such times required that those duties be made into solemn commitments to powerfully providential, sanctioning deities.

Socrates did more than take note of this pious initiative on the part of the young lady. Swearing himself by the gods in general, and asking the gentleman to go through the first thing that he taught his wife, the philosopher declared to Ischomachus that he would listen to the gentleman's report of his education of his wife with greater pleasure than if the gentleman were to give a report of the noblest sort of gymnastic or horse racing "contest" (*agōn* 7.9). Ischomachus did not pause to question this outré comparison. Why in the world should Socrates associate the gentleman's education of his wife with noble contests to win victory—and to avoid defeat? (Could one place a bet on the outcome of this education—on who was to win and who lose?) It is true that Ischomachus was prodded this much: to assure Socrates that he had not commenced the young lady's education until "she was accustomed to be managed/handled (*cheiroēthēs*) by me, and was tamed (*etetithaseuto*), so as to be able to enter into dialogue."[16]

## THE INITIAL STAGE IN THE WIFE'S EDUCATION

Socrates reports Ischomachus as having said that he began by asking his bride, "have you given thought to what ever could be the purpose of my taking you, and your parents giving you to me?" (7.10)—and then, without waiting a moment for any reply from her, launching into his own explanation.

As a preliminary, Ischomachus ruled out erotic love, doing so in a somewhat rough[17] male manner.[18]

Then Socrates reports the gentleman having declared to his young wife (7.11–12) that he for his own sake, and her parents for her sake, made their complementary choices after deliberating as to whom they might take as the best partner (*koinōnon*) in household, and also in children. But Ischomachus immediately set aside the children, declaring that "for now, indeed, what is common for us is the household." As regards children he noted only that "this also is a common good for us, that we obtain the best possible allies, and caretakers in old age," and for this reason, or with a view to this good shared by the two of them, "we *will* deliberate regarding how we will give them the best possible education"—but only if and when "a god grants that they come to pass for us." The gentleman sees children as an uncertain product of divine favor; he was not, however, moved to suggest that he and his wife pray for children. And Ischomachus did not at first mention to his bride what he soon was going to teach her to be the divinely planned purpose of children: preservation of the species. He at first spoke of children only as a common good for himself and his wife. Accordingly, he certainly did not speak of the household as being for the sake of the children. The gentleman as portrayed by Socrates does not live for the sake of his children; he sees the primary common good of free husband and free wife to be their sharing in the household itself, whether there be children in it or not.

Materially, the gentleman noted to his wife (7.13), he continuously contributes much more to this common good than she has done through her one-time dowry; but (Ischomachus magnanimously declared), rather than "calculate which of us contributes more" in *that* sense, "know well that whichever of us is a better partner is the one who contributes the more deserving things" (*ta pleionos axia*).

The response that Socrates has Ischomachus reporting his bride giving to this introduction (7.14) makes clear her ingenuous astonishment (and her acceptance, without a murmur, of the secondary status of children, as part of the couple's common good): "But what could I with you (she said) be capable of in action? What power do I have? Everything is in your power!"[19]—"Mother said that my task was to be moderate/sensible (*sōphronein*)."[20]

Socrates says Ischomachus reported that he answered his young wife by emphatically and vastly expanding, and by in effect making "gentlemanly," or equal to his own moderation, her conception of the "moderation" appropriate to her station (7.15): "Yes, by Zeus! Father said the same to me"—but "it belongs to the moderate/sensible (*sōphronōn*), both a man and a wife, to put their property in the best possible condition and in addition to make it increase, as much as possible, through noble and just means!"[21] When the young woman, in her unabated astonishment, asked if her husband really discerned something that she could do to help increase the household wealth (she did not repeat the gentleman's limitation—by noble as well as just means), Ischomachus replied with continued emphasis: "Yes, by Zeus! Try to do in the best possible way the things for which the gods have given you the natural power (*ha te hoi theoi ephusan se dunasthai*) and which the law joins in praising."[22] In the gentleman's teaching, as reported by Socrates, the dedication to increasing the household wealth within the limits of noble and just means[23] is closely linked with experiential belief in a supporting, divinely providential nature, seconded by the honor bestowed through the human law of nations (the unwritten, universal law that later came to be called the *ius gentium*—see also 7.30). In the gentleman's understanding, the noble and the just and the lawful, conceived primarily as limitations on and elevations of self-aggrandizement, do not stand alone. Divinity is experienced primarily as the transhuman support for human nobility and justice and law. Would it be idle questioning, or would it be essentially Socratic-dialectical, to inquire: Which is ultimately more important and fundamental for the gentleman (and why)—human lawful morality, or supportive natural divinity and what the latter bestows? Such inquiry is not carried out explicitly in the *Economist*.

When his bride, in her deepening wonderment, asked what these powers and functions of hers might be, Ischomachus proclaimed to her that she was to hold a position in the household like that of the queen or "leader"[24] in a beehive; and then he supported this proclamation by elaborating in an eloquent minioration his conception of the human couple's situation in a divinely designed nature.

## THE GENTLEMAN'S THEOLOGICAL TEACHING

The theology that Socrates now says the gentleman recalled laying out to his recent bride is a natural theology, not a revealed theology (Ambler 1996, 117): Ischomachus based his "opinion"[25] on no claims to communication from divinity through "omens, sayings, portents, or sacrificial victims," or through dreams, or visions, or answers to prayers, or guidance by any *daimonion*; nor did he invoke any priestly or poetic authority (contrast *Memorabilia* 1.1.3–4 as well as Plato's *Apology* 33c), or any divine law (contrast Sophocles, *Antigone* 450–57). By the same token, Socrates has the gentleman recall making no reference to Earth, or to Zeus, or to any other Olympian or infernal Greek god or hero or *daimon* (the divinities to whom the gentleman and his young wife had a moment ago presumably been sacrificing, praying, and vowing). The gentleman now broadened and enlightened very considerably his young wife's theological horizon. He situated marriage and its duties in a trans-Hellenic theology; he testified to a religious consciousness, and perhaps a religious experience, that can readily be conceived as acceptable to and articulated by reflective, somewhat enlightened gentlemen in any and every civilized age or culture.[26] This gentlemanly natural theology obviously foreshadows the natural teleotheology that the mature Socrates promulgated in various versions and venues.[27] Xenophon provokes us to wonder whether Socrates's later teleotheological teaching was not inspired, at least in part, by what he claims that he heard on this momentous occasion. Certainly, from listening to Ischomachus Socrates learned how very receptive gentlemen could or would be to a philosopher's naturalistic, trans-Hellenic teleotheology.

Socrates reports the gentleman as having started from a perspective that was as comprehensive as it was unmythical. He expressed his "own opinion" (*emoi dokousi*) that in animate nature as a whole "the gods too" have taken careful thought to putting together "this yoking called male and female" so that "it would be most beneficial *for itself* with a view to *its* community."

Yet the only specific benefit the gentleman adduced—procreation—he spoke of not as benefiting or perpetuating each sexual couple, or their own intimate community, but instead as perpetuating and thus benefiting the many species (*genē*); the couples might even appear to be only means to that divine-natural end (7.18–19).

And how could the gentleman, as a farmer, be unaware that many or most animals, especially herd animals, do not naturally live as couples (see 10.7)? "Ischomachus' gods of nature have ensured that male and female will come together; they have not, however, ensured that particular couples will stay together" (Ambler 1996, 120).

These grave difficulties or perplexities in the gentleman's vision of the divine-natural order were at least partly submerged when the gentleman quickly narrowed his focus from animate nature as a whole to the human couple: for, he said, in their case "at least" (*goun*), "the acquisition *for themselves* of caretakers in old age is provided" (7.19). Ischomachus refrained from indicating whether in his opinion this was a secondary, or only an incidental, part of the gods' universally planned arrangement of sexual procreation. Certainly, "the gods' first concern [species replication] can be satisfied even if" Ischomachus's and his wife's "children should neglect them in their old age" (Ambler 1996, 119). But what Ischomachus had stressed from the outset was the value for himself and his wife of divinely allotted children as allies and caretakers in old age (recall 7.12).

Socrates's narration has the gentleman ascending, in the third place, to what he said "clearly" (*dēlon*) distinguishes human life from the life of other animals (the gentleman does not see procreation as doing this so clearly): humans live not "in the open air," as do "the herds," but rather "with a need of roofs" (*stegōn deitai*)—"although" (*mentoi*) humans do also need outdoor work (specifically, ploughing, seeding, growing, and herding), as a means to acquiring and bringing in under roofs what is needed for human life. It is this that entails the sexual division of labor for humans. After we hear that Ischomachus added the consideration that care of the newborn children needs also to take place indoors, we begin to see more clearly how his oration was meant to prove to his wife that she should expect to be "leader" not only in, but of or over, the household (7.19–21). For the indoor, feminine works sound closer to being the realm of human *ends* than do the outdoor, masculine works, which sound more like the provision of *means* or material. Accordingly, the gentleman declared it to be his personal opinion (*hōs emoi dokei*) that "the god" (sing.—might Ischomachus speculate that the human realm is under the special care of a single one among the many natural divinities?) has "made the *nature* of woman for the indoor works and cares" and has "by *nature assigned* (*phusas prostaxai*) to her the indoor works," whereas Ischomachus opined only that the god has "prepared the body and the soul of the man to be *more able to endure* cold and heat and marches and military service" and so has "*imposed* (*epitaxen*—see also 9.9) on him the outdoor labors."[28] Similarly, Ischomachus taught that the god, in "knowing that He has instilled by *nature* in the woman, and has assigned to her, the care of the newborns, has also allotted to her greater love of the newborns." Ischomachus added that the god allotted more fearfulness to the woman because He knew that anxiousness aids her in her assigned function of guarding the things brought inside—whereas the reason why the god allotted more boldness to the man is because the latter's outdoor labor incurs the risk of needing to defend himself against unjust assault. As regards memory and attentiveness, the gentleman taught that the god equalized the sexes, such that (Ischomachus recalled saying to his wife) "you would not be able to decide which tribe, the female or the male, *gets the better* (*pleonektei*) in these respects." Similarly as regards self-control: "the god allowed to whichever one of the pair is superior, be it the man or the woman, to *get more from* this good"—so, in the gentleman's view, these virtues benefit primarily the perhaps somewhat competitive individual husband or wife, and only derivatively the couple as couple. Summing up, the gentleman recalled stressing to his young wife the complementarity of the "nature" of human male and female, for the greater benefit of "each" (*heautō*—not of "both"); and his having urged her to apply to their marriage his general teaching about the assignments given by "the god" (7.24–29).

Xenophon has Socrates provoke his audience to wonder: Was the gentleman's failure to articulate, in the divine scheme of nature, a clear place for himself and his own activity as the flourishing fulfillment of human nature—as the end or purpose of household management—due to a deliberate effort on his part to enchant his young wife with her status, by obscuring or diminishing his own? Or, was this indicative of a deep, existential unclarity in the gentleman's mind regarding the (divine and natural) purpose of his life and of the human household? Or some of both?

Socrates reports the gentleman recalling that he continued by teaching that law/convention (*nomos*) contributes important additional weight to the divinely natural plan (7.30–31). He said that he told his bride how the universal human *nomos* supplements the providential "partnership in children" with an additional, *conventional* "yoking" as well as "partnership." Above all, he told her how the *law* adds "praise" for fulfillment of the divine assignments (the gentleman does not look for praise from *natural* divinity; recall 7.16); indeed, he went on to teach that "the law shows forth as noble/beautiful those things that the god has by nature made each more capable of." The gentleman's silence here about the city's gods, about the gods of the poetic tradition, about Zeus and his entire Olympian regime, as well as the infernal deities—about the gods to whom he and his wife previously sacrificed and solemnly swore oaths—is remarkable, and puzzling, and may well betray the gentleman's own puzzlement or uncertainty as to the overall structure of the pantheon. This much is clear: the gentleman sees the noble or beautiful (*kalon*) entering through law or convention, as an essential supplement for (and thus not spontaneously present in) the divinely planned order of *nature*. Here too, however, the gentleman circumscribed a slight but significant legal-conventional distinction between the sexes: while for the woman, the law "makes it nobler [more beautiful] to remain indoors rather than spend time outdoors," for the man, the law "makes it more shameful [ugly] to stay indoors rather than to take care of things outside." Socrates has Ischomachus thus expressing to his wife an awareness that both the *nomos* and providential nature contend, not altogether successfully, with some recalcitrant male humans who succumb to an attraction to staying indoors and to doing indoor work—who do not find outdoor male work (with its previously noted risks and endurances) sufficiently attractive. Is this because such men, in some cases at least, have much more attractive indoor activity? Socrates reports Ischomachus telling him that he went on to spotlight such men: "if someone acts against what the god [sing.] has made natural, *perhaps* in bringing about some disorder he does not escape notice of the gods [pl.] and pays a just penalty for neglecting his own work or doing the work of the woman" (7.30–31; could "the gods" in this statement be Zeus and the Olympians? Could Ischomachus conceive them to be the not-altogether-reliable "enforcers" of the design of the god of nature?). This warning about men who stay indoors and neglect their outdoor work or do the work of the woman was a singularly inapt pronouncement with which to culminate the gentleman's first educative address to his young bride, about *her* role! Could Xenophon's Socrates be presenting Ischomachus as having been thinking, for a moment at least, of what he had heard or gathered about the unmanly, indoor (*phrontisterion*) way of life of his interlocutor Socrates? Is Ischomachus presented here as injecting a gentle admonition to his odd philosopher-student?[29]

## THE GENTLEMAN'S INITIAL TEACHING ON RULING AND BEING RULED

Socrates has Ischomachus report that when he referred again to his likening of his wife's role to that of the bees' leader (now understood as appointed by "the god"), the young lady expressed her continuing wonder at the comparison.[30] This prompted her husband to give a (rather wondrous) elaboration: the queen bee is to serve as model not only in that she supervises the indoor work, and cares for the upbringing of offspring, but that "while remaining within the hive, she does not allow the bees to be idle, but sends out to their jobs those who should work outside," and knowingly receives and saves, until needed, their products—in the timely use of which "she distributes what is just, for each"; "and when the young are raised and capable of work, she sends them out as a colony, under some leader of them, as followers" (7.33–34).

The young lady's astonishment understandably grew. "For me, then (said the wife) it will be necessary to do *these* things?!" (7.35). It is not yet clear whether she was speaking in uneasy or in pleased anticipatory wonder.

Socrates has the gentleman recount how he responded by explaining to her that while remaining indoors, she was indeed to send out the farm servants, and to supervise the indoor servants, and also to look after the reception and expenditure and distribution of the inflow so as to insure an annual favorable balance, while seeing to it that the needed clothing was made and the grain kept in good condition. Ischomachus added—perhaps consciously or unconsciously drawing attention away from some obvious big questions that all this might provoke about his own place in the rule in the household—that there was one responsibility that he feared might seem to his young wife rather disagreeably thankless (*acharistoteron*): she must, he told her, care for any and all of the servants who become ill, male as well as female (7.35–37).

The gentleman could not have been more wrong about his wife's reaction to this last. For Socrates has him relating that it elicited from her a burst of enthusiasm. Swearing the manly-profane oath "By Zeus!"[31] she said this would be "most agreeable" (*epicharitōtaton*), if or since "those who are going to be nobly cared for will feel gratitude and will be more well-disposed in mind than before!" (7.37). The young lady gave evidence of having a taste for—she foresaw gratification in—nobly generous rule inducing good will in the ruled. Such rule no doubt appeared to her as contrasting vividly to the status of being ruled that she had herself always before experienced in her loving parents' home: consider here *Memorabilia* 2.1.10.

Socrates has Ischomachus report that he responded, "in pleasant amazement at her answer," by asking if it wasn't on account of "such forethought on the part of the leader in the hive" that "the bees are so disposed toward her that when she departs, not a single one of the bees thinks he ought to remain, but all follow?" (7.38). This, Socrates says the gentleman told him, provoked his wife's first (quite understandable) demurral: "I should be amazed (she said) if the deeds of the leader [masc.] were not your affair rather than mine." But when the young lady added her reason, it was evident that she was quickly learning to welcome the very considerable scope of her future authority and importance: "for my guarding of the things inside, and my distribution" (she dropped any mention of the *justice* of her distribution) "would be something laughable, I think, if you for your part did not take care that something would come in from the outside!" (7.39). To say the least, this formulation does not provide unambiguous grounds for the husband's supreme leadership in the household (Ludwig 2010, 86). But this formulation was not in disaccord with her husband's previous teaching—except that all reference to divine providence, natural or traditional, was dropped, along with all reference to justice; this despite the fact that the young lady had so intently invoked the gods and their sanctions for her performance of her duties at the outset (7.8); but that was prior to hearing her husband's teaching, which had in the meantime made her (ruling) duties unexpectedly attractive and imposing.

Perhaps because he sensed that he was at some risk of cutting the ground out from under his authority as husband, the gentleman (in Socrates's telling) gave a reply that took a big step back from his beehive analogy. He dropped his previous reference to his wife's administration of distributive justice, and spoke only of how laughable a sight his outdoor work would become if "there were not *someone* who saved the things brought in" (yes, but need this "someone" be a wife? Had not "someone"—probably a slave stewardess—been doing this in the years during which Ischomachus had been unmarried?). To bring home how fruitless his outdoor work would become without an indoor storage manager, Ischomachus invoked as an analogy the pitiful condition of those proverbially said to draw water in a perforated jar (7.40). This image rendered his wife's future role still more unclear.

Her response—the last response Ischomachus is said to have reported from her to this primary stage of his teaching—was very brief but poignant: swearing again by Zeus, in manly-profane fashion, she declared that "they are even miserable, if they do this!" (7.40). The image of water carriers is very likely to have reminded the young woman of onerous, conventionally feminine, household duties that she had been compelled to perform as a daughter: "carrying water was usually a woman's chore."[32]

Socrates has Ischomachus switching to a cheerier note, telling his young wife about other future responsibilities that he supposed would be pleasant for her: she would transform those who are ignorant of household tasks into knowers, thereby making them double in value "to *yourself*"; she would reward "by *yourself*" those who are moderate and beneficial to "*your* household," while she would "by *yourself* be able to punish anyone who appears wicked."[33] But "the most pleasant of all" would be "if you are manifestly better than me" and "for *yourself*[34] make me your servant": thus "you" would "not have to fear that as you age you will become more dishonored in the household" but instead may trust that, "by becoming better as a partner for me and as a guardian of the household for the children, you will be more honored in the household." "For" (Socrates has Ischomachus reporting that he continued) "the gentlemanly/noble-and-good things (I said) increase for humans in life not through youth's bloom but through the virtues" (7.41–43). The peroration of the gentleman's primary teaching of his wife thus continued to leave cloudy or even questionable his title to lead or to rule the household, over and above his wife and partner, if and when she acquired the virtues and, through them, the "gentlemanly things." In educating his young subordinate to gentlemanly rule, the gentleman ruler would seem to have been unwittingly creating a potential rival and even a replacement.

Also rendered somewhat nebulous, by the gentleman's last statement as narrated by Socrates, was his conception of the precise relation between the virtues, on one hand, and the gentlemanly (noble-and-good) things on the other. He surely did not mean that the former are only or simply means to the latter. But precisely what *did* he mean by the latter? Did he not mean virtuously prosperous rule, through which the virtues are put into honored or even glorious action and thus most felicitously realized and most fruitfully enjoyed? As such, to what extent do "the gentlemanly things" constitute a/the *common good* between a gentleman and his wife—or, for that matter, among gentlemen? Are they more coherently understood as the prize an individual wins in a common *competition*? Consider *Memorabilia* 2.6.16–28. Has this question been faced by the gentleman? What would happen if Socrates made him face it? What happens to Xenophon or to other alert and thoughtful members of Socrates's audience when *the* Socratic discourse makes *them* see the need to face, by and for themselves, this question about the common good?

## THE FIRST PART OF THE GENTLEMAN'S TEACHING ON ORDER (AND DISORDER)

Ischomachus's failure to report any response from his young wife is underlined, and even rendered ever so slightly ominous, by the fact that Socrates reports that he had to ask (presumably after a pause) whether Ischomachus "had noticed *any sign* that she was moved, on account of the preceding, more toward responsible care (*kekinēmenēn mallon pros tēn epimeleian*)?" To this rather surprisingly skeptical question, Socrates has Ischomachus replying with startling brusqueness: "Yes, by Zeus!" (8.1)—and then immediately transitioning to another subject (XSD 140). A profane expletive in reply to a question, followed by a change of subject, may well signal a desire not to be pressed further about the (touchy) matter being interrogated. Could it be that the manner in which the young lady responded, in taking over responsibility for the household, was not entirely pleasing for the gentleman to recall or to report?

In any case, what Socrates has Ischomachus proceed to recall with enthusiasm is his teaching on order (and disorder)—a subject about which Socrates depicts himself as not having asked, but which we soon see is of very lively concern to the gentleman. The occasion was an incident in which his wife, while blushing intensely, could not deliver up to him something that had been brought inside and that he was asking for (she was now in charge of the household items). Ischomachus immediately assumed that her deep blush indicated that she was "vexed" and "discouraged" by her having lost track of the item. (The gentleman of course did not for a moment entertain the possibility that her blushing might signal something less candid, but we for our part cannot avoid recalling that Socrates had the young lady—like Socrates himself when he later taught Critobulus—drop or ignore her husband's insistence that one should increase one's property only by noble as well as just means.)[35]

Socrates narrates how Ischomachus magnanimously comforted his wife by himself assuming the blame, for having failed "to provide the order" when he handed over to her the placing of each thing where it needed to be (8.2). He proceeded to deliver a monologic lecture on the importance of order (*taxis*) in general and, in that light, on the importance of an orderly arrangement of the household possessions so as to have them ready at hand. Socrates does not have Ischomachus report a word of question from, or back and forth dialogue with, his wife during this lengthy monologue (XSD 140), but Socrates has him conclude by saying, "as regards the ordering and use of implements, I seem to remember having *carried on a dialogue* with her in such terms" (*toiauta autē dialechtheis*—8.23, repeating what he had said at 7.43). Does Socrates picture Ischomachus as so transported by his warmth in recalling for and to Socrates his "dialogue" on order that he "edited out," as unnecessary interruptions, his wife's questions or responses? Does Socrates prompt his audience to wonder whether the young lady might not have asked some troubling or difficult questions that Ischomachus preferred not to recall?

Socrates tells how Ischomachus reported that he began his "dialogue" by proclaiming that "there is nothing, oh wife, so usefully good or so beautiful for human beings as order!" (8.3; the stress on human beings circumscribes Ischomachus's very surprising, utter failure to refer to divinity or to the natural teleotheology that he previously taught). What the gentleman first emphasized was order's beauty rather than its utility, or more precisely the displeasure of contemplating ugly disorder in (nonutilitarian) motion vs. the gratification of contemplating order in such motion: his leading illustration was witnessing a dancing and singing chorus—which, he rather oddly stressed, is "composed of human beings."[36] When he turned in the second place to adduce, much more elaborately, the example of ordered motion of an army, he continued to stress the gratification (and unease) afforded *onlookers*. He characterized an army's disorderly marching as "for enemies easy to handle, but for friends most inglorious to behold," as well as "most useless"—for if disordered, "how could they proceed?" and if the army "should also have to fight, how would it fight in that condition?" On the other hand, he declared that "many hoplites proceeding in order" and "cavalry proceeding in ordered ranks"—"all marching calmly in unity"—are "most beautiful to behold for friends, and most disagreeable for enemies" (8.3–7).

Ischomachus said almost nothing about an army putting its order to use in actually fighting a battle, parallel to a chorus actually performing.[37] And when Ischomachus adduced as his third paradigm a warship, "full of humans," he again made no mention of a warship putting its order to use in actually fighting a naval engagement.[38] Did he avoid reference to battle because he felt that the deadly horror of the disorder in which battle order culminates was inappropriate for a speech to his young wife? But then why in the world did he get involved in expatiating on military order, in a speech to his sheltered young wife about her indoor household affairs?![39] The answer is not hard to figure out. Military discipline, essential to warding off, while inflicting, the terrible chaos and death of defeat, is naturally the order (and disorder) whose urgent necessity and importance is uppermost in, not to say haunting, the male citizen-soldier's mind (see also 20.6–9). So: Is not the gentleman's silence about the tenuous order of armies engaging in actual battle caused by the fact that, even or especially for Ischomachus as a citizen-soldier, who is naturally preoccupied with his city's militia and naval discipline, the gruesome carnage that is the goal of all armies and navies in their battle-order is something about which he both thinks and does not want to think? To put it another way: Socrates portrays the gentleman as having praised humanly constructed order against the somewhat veiled but still visible backdrop of a looming, terrible disorder that the human order strives to anticipate and to control or to prevent.[40]

Certainly, when Ischomachus proceeded next to impress upon his wife the meaning of disorder, he abruptly dropped all reference to the military, and rather cheerily illustrated disorder by an example lying as far as possible from the battlefield (8.9): he portrayed a preposterously stupid farmer making a disastrous blunder in the storage of his grain, mingling different species, which required him to engage in a risible task of "dialectical" separation (*dialegein*) of the grains one by one.[41] On the basis of this comic image, Ischomachus addressed his wife directly once again, now focusing on the *usefulness* of order rather than on the pleasure of beholding its *beauty*: "And you, therefore, wife, would not be in need of such confusion, and [if][42] you would wish to know how to manage the belongings [things-that-are, *ta onta*][43] with precision, and to lay hold easily of whatever item of the belongings [things-that-are, *tōn ontōn*] you need to use, and to give in a way that gratifies me if I ask for something, let us select with care the place that is fitting for each (*chōran tēn prosēkousan hekastois*), and setting it in that, let us teach the maid servant (*tēn diakonon*)." In that way, the gentleman said he continued, "we will know the belongings [things-that-are, *ta onta*] that are saved and those that are not—for the place itself will be longing (*pothēsei*) for that which is not [the not-being, *to mē on*]."[44]

Immediately after having had Ischomachus thus enunciate this flurry of references to *ta onta* (and *mē on*) in the context of stressing the utility of order, Xenophon's Socrates has the gentleman do something quite startling. Suddenly—as though carried away by his theme of order and its beauty as well as utility—the gentleman temporarily left behind the account of his education of his wife and, instead, delivered a brief and pointed didactic monologue directly to the philosopher:[45] "but it was my opinion that I saw the most beautiful and most precise order of equipment once upon a time, oh Socrates, when I went onto the great Phoenician ship[46] to take a look; for I beheld a very great amount of equipment set in distinct places in a very small containing area" (8.11). After sketching the details of the big ship's marvelous ordering of implements, Ischomachus added that the pilot's mate—"he is called," Ischomachus informed his fellow landlubber Socrates, "the prow-man of the ship"—knew so perfectly where each thing fitted that he could tell you even when he was away from the ship, just as "the knowledgeable grammarian would say of the name 'Socrates' both how many letters it has and the ordering of each" (8.14). But it turned out that this last, quietly harmonious, spelling analogy was somewhat of a disanalogy. For Ischomachus, in Socrates's telling, went on to confess that he had been surprised to see the "prow-man" spending his "leisure time" inspecting everything on the big ship; and when the gentleman asked the prow-man what he was thus doing, the Phoenician—addressing his Greek-landlubber questioner as "stranger"—informed the gentleman that there was urgent need for such constant supervisory inspection because the marvelous order is by no means self-sustaining. Things go missing; things get awkwardly situated. And this is very dangerous because, "when the god raises a storm in the sea," there is no time to search for what is needed, or to get out something that is awkwardly placed. "The god threatens and punishes the lazy!" In fact, continued the boatswain, "if He only does not destroy those who have done nothing wrong," it's a godsend,[47] and "if He saves those who have very nobly served, much gratitude (he said) is owed the gods" (8.15–16).

The expert mate is portrayed as evidently conceiving of his own and his fellows' careful and industrious seamanship as pious, humbly devoted service to frightening divinity—which holds out to those who thus devotedly serve it a hope for, but not a guarantee of, salvation, in the terrible tests unpredictably imposed by the divinity. This "shocking or savage" (XSD 162) theological teaching of the pious barbarian boatswain (who of course did not voice any profane expletives) goes far beyond the allusions to the background of fearful military disorder that we discerned in the gentleman's previous paean to order; nevertheless, the gentleman, in reporting the theological pronouncement of the Phoenician to the philosopher, "finds no fault with it" (XSD 142 and 162); the gentleman is portrayed as having indelibly remembered this theological teaching, and as having been moved to interrupt his account of his education of his wife in order to convey it to Socrates—but not, it would seem, to his wife. To her, the only theology Ischomachus seems portrayed by Socrates as having conveyed was the one he previously sketched, about divinity's purposefully beneficial ordering of all animate and especially human sexual nature. It is amazing that in his speeches on order to his wife and to Socrates, Ischomachus made absolutely no reference to that naturalistic teleotheology that he had previously laid out for his wife. Indeed, his lecture on order makes no reference whatsoever to nature (XSD 152). Ischomachus shows "in the section on order that men can and to some extent even must improve on nature" (XSD 156). And "in the whole chapter, order is not presented as in any way rooted in something divine; it is presented rather as being altogether of human origin; the gods are mentioned only as disturbers of order" (XSD 143). It is as if the gentleman's earlier venture into naturalistic teleotheology became eclipsed by his recalling the impression made on him by the pious barbarian's "shocking or savage" theology—and perhaps by a certain profound affinity of that barbarian theology with the Greek city's belief and worship, and the accounts given by the Hellenic poets (above all Hesiod) in their inspired singing about Dionysus and Zeus and Ares and Hera and Eros and Chaos, not to mention even worse divinity that was revealed by the Muses to Hesiod.

Socrates has Ischomachus returning to his report of his educative lecture to his wife by saying to Socrates that it was the "seeing of this precision" of order on the large Phoenician ship (Ischomachus does not refer to what he heard the boatswain say about divinity and humanity's relation to divinity) that led him to say to his wife the following: "it would be very lazy of us if those in ships [pl.], which are *small*, find places, and, when strongly tossed about, nevertheless preserve the order, and even when terrified nevertheless find what they need to take," while we, "with *large*, separate storage chests in the house for each thing, and a house firmly seated on land, fail to find a beautiful and easily located place for each thing!" (8.17; the fact that the *large* Phoenician ship is such an apt example of the ordering of implements, and Ischomachus is teaching his wife about the ordering of implements, makes it all the more striking that Ischomachus did not tell his wife about his visit to that very large ship,[48] let alone about his dramatic encounter with that ship's boatswain and his theology).

Socrates has Ischomachus then signal a turning point in his lecture to his wife. Declaring that the goodness, advantage, and ease of ordering the implements of the household had been stated, the gentleman burst into a rapturous salute to the beauty of the appearance of that order—this despite the fact that he had by no means previously focused exclusively on the useful goodness of order but had already stressed the beautiful appearance of order. Nevertheless, Ischomachus was apparently sure that he had yet to do full justice to the beautiful appearance of distinctly ordered placement of household implements, and he proceeded to wax eloquent on this theme, using the word for "beautiful" (*kalon*) no less than ten times in as many lines (8.19). Ischomachus is presented by Socrates as having an enthusiast's appreciation for the beautiful appearance of distinctly ordered human implements—even or especially the humblest, and this as regards not least what he called the "gracefully rhythmic"[49] and "well-distinguished" (*eukrinōs*) placement of pots. Ischomachus was aware that this last would provoke laughter from "one of your elegant wits" (*kompsos*)[50] but not from "one of the august" (*semnos*—like Ischomachus himself).[51] Indeed, it was "from this" that he concluded that "all other things" (he seemed to mean things of human art, not nature) "manifest themselves as more beautiful when they lie placed according to adorning order (*kata kosmon*)." He declared that each sort of implement when arranged in orderly distinctness appeared as a chorus—like the beauty of a circular (i.e., Dionysian dithyrambic) chorus surrounding the beautiful "purity" of the space left vacant by the precisely situated members in their choreographed dance arrangements (8.20).

Then, as if he detected some doubt in his wife, Ischomachus said: "But if these things I am saying are true, it is possible (I said), O wife, to make trial, without suffering some penalty or undergoing much labor." He concluded by reassuring his wife as to the ease with which they could find servants who could learn where each thing belongs—pointing to the facility with which her servants were able to locate what she ordered them to buy from the market (she had already taken charge of purchases). In an odd addendum, the gentleman ended on a note of disorder—remarking with some chagrin that since the individual human beings in the city have no assigned place, it is not so easy to succeed in locating them when one needs to. Only for very brief times, in Dionysian choral worship, are (a few of) the citizens well-ordered in place, according to the frustrated gentleman (8.21–23).

## THE SECOND PART OF THE GENTLEMAN'S TEACHING ON ORDER (AND DISORDER)

Once again, Socrates portrays himself as having had to ask the gentleman how successful his attempt to teach his young wife actually was—and once again, Socrates has himself phrasing his question in surprisingly skeptical terms: "And so what, then? Did the lady seem to you (I said), Ischomachus, *in any way* (*pōs ti*)[52] to pay heed to the matters about which you were so seriously teaching her?" Socrates makes it sound as though he continued to have doubts about the young lady's docility—as well as about her sharing in her husband's very earnest enthusiasm for order. The reply Socrates ascribes to Ischomachus is somewhat ambiguous: "she was promising, at least, to take care; and she was manifestly strongly pleased, as if she had found a good way out of a dilemma—and she beseeched me to bring about the distinguishing order as I had described, as quickly as possible" (9.1).

Socrates says that when he then asked Ischomachus how he had brought about the distinguishing order for his wife, Ischomachus explained that he first showed her the capacious design of the house—which, he stressed to Socrates (addressing him by name), was not ordered/adorned (*kekosmētai*) with decorations but constructed with a view to making the rooms "most advantageous as receptacles" (9.2). As we listen to the gentleman's elaboration of his home-architectural principles, we see that Xenophon's account in the *Memorabilia* (3.8.8–10) of what Socrates later taught as principles of "beautiful" house building follows in some measure Ischomachus's teaching[53]—except that the philosopher stressed much more the importance of affording beautiful pleasure to the inhabitants, and did not at all share the intense concern of the gentleman to have the sleeping quarters of the slaves locked down in sexual segregation so as to enable the master and mistress to bring order to *eros* or to the "making of children" (9.5; XSD 146–47).

Having completed his explanation of the utilitarian design of the house, Ischomachus proceeded with his young wife to "separate the articles according to tribes." They began with a fundamental distinction that would have been approved by the pious boatswain: grouping together all the diverse items used in sacrificing to the gods (9.6). In Socrates's account the careful separation between pious and profane is foremost in the gentleman's conception of household order.

Secondly, keeping to the same sense of priority, they set apart the wife's adornment for religious festivals, and the man's clothing for those festivals—and for war (for a man, the activities of worship and war have some crucial affinity: for an elaboration of the reasons, see the *Skilled Cavalry Commander*).

They then proceeded to divide other cloth items along lines governed by function and by the sex of the users: bedding for females, and then for males; shoes for females, and then for males. Skipping to utensils, Ischomachus recalled that they separated first the "tribe" of weaponry, then the tribes of tools for spinning, for bread making, for cooking, for kneading dough, and for table service. He recalled that they then made a cross-cutting dichotomy of "all these" utensils, into (1) those "needed all the time" (*aei dei*) and (2) those associated with religious festivals (9.7).

After also setting apart the monthly from the annual disbursements, they carried each separated "tribe" of their belongings to its fitting place (9.8).

Does Socrates represent Ischomachus as having *forgotten* to say that he and his wife set apart male and female clothing for *daily* use? *Or* are we perhaps to understand that the gentleman regarded those two "tribes" as unworthy of mention after the setting apart of religious and war clothing, and of weaponry?

Some of the weaponry, Ischomachus indicated, is "needed at all times": the threat of violence is never far from the pious gentleman's life and consciousness; after all, he lives surrounded by robust and sexually frustrated male slaves.[54] Here again we see that order is brought about against a background of frightening disorder, and of intense attentiveness to traditional providential (protective) deities.

If we step back and survey the theological-cosmological-ontological implications of the gentleman's unfolding thus far of his education of his wife, we observe the following movement. Socrates has Ischomachus begin by leading his wife in sacrificial, prayerful, conventionally ritualistic imploring of providential help from the traditional civic deities. Ischomachus is then shown striving to educate his wife in his own rationalistic, humanly beneficial teleotheology of nature, which ambiguously transcends, without replacing, the traditional, lawful Greek deities. But, when the gentleman is portrayed turning to his teaching on order and disorder, of *ta onta*, this natural teleotheology is not sustained; it seems, so to speak, evaporated by the friction and heat of humanity's desperate struggle to forge and to maintain beautifully artful order as a way of contending with a reality whose underlying, ugly disorder in motion makes more plausible the rule of and by a frighteningly mysterious divine willfulness. The latter becomes only somewhat less alien when it is worshipfully experienced in Greek festivals, including beautifully ordered (Dionysian) choral worship, to which Ischomachus is shown returning emphatically when he actually orders *ta onta*.

Xenophon thus has his Socrates make as stark as he can the fundamental, confounding ontological perplexity and hence theological challenge that Socrates, in part by listening to the gentleman, came to understand philosophic rationalism and naturalism as such to be up against. The question is thus provoked: How if at all does the Socratic transformation of the philosophic life (the turn to political philosophy or to the study of the gentleman) *dispose* of this challenge—the challenge of the possible reality of profoundly alien, willful, suprarational, nonorderly, ruling divinity? How does Socratic political philosophizing go beyond merely recognizing and acknowledging the awesomeness of the challenge? The next topic that Socrates presents is the gentleman recalling and explaining—in a notable digression—how he and his wife selected their chief subordinate and then educated her in the moral virtues, above all justice. Is this digression, which occurs at almost the exact center of the *Economist* as a whole, a pointer to the answer?

A more obviously intelligible answer is given by the teleotheology adumbrated by Socrates in the *Memorabilia* (especially 1.4 and, more anthropocentrically-exoterically, 4.3): a cosmic divine "economy" or "household management" (*oikonomon* 4.3.13) intended to benefit mankind, which purportedly becomes evident to the philosopher through interpretation of empirical observations of meteorological phenomena and of animal, including of course human, nature. These passages in Xenophon became the well springs of a great tradition of teleological natural science.[55] Does not Xenophon signal that Socrates achieved a "piety which emerges out of the contemplation of nature and which has no necessary relation to law" (OT chap. 7, para. 3), and that Socrates did so by working out a cosmology of intelligent design that was a far more adequate and convincing version of the gentleman's ultimately rather frail and fumbling attempt—an attempt that nonetheless provided the inspiration for the Socratic achievement?

But does the Socratic teleological cosmology overcome the difficulties indicated here in the *Economist*, where, "in the section devoted to 'order,' there is" found "even less support for the teleotheology than before?" It has been suggested,[56] following the playful spirit of Xenophon, that Ischomachus's "separating his indoor things according to tribes in order to establish order within his house reminds us of" Socrates's "dialectics," by which the founder of political philosophy is seen to be "attempting to discover the order of the whole by distinguishing the kinds of beings that make up the whole and by finding out what each of the kinds is"—"forcing us to wonder whether" Ischomachus's "separating his indoor things according to tribes is not the model for the peculiarly Socratic philosophizing." To be sure, this suggestion is all a "deliberate exaggeration," since "every child can see the difference." Most massively and obviously, the "order according to tribes" that Ischomachus teaches his wife is an order "among artifacts" and an expression of artfulness or *technē*—an emphatically human, not a divinely teleological, artfulness. But could this be a serious (if exaggerated) clue to an important dimension of the Socratic "forms"? We are reminded of a crux statement of Aristotle: "it is necessary that there be also in the soul an intellect such as makes all [forms], as a certain disposition, like light; . . . the soul is as the hand; for the hand is the tool of tools, and the intellect the form of forms, and perception the form of perceptibles" (*On Soul* 430a14–15, 432a2–3). Are not the Socratic forms in part *constituted* by the human mind, in response to its human needs?

## CHOOSING AND EDUCATING THE CHIEF SUBORDINATE RULER IN THE HOUSEHOLD

Socrates narrates how Ischomachus recalled that after the organization of the implements, he and his wife showed to the servants the places of the ones employed on a daily basis (9.9), while "those that we use for festivals, or entertainment of guests, or on certain occasions, we turned over to the housekeeper" (*tamia*). To her they "showed the places for them, and, counting and writing down each of them," they turned over to her their supervision and safeguarding (9.10).

Having thus incidentally introduced this most important subordinate ruler within the household, the gentleman (in Socrates's telling) rather casually digressed from his account of his education of his wife about order and embarked on an account first of the housekeeper's selection—on the basis of her moral and intellectual character—and then of the housekeeper's moral and intellectual education over a long period of time. Both the selection and the education, he said, he carried out together with his wife. Socrates has Ischomachus offering no explanation of how his wife became educated to be his partner in the selecting and educating of this key subordinate. Was the gentleman careless about such education of the educator? Or, by including his wife in the process, did he in effect thereby give her a sort of "on the job" training in these delicate matters of moral and intellectual education? Or a bit of both?

At any rate, Ischomachus is reported telling Socrates that they made their selection after quite a thorough investigation, by which they found a (slave) woman who was most self-controlled as regards food (recall 7.6), as well as wine, sleep, and sex, and who was intellectually possessed of a good memory, along with a capacity to foresee her punishment by her owners if she were careless and her being honored by her owners if she pleased them (9.11). The gentleman's failure to attend to the woman's *piety* is made conspicuous by Cicero, who in his Latin translation[57] inserted such a concern. Does Xenophon's Socrates present the gentleman as having assumed (maybe only half-consciously) that a human supervision as close as theirs would be, along with the housekeeper's self-control, her prudent fear of their punishments, and her desire for their rewards and honors, would together render superfluous her belief in being also under the supervision of superhuman masters and mistresses whose punishments and honors or rewards supported those of the human master and mistress? Does the gentleman's felt need of, hence his experience of the presence of, the gods recede somewhat insofar as he feels confidently in control? Or: Does Xenophon's Socrates want us to wonder whether the gentleman was not (again, maybe only half-consciously) uneasy lest divinity might heed the prayers of a pious slave as rivaling or even taking priority over the prayers of punitive and rewarding human masters and mistresses? Does the gentleman's experience of the ruling presence of the gods recede insofar as he feels somewhat doubtful about the justice of his mastery? Does the absence or forgetting or repression of thought about the just entail the eclipse of the experience of the gods?[58] Or: Does not Xenophon prompt us to think of *both* these psychological possibilities (which are by no means mutually exclusive)? Certain it is that Xenophon's Socrates has the pious Ischomachus, whose concern for the gods has up until now been so conspicuous, make no mention whatsoever of having sacrificed or prayed to the gods for a good outcome from, or help in, his and his wife's selection, lengthy education, and management of their most important household subordinate.[59]

Suddenly ascending to a long-range temporal perspective on the education of the housekeeper, the gentleman told how he and his wife "taught" (*edidaskomen*) the housekeeper to become, over considerable time, emotionally good-willed towards them, by making her a sharer in their joys and sorrows, and how over time they "gave her an education" (*epaideuomen*) in being eager in spirit to increase the household, by "making her a *knower* of it, while sharing with her its prospering" (9.12). But all this did not yet suffice. Ischomachus evidently felt that a housekeeper encounters temptations, and is called to duties, such as are not reliably resisted or sustained without a more truly moral compass. So, most impressively, Ischomachus claimed that, over time, "the virtue of justice/righteousness (*dikaiosunē*) we instilled in her." This is the first mention of the virtue of justice or righteousness (*dikaiosunē*) in Socrates's account of his dialogue with Ischomachus.[60]

They achieved this, the gentleman reported, "by making just men more honored than unjust, and showing that they live lives richer and more free than the unjust." "And," Ischomachus concluded, "her in this place we put in order" (9.13). Our author has made these last words provocatively ambiguous: the phrase could have either the amoral and quite redundant meaning of "we installed her in the (slave) office [of housekeeper],"[61] or alternatively, it could have the pregnant moral meaning of "we put her in the category and situation of a just person, whose life we ordered morally so as to become deservedly richer and freer than the lives of the unjust." The latter might well seem to imply that the housekeeper should eventually be freed and given a decent economic basis of her own.[62] But Socrates has Ischomachus expressing no hint of such a prospective manumission. Xenophon delicately indicates the question: Is not the gentleman's own teaching, delivered to his most trusted indoor slave, on the deserved consequences of the virtue of justice, contradicted by his practice of that virtue, toward that very slave? But would not a strict practice of justice (as the gentleman teaches it), in regard to his just housekeeper and his other just slaves, entail unacceptable loss or sacrifice for him? In Ischomachus's report of his moral educating of his housekeeper, there is no reference to the noble (*kalon*)—that is, to self-transcending, even self-sacrificing, devotion to the deserved good of others or to the common good, or to justice itself (recall the opening of Virtue's speech to Heracles in the *Memorabilia*). Ischomachus neither called for the noble from his housekeeper nor committed himself to the noble in his treatment of her. He tried to articulate and to teach a virtue of justice apart from any noble sacrifice, a justice of self-interest prudently understood. It is remarkable, again, that Xenophon's Socrates has the otherwise very pious gentleman make no mention of divine providence helping to support this teaching on justice, a providence that would insure that somehow or other the just ultimately do in fact "live lives richer and more free than the unjust" (recall, in sharp contrast, 5.12—the only previous mention of the virtue of justice, and of education in that virtue). One might expect such a reference especially here, since, without divine assistance, the gentleman's moral responsibility and the grave difficulty of his striving to insure that deserved rewards accrue to those who are just under his supervision becomes much greater—and simultaneously the tension at the heart of the gentleman's teaching on justice increases, with the potential risks or costs, to him and his household, of such striving to insure distributive justice. Is it the absence or forgetting of thought about the noble that brings with it the eclipse of the experience of the gods? Certainly Xenophon's Socrates has the pious gentleman Ischomachus give the impression that neither he nor his wife sought or experienced a lively presence of divinity during this very important, and long-lasting, part of their household rule, when they selected their housekeeper and then carried out, over a protracted time, her moral education.

## THE GENTLEMAN'S POLITICAL REGIME

Emphatically returning back from his account of the education of his housekeeper to his account of his education of his wife (9.14), Ischomachus told Socrates (addressing him by name) how he expanded his teaching on order by reminding his wife of her responsibility for supervising the maintenance of the ordering of the household's human as well as inanimate tools. Without such total supervision on her part (he told her), there would be "no benefit" from "all" that had been put in order (including the well-educated housekeeper—the gentleman was not fully confident even or especially about the sufficiency of the virtue of justice that they had instilled in their housekeeper[63]). The supervisory queen-ruler remains essential. The silence on the gods and divine providence continues.

But now Socrates has the gentleman saying that he "taught" his wife what he conceived to be the close parallel between her required rule in the household and rule "in the cities well governed under law" (*en tais eunomoumenais polesin*): "to the citizens it does not seem sufficient if they will formulate, in writing, noble laws; but they also select law-guardians (*nomophulakas*),[64] who carry out surveillance by which they praise the one who does the lawfully conventional things, but if someone does what is against the laws, they punish" (9.14). Ischomachus bade his wife consider herself "law-guardian" of the matters in the house—not only "inspecting the implements as the commander inspects the guards," but "testing to see if each thing is nobly situated, as the council tests horses and knights," and "praising and honoring the deserving, as a queen (*basilissan*)," while "reviling and punishing anyone needing this" (9.15). In articulating this civic analogue Ischomachus naturally had to begin to refer to the noble (*kalon*), especially when speaking of the cavalry—for they (and Ischomachus as one of them) must be prepared to sacrifice their very existences for the city.

The political regime Socrates has Ischomachus thus sketch, as an analogue to his household, is an aristocratic regime, where a citizenry restricted to the minority of gentlemen—analogous to Ischomachus and his wife—rules through noble laws and a council, and constituting a board of law-guardians or censors enforcing a high moral tone, all unimpeded by any vulgar democratic assemblies. The gentleman seemed to find no difficulty in the implication that the ruled noncitizens in such a gentlemanly regime—the vast majority of inhabitants—have a status analogous to that of servants or slaves in a gentlemanly household. But there is this disanalogy: in the aristocratical *civic* regime, citizens as well as noncitizens are unambiguously under a rule of law; the ambiguity in the lawfulness of the household regime is due to the chief difference between the gentlemanly civic regime and the gentleman's household: in the latter, citizenship is restricted to the husband and wife alone; the aristocracy shrinks to a dyarchy. The meaning of this last was made vivid when the gentleman went on to "teach" his wife that it would not be "just" of her to be annoyed at his supervisory assignment to her of more duties regarding the possessions than he assigned to the servants, given that the latter partake of their owners' wealth only insofar as that wealth is to be transported, cared for, and guarded, and *not* insofar as it is to be *used*—unless permission is granted them by "the sovereign" (*ho kurios*, masc.). In contrast, "the master" himself can use each and every thing as he wishes. And "to him who derives the greatest benefit from their preservation, and the greatest harm from their destruction, to this one" it is justly appropriate to assign the greatest supervisory care (9.16–17). This gentlemanly teaching on regime justice that Xenophon's Socrates puts in the mouth of Ischomachus provokes the question: How does the gentleman-king understand his justice in relation not only to his junior partner(s), but also to his subjects—not only in the gentlemanly household regime, but also and especially in the gentlemanly civic regime? How does the gentleman understand his regimes, household and civic, to exhibit justice in the sense of the common advantage of the *whole* community, of *all* the inhabitants?

What Socrates was eager to hear (9.18) was how the young wife responded to this remarkably ambiguous new formulation by her husband of her role in the household regime. Ischomachus replied (9.19) that his wife responded by saying that he did not correctly know her if he supposed that he was ordering her to harsh duties when he "taught that she must take care of *their* properties (*tōn ontōn*)"; for "even as it seems natural[65] for a sensible woman to care for, rather than to neglect, children that are *her own*, so also (she said that she believed), a sensible woman takes more pleasure in caring for than in neglecting as much of her property as she takes delight in as belonging to her *individually* (*hosa idia onta*)."

Socrates reports that when he heard that the young wife had answered in these terms, he swore by Hera that Ischomachus had shown the "manliness" of "the wife's thinking."[66] Socrates's swearing of a womanly oath,[67] which he sets off in the wording of his narration—" 'By Hera!' (I said) 'Oh Ischomachus, . . ."—indicates that he regards his own thinking (*dianoia*) as *not* manly,[68] unlike the young wife-ruler. Xenophon certainly does not present the philosopher as posing any rivalry to Ischomachus's royal preeminence in his household (or in his civic) regime.[69] For his part, Ischomachus took Socrates's outburst as a compliment, which he turned in a direction flattering to his own predominance in the household: he expressed his willingness to show other marks of what he called his wife's "full greatness of mind" (*panu megalophrona*), manifested in her swift obedience to the very first utterance of each of his various admonitions.

## XENOPHON AND HIS SOCRATES AS DRAMATIC ARTISTS

This, Socrates reports, so intrigued him that he urged Ischomachus on, avowing that he was taking much more pleasure in learning from the gentleman about the virtue (*aretēn*) of a living woman than if the famous painter Zeuxis were to display a painting he had made of an image of a beautiful woman (10.1).[70]

Here (10.2) our author suddenly and bizarrely intrudes himself (XSD 130). The next line Xenophon indites as follows: "at this point indeed Ischomachus says (*legei*)." Xenophon momentarily writes as if he were relating directly the story of Ischomachus's dialogue with Socrates, rather than through the past tense, in a ventriloquized narration by his character Socrates. Xenophon then immediately and emphatically subsides back into his self-effacing employment of Socrates as narrator: "so I, he said (*ephē*), seeing her once, oh Socrates, having been painted with a lot of white lead. . . ."

What is our playful author up to, here?

Xenophon momentarily brings his authorship to the fore and thus contrives gently to remind us that he too is a painter—in or with words—who has been painting for us an image of Socrates engaged in painting an image in or with words, as a major dimension of his practice of his "unmanly" philosophic-didactic art. But that art is here exercised in depicting a gentleman acting as a painter in or with words of an image of his education of his wife; it is that artistic activity, of that exemplary human type, that is the cynosure of *the* Socratic discourse.

## THE GENTLEMAN ON APPEARANCE AND REALITY (BEING)

We readers now keenly anticipate—sharing in what we are led to believe was the disposition of Socrates at this point in the drama—hearing how the gentleman went on to relate a number of other manifestations of his wife's "full greatness of mind," shown through her prompt obedience to her husband's lessons. Do we not expect some impressive accounts of how, through obedience, she managed, ruled, and increased the household indoors, as her husband's subordinate partner, perhaps especially after children were born?

But in fact, Xenophon's Socrates contrives to make his "remark about a woman painted by Zeuxis and a living woman remind Ischomachus of a time when his wife had painted her face" (Pomeroy ad loc.), and so, instead of what we are led to expect, Xenophon's Socrates wryly presents the gentleman's account of his education of his wife culminating, to our amused amazement, in a light comedy (unintended and unselfconscious on the gentleman's part) about cosmetics and sexual attractiveness. Socrates makes a point of highlighting his deliberate cutting off or postponement, at this point, of what were expected, further, earnest reports from Ischomachus about his education of his wife.[71]

We may descry the serious message that Xenophon's Socrates conveys through this comicodramatic veil if we take due note of the following aspects of the dialogue that Socrates has the gentleman now relate. Socrates first (10.2–3) has Ischomachus telling how, in reaction to his wife's attempts to enhance and thus to disguise her appearance as it is—in "truth," and by "nature"—he brought home to her how "undeserving of loving affection" *he* would be, as "a partner in *property*," if he failed to show her what *truly* belongs to him ("the things-themselves-that-are"—*auta to onta*), without any refined boasting, and without any concealment (of the things-that-are—*tōn ontōn*), and if instead he were to try to deceive her by claiming that there belonged to him more of the things-that-are (*tōn ontōn*), and to trick her by showing counterfeit money and gilded wood necklaces and clothes with phony dye as if it were dye that was true (*alēthinas*).

His wife expressed her manliness of mind (XSD 155) by ardently interrupting—as if the very idea of such deception about their *property* were blasphemy: "Hush! Avoid profanity!" (*euphēmei* 10.4).

In the second place (10.5), Socrates has Ischomachus telling how he then asked his wife whether he would be deserving of loving affection as a *physical* partner if he used cosmetics to effect deception as regards the health and strength of his body.

The young lady replied, with notable lack of ardor, that she would not find it more pleasant to touch and to behold her husband in cosmetics than without them (10.6).

Then (10.7) the gentleman stressed his own corresponding sexual delight—derived, he explained, from the gods' design for male herd animals such as horses, cattle, and sheep (!)—in his wife's unadorned body, free of "deceptions." He added (10.8) that such deceptions can go "unrefuted" in relations with "outsiders" but come to be "refuted" in relations of "intercourse."

Socrates says he exclaimed (presumably managing to keep a straight face: 10.9): "How—before the gods!—did she respond to *these* statements?"

Ischomachus complacently assured Socrates that she permanently complied and, what's more, asked for his advice as to how she might "appear beautiful in reality/being (*tōi onti*)." Then, after relating how he recommended various exercise routines for her to perform "with the help of the gods," so that she would "appear ruddier in truth," Ischomachus remarked—whether only to Socrates or also to his wife is unclear—that as a result, in competitive comparison (*antagōnizētai*) with the slave girls, his wife's appearance, when unadorned and fittingly dressed, won out in being sexually arousing to him, especially with the added consideration of her willing sexual compliance, versus the slave girls' compelled submissions (10.10–13).

The gentleman as delineated by Xenophon's Socrates is not exactly a "romantic" when it comes to erotic love.[72] Despite what he taught his young wife back at 7.42–43, it did not occur to Ischomachus here to say to her anything about being deserving of loving affection as a *spiritual* partner, by transparently manifesting one's health and strength of *soul*, capable of devotion, without any hint of refined boasting or concealment or deception. Just as the gentleman insufficiently appreciated the importance and the difficulty of noble devotion when "instilling the virtue of justice" in his housekeeper, so he insufficiently appreciated the importance and the difficulty of noble devotion in the erotic education of and partnership with his wife.[73] The gentleman as presented by Xenophon's Socrates does not think much about, does not confront the problem of, noble erotic devotion. We note that *eros* is not at all a theme of Aristotle's *Ethics* and its portraits of the gentlemanly virtues.

Yet we can be sure that the gentleman is deeply attached to the authenticity of his appearance as a spiritually true gentleman: for in what immediately follows (11.1), Socrates recalls saying to Ischomachus that the latter "will be pleased by relating the deeds for which you are highly reputed"—the deeds of "the real man (*andros*) who is a gentleman [noble-and-good]," about which Socrates expects to hear from Ischomachus "in perfected fashion" (*teleōs*);

and then Socrates reports the gentleman replying emphatically, swearing by Zeus, that he would indeed be "altogether pleased" to relate the things he spends his life doing, "in order that you might also set me straight, if I seem to you not to act in a noble fashion." If or to the extent that the gentleman Ischomachus were ever shown, through being refuted by Socrates, that the moral principles by which he lives, and above all his conception of the just and the noble, were confused, incoherent, radically deficient, or false, the effect on the gentleman, on his soul, on his experience of all that is most important in his life, would be shattering. But to repeat: Xenophon's Socrates provides only a glimpse of these dark potential depths of the gentleman's spirituality, through a light intermezzo.

CHAPTER FOUR

# Teaching Socrates the Activities of a Gentleman

When Socrates asked Ischomachus to teach him about the gentleman's own activities,[1] Ischomachus replied with gracious modesty, saying that he would be altogether pleased to do so, in order that Socrates might also set him straight if he seemed in some way not to act in a noble fashion (11.1–2). Socrates proceeded immediately to set Ischomachus straight—not, of course, as regards the nobility of Ischomachus's action, but as regards his vast overestimation of the moral competence of Socrates to render such judgment. "How could I with justice set straight a man who is a complete gentleman?!—I, who am a man reputed 'to engage in idle chatter'[2] and 'to measure the air'[3] and (what seems the most mindless accusation of all) I am called 'impoverished!'" (11.3). Here Xenophon's Socrates gives a brief glimpse of what the Socrates of Plato's *Apology* (18c–19c) identifies as the charges levelled by his "first" or "old" accusers, led by Aristophanes. These are the most dangerous accusations, Plato's Socrates declares, because "those who hear them hold that those who investigate these matters do not believe in gods" (see also *Laws* 967a).

But Xenophon's Socrates, having given us this reminder of those most dangerous charges, immediately obscures them by focusing attention on his response to the comparatively harmless accusation of poverty (an infirmity sometimes shared by the very pious, of course—see, e.g., *Symposium* 4.49). Socrates once again presents himself as one who, at the time that he sought out Ischomachus, was emerging from a cocoon of unworldliness. Socrates says that he told Ischomachus that he "would have been in despair" over this accusation of being poor (as if he realized for the first time that his indigence was indeed something of a conventional disgrace), had he not discovered, by way of a very recent encounter with an admired horse and its groom, that "it is sacred law (*themiton*) for even a horse lacking possessions to become good if it should have a good soul by nature," and "therefore" (Socrates concluded, with rather preposterously dubious legal reasoning), "it is sacred law (*themiton*) for me also to become a good man." And on that playfully solemn basis, Socrates urged Ischomachus to relate his doings completely, so that Socrates could try to imitate them "starting tomorrow, a good day to begin being virtuous" (11.4–6).

While explicitly claiming that he was guided by the lawfully sacred (*themiton*), Socrates in jesting implicitly suggested that at the time he sought out Ischomachus he was not only penurious but, what is much more grave, lacking in both the knowledge and the practice of gentlemanly virtue—and had had, in his previous life, no interest in remedying these deficiencies. Yet despite this, he had established that his soul was by nature good (XSD 160–61).

Socrates reports Ischomachus as having given no indication of being perturbed by all this, evidently because he assumed that (as he said) Socrates was "joking." Still, the gentleman went on to betray a hint of mild umbrage at his interlocutor's lack of due seriousness regarding the gentlemanly life and its deeds: "but I, on the other hand, nevertheless, will go through for you the things that I, as much as I am able, try to spend my life accomplishing" (11.7). What's more, Socrates has Ischomachus then begin (implicitly delivering a gentle reprimand) by invoking with unqualified seriousness "sacred law" (*themiton*) as legislated by the gods. The gentleman declared to Socrates that he believed that he had learned that while "the gods have made it not lawfully sacred (*themiton*) for humans to prosper without knowledge of the things that need to be done and without taking care that these be accomplished," still, among "those who *are* prudent and *do* take care, they grant only to *some* to become happy, and to *others* not"; "therefore *I* begin by serving the gods,"[4] and "I try to make it so that it will be lawfully sacred (*themiton*) for me, by praying, to obtain health, and bodily strength, and honor in the city, and goodwill on the part of friends, and in war noble salvation, and increase of wealth through noble means" (11.8).

## THE GENTLEMAN'S MAGNIFICENCE

Socrates reports himself as having made a response that highlights still further the "economic" and thus moral gulf between the philosopher and the gentleman: "so you then are concerned, Ischomachus, to be wealthy, and, by having much money, to have the many troubles involved in caring for it?"

Socrates has the gentleman answering by stressing the pleasure of the practice of the moral virtues of magnificence and generosity, first and foremost in "greatly honoring" the gods, then in helping friends, if they need anything, and then in "adorning" the city. (Wealth is the essential "equipment"—as Aristotle says—for the most resplendently generous moral and civic virtues.)

This answer Socrates immediately characterized (addressing Ischomachus by name) as "noble," and as befitting men of power, who make a surplus so that they can adorn the city and support friends—unlike those who are pleased if they can provide enough to support their own families. In return for the magnificent deeds of gentlemen such as Ischomachus, "we hoi polloi" (Socrates said) can only offer "our" praise.[5] Socrates spoke as a respectful plebian—except that, in rehearsing the gentleman's praiseworthy employment of money, Socrates dropped all reference to "greatly honoring the gods."[6] This went with the philosopher's silence as regards Ischomachus's previous, emphatic insistence on the crucial importance of prayerful service to divinity. Indeed, Socrates proceeded to lead the gentleman insensibly into an eclipse of that stress on the need for prayer, by way of making bodily exercise the focus instead: Socrates asked Ischomachus to tell how he cared for his health and strength of body and to explain also "how it is lawfully sacred" (*themiton*) to be "nobly saved in war"—to which the gentleman was led to reply by speaking (only) of the efficacy of sound human practice, including not least military practice (11.11–12).

Socrates, in line with *his* "way," asked the gentleman, addressing him by name, to postpone talking about his money making and to focus on giving exemplary advice about how he cared for his health and strength of body and noble safety in war. *These* are goods for which Socrates shares with the gentleman a real concern. But the gentleman, in line with *his* "way," is reported insisting—addressing Socrates by name—that "all these things are linked together," and so, just as correct practice brings about the other goods "more," so it "makes more likely the increase of the household" (11.12).

Socrates replied, again addressing Ischomachus by name, that he could "follow [only] this far": "that you are declaring that a human by exercising, and taking care, and practicing, happens more upon the good things."

Nonetheless, Socrates went on to say that he would with pleasure learn not only what sort of exercises the gentleman employed for health and strength, and how he practiced for war, but also how he "took care to make a profit so that he could succour friends and strengthen [Socrates did not say "adorn"] the city" (11.13).

When the gentleman obligingly related the rigorous routine of his daily morning activities, Socrates reacted with an outburst of naively astonished, quasi-feminine admiration for the way in which the gentleman did indeed combine exercise for health and strength, practice for war, and supervision of his slaves' profitable farming: " 'By Hera! (I said) Oh Ischomachus! You do these things in a way that does impress me!" While Socrates thus spoke as if he previously had had no idea how a gentleman spends his mornings, he added that the *results* of this manly morning routine were already known to him, as well as to other plebians (and to women): "*we* observe" the health and robustness exhibited by Ischomachus generally (with the help of the gods), and "we know" that Ischomachus is "said to be one of the foremost cavalrymen, as well as one of the most wealthy" (11.13–20).

## THE GENTLEMAN AS SPEAKER AND REASONER

A glowing portrait of the gentleman's active, flourishing, superior life was thus emerging. But a shadow abruptly fell upon this picture. Ischomachus declared, Socrates reports, that he was badly beseiged with false lawsuits by many litigious graspers at his money—"though you probably thought that I would tell," he said, with a hint of rue, "how I am hailed by many as a gentleman!" (11.21). Ischomachus is naturally chagrined by the deficiency (in democratic Athens) of the public honor that he is sure a gentleman-knight like himself deserves, and he has received the impression that Socrates is one who, while having himself the proper respect for his superiors, is somewhat naive about those superiors' beleagured status in the city.

Socrates in reply showed that in fact he was not entirely naive in this regard. He said that he had been about to ask if Ischomachus took some care to be able to give, and to take, an account (*logos*) of himself, whenever needed (11.22—Socrates of course does not present himself as having spoiled everything by launching an attempt to make the gentleman give to the philosopher a justifying account of himself and of his life).

Ischomachus's response (11.22) revealed that it had not escaped his notice that he had been for some time an object of Socratic observation: "now don't I seem to you (he said), oh Socrates, to take care ceaselessly about these very things—making my defense/apology (*apologeisthai*), through doing injustice to no one, while I do well to many, as much as I am able?" And "do I not seem to you to take care to lodge accusations against humans, when I learn of some who are unjust to many in private, and to the city, while doing good to no one?" We learn from the *Apology*[7] that when Socrates was indicted, and was asked by Hermogenes why he was not preparing a defense speech, he replied: "Don't I seem to you to have gone through life attending to the making of a defense?" And when Hermogenes then asked in puzzlement, "How?" Socrates answered: "In that I have been all along doing nothing unjust: which I believe to be the noblest attention to the making of a defense." According to the more defensively civic-spirited *Memorabilia* (4.8.4), Socrates replied to Hermogenes "that he all along was doing nothing except investigating the just things and the unjust things, doing the just things and refraining from the unjust things." Even this latter falls far short of the gentleman's spirited, accusatory police work for the city.[8] Is there any risk that this police work might someday lead Ischomachus to become—like the gentleman Lycon—one of the accusers of Socrates?

Socrates tells how he next asked the gentleman if his care for his defense of himself included also any care "to give an interpretation in speech" (*hermēneuein*) of the deeds by which he vigorously enacted justice and prosecuted injustice. Ischomachus made it clear that the answer was "No." The gentleman saw no need to give any such "interpretation in speech" concerning those previously listed deeds; their meaning he finds obvious; he certainly does not imagine it necessary to ask the Socratic question, "what is just, what is unjust?" So, instead, he responded by assuring Socrates that "I never cease caring about speaking"—either by refutative questioning (*elenchein*) of servants who have lodged accusations and servants who are defending themselves against accusations;[9] or by engaging in blaming and praising, before friends; or by reconciling some useful associates (*tōn epitēdeiōn*), trying to teach them how it is more advantageous for them to be friends than to be enemies; and when "we" (gentlemen) are around a general, "we" censure someone, or defend someone unjustly blamed; or "we make accusations against one another if someone is unjustly honored." And "frequently deliberating about things that we desire to do, we praise these, and what we do not want to do, these things we blame" (11.23–24). The gentleman's *logos* is investigative-refutative (only) with a view to establishing guilt and innocence; it is didactic (only) with a view to reconciling associates; its chief preoccupation is with rhetorical praise and blame, honor and dishonor, of policies and especially of persons—who are assumed to have full moral responsibility for their actions, which are thereby deserving of reward (honor) or retributive punishment (dishonor). The gentleman does not feel any need to raise, let alone to pursue, the question "what is noble?" or "what is honorable?" or "what is virtue?" (XSD 176 n. 4 and context). If he ever did, helped by Socrates, he would run up against the most famous Socratic moral thesis: all crime or evildoing is due to ignorance, and is thus deeply involuntary and deserving of pity and educative assistance, not at all retributive justice (*Memorabilia* 3.13.1; *Apology* 28).

The stress on argumentation over guilt and innocence, and praise and blame, led Ischomachus to generate an uncharacteristic bubble of rather penetrating levity, which reintroduced into the dialogue his relationship with his wife (now described no longer at the time of the start of their marriage but at the time of this encounter with Socrates). "And at the present time (he said), oh Socrates, I in particular am often under judgment as to what I ought to suffer or what penalty I ought to pay." Socates fell for the joke, asking in surprise: "By whom, I said, oh Ischomachus?! For I have failed to notice *this*!" (Again we see that Socrates had been observing the gentleman for some time.) "By the wife," Ischomachus dryly and wryly answered (11.25).

Our previous suspicions as to the young lady's "manly" (and potentially successful) ambition to rule are confirmed, and we catch a glimpse of why Ischomachus was earlier reported to be not eager to elaborate on how his education of his wife turned out.[10]

When, Socrates says, he then asked Ischomachus how he fared in the "contesting" with his wife (*pōs agōnizei*: recall Socrates's seemingly bizarre reference to the gentleman's education of his wife as an *agōn* at 7.9), the gentleman replied that he fared well, so long as it was in his interest to speak true things—and then, revealing for the first time his awareness of the dubiousness of Socrates's reputation as a teacher of deceptively tricky rhetoric, Ischomachus said: "but when it is falsehoods [that it is in my interest to speak], then, the weaker argument, oh Socrates, I am not—by Zeus!—no, *not* able to make the stronger!" The fact that this grave and notorious[11] accusation of Socrates—that he "makes the weaker argument the stronger" and teaches others to do so—occurs in the *Economist* only by way of a gentlemanly jest shows both the elastic magnanimity of the gentleman toward the philosopher (for the time being at least) and the cloud of risk that is visible on the horizon. Socrates depicts himself replying as if he had not noticed the veiled imputation and, indeed, as if he were naively unfamiliar with the business of deceptive rhetoric, or "making the weaker argument the stronger": "For probably, oh Ischomachus, the false you are not able to make true!" (11.25). For how could anyone do that? Yet according to Xenophon, this is at least attempted, with some success, even by certain trouble-making hunting dogs: the *One Skilled at Hunting with Dogs* 3.9.

## SOCRATES MAKES A MISTAKE

At this point (12.1) Socrates relates that he voiced to Ischomachus a concern that he might be detaining the gentleman, when he probably wished to depart. Xenophon thus has Socrates portray himself having spoken as if he were politely seeking to end the conversation—as if he thought that he had learned or confirmed all that he needed to from this conversation with a perfect gentleman (XSD 167). Xenophon certainly seems to signal that it is the sections in which Socrates learns about the gentleman's education of his wife and about the gentleman's own daily activities that are the most important parts of the reported dialogue with Ischomachus.

Yet Socrates's assumption, or inclination to suppose, that he had little or nothing more to learn from this conversation proves to have been a rather grave mistake. Again we see that Socrates depicts himself learning from Ischomachus at a time when he was not yet the mature Socrates, the great dialectician, but only that being *in statu nascendi.*

One could well wonder why the famous *daimonion* did not signal to Socrates that he should refrain from trying to bring the conversation to a close (consider Plato's *Euthydemus* 272e). This provokes us to note once again that the *daimonion* is never mentioned in the *Economist*. The *daimonion* is missing also from the *Symposium*, but there, of course, the *eros* of Socrates is pervasive, and Plato teaches us[12] that Socrates's *daimonion* and his *eros* are identical, or at least are facets of the same spiritual phenomenon. Similarly, in light of what we learn from the *Symposium* about the relation between Socrates and Critobulus, and what we may deduce from Xenophon's Socratic writings about the relation of Socrates to Xenophon, we may say that Socrates's *eros* (and thus his *daimonion*) is pervasively present, if in a muted and implicit way, throughout the conversation with Critobulus, and thus in the *report* to young Critobulus (and to young Xenophon) of the conversation with the gentleman. But *within* that reported conversation, *during* Socrates's reported conversational engagement with the perfect gentleman, I venture to suggest that Socrates's *eros*—as aroused by a fellow human—is rather quiescent, and that fact may be highlighted by the prominent mention of the arousal of Critobulus's *eros* (for becoming a gentleman) immediately prior to the beginning of Socrates's report of his anerotic conversation with the gentleman (6.12). Ischomachus himself is indeed reported to have referred emphatically to *eros*—but as a source of disorder in slaves, needing severe repression (12.13–14; also 9.5 and 9.11, and recall 7.11); the remarkable exception was, we will soon see, the gentleman's strong approval of the *eros* for gain or profit (12.15). The gentleman as such comes to sight both as relatively anerotic and as not arousing the *eros* of Socrates.

In response to Socrates's suggestion that he probably was wishing to depart, Ischomachus replied—swearing rather solemnly by Zeus—that he certainly was *not*: he would not contemplate leaving until the last person had quitted the agora (i.e., at the noon closing[13]). This instigated Socrates to indicate, swearing by Zeus, his surprised admiration at the strength of Ischomachus's concern "to guard lest he cast away the repute of being called a noble-and-good man"—"for while there are probably many of your affairs in need of care, nevertheless, because you made a promise to the strangers, you keep waiting for them, so as not to have spoken a falsehood!" (12.2).

What is remarkable about this statement is that it reveals that Socrates had not at all presumed that the gentleman would be thus so fastidious about his reputation for keeping promises that he would for its sake make substantial sacrifice of his affairs, even for a few hours. Socrates here seemed to be learning that the gentleman's famous virtues of truthfulness and righteousness are expressed not only in his (even playful) defensive argumentation but in his completely serious and even sacrificial fidelity to promises.

Although Ischomachus did not demur as regards this ascription to him of such categorically serious concern for promise keeping, he assured Socrates that in this particular case his affairs would not be neglected (he would undergo no great sacrifice), because of his field overseers (12.2—*epitropous*; Chantraine translates "chefs de culture"). Does Xenophon thus provoke some slight question about the categorical character of the gentleman's fidelity to promises? If Ischomachus *had* lacked a trusty overseer, might he have felt that he *did* need to depart? Or is that the sort of question a gentleman does not ask himself?

CHAPTER FIVE

# Teaching Socrates How a Gentleman Educates His Overseers

Ischomachus's mention of his overseers, reminding us of the earlier account of his housekeeper, evidently moved Socrates to see if there was an opportunity here to learn more about how the gentleman conceived of himself as an educator (education, as "the greatest good for human beings," is *the* major "business" of Socrates, both before and after his "turn"—*Apology* 20–21; XSD 161). Socrates says that he asked: "when you need an overseer, do you learn where there might be a man skilled in overseership, and try to buy him, even as when you need a carpenter," or "do you yourself educate the overseers?" Ischomachus replied in no uncertain terms: "I myself, by Zeus! (he said)—oh Socrates!—try to do the educating." And then Ischomachus made clear how high in rank the overseers are (much higher than the housekeeper): each overseer is to be made capable of taking the master's place when he is absent and so (Ischomachus stressed) ought to acquire, by being taught, the very same knowledge that the master himself possesses (12.3–4). Eventually Ischomachus will claim that in fact he educates some of his overseers to become gentlemen—"noble-and-good"—and these he treats as "free men" (14.9; see also 12.20). Yet strangely then, or revealingly, "Ischomachus is completely silent about what one may call the intellectual qualities—about qualities which he had not failed to mention when speaking of what is required of the housekeeper" (XSD 176; see 9.11).

## IN GOOD WILL TOWARD HIMSELF

No doubt partly because Socrates remembered that good will was the first thing that Ischomachus had said he needed to teach the housekeeper (recall 9.12), but even more because Socrates was himself already something of an expert in education, the philosopher offered a major supplement to, verging on a substantial correction of, Ischomachus's characterization of his education of an overseer (12.5). Socrates pointed out that it was not an education in any *knowledge* that was fundamental for an overseer: "well, as the first thing, it is goodwill (I said) that he will need to have, toward you and yours, if he is going to substitute adequately for you; for without goodwill, what benefit is there in any overseer's having any sort of knowledge!?"

Socrates presents himself as having already known that the cornerstone of virtue, at least in an overseer who is to be capable of substituting for a gentleman master who is absent, is certainly not knowledge.

Ischomachus immediately and heartily agreed, swearing by Zeus—and then declared that this was indeed the "first thing" in which "I try to educate."

Socrates reports that he responded with awed (or skeptical) wonder (12.6): "And how (I said)—before the gods!—do you teach, whomever you wish, to have goodwill towards you and yours!?" Evidently Socrates held that it is one thing to be able to teach a *housekeeper* to have goodwill toward her master and mistress, with whom she lives in intimacy, sharing their joys and sorrows (recall 9.12); it is a much, much taller order to instill the same in field overseers.

Socrates has Ischomachus giving a reply that brims with confidence: "Through treating them well—by Zeus!—whenever the gods grant me abundance of some good!" (12.6; recall that this sort of generosity was employed by the gentleman and his wife toward their housekeeper, but *not* as a way to "teach her *goodwill*" toward them; rather, only as a way of "educating" her to be eager to help increase the household fortunes—9.12).

Socrates again expressed his (skeptical) amazement, now at this specific claim of the gentleman regarding his mode of successfully inculcating goodwill in his chief subordinate slaves (recall 9.16–17).

Retreating slightly but significantly, the gentleman replied: "For this, Socrates, I see to be the best tool for goodwill!" (12.7—Ischomachus was forgetting, it seems, what he had at 9.12 taught in regard to his educating of the housekeeper).

"The Socrates who was notorious only as an idle talker and as a measurer of the air is not as sanguine or as simple-minded as Ischomachos" regarding the possibility of instilling goodwill in servants towards their master (XSD 167–68). This excessive sanguinity of the gentleman as moral educator is one manifestly new thing that the philosopher would seem to have learned about the gentleman from the latter's acount of his education of his overseers.

Xenophon instigates us to ask: What could be the basis of the gentleman's overconfidence as a moral teacher?

On reflection, we can surmise that a major part of the basis is what (as we have already remarked) will be stressed by Ischomachus in his impassioned closing "sermon." The gentleman's self-understanding is centered on the hopefully noble belief that he rules over his household inferiors as a godlike king over the willing, and thus is situated at the opposite pole from the divinely damned tyrant ruling over the unwilling (see again 21.12). If this belief in the quasi-divine justice of his rule over his subjects were to be seriously shaken, the experience of the gentleman as being a gentleman, or his gentlemanliness itself, would totter (Ambler 1996, 125–26). And we begin to see that a deeper level of what Socrates learned from the gentleman's account of his education of his overseers is the problematic character of the gentleman's understanding, or presumption, of the justice of his rule over his highest ranked slaves.

A crucial and major corollary to the previous is the gentleman's pious belief in, and gratitude for, the fact that whatever abundance he acquires is granted by the grace of powerfully supportive, if unpredictable, divinities (consider OT chap. 7 and esp. the final paragraph). Socrates, we note, presents himself as having dropped the reference to divine grace when he paraphrased, in skeptical amazement, the educative claim about goodwill made by Ischomachus. The fact that Ischomachus was not fully conscious of this pious psychological basis within himself for his confidence about his success in instilling goodwill in his chief servants would seem to be indicated by the following amazing fact: he is presented by Socrates as never once mentioning any effort on his part to try to educate his overseers in *piety*—in his own foundational faith in the divinity supporting him in his acquisition of abundance and in his rule over the overseers. Nor does Ischomachus ever even allude to prayers or to sacrifices as a crucial prelude to his education of his overseers—after having stressed, only shortly before, the crucial importance of beginning *all* his activities with prayer (11.8; recall similarly 6.1 and 7.7–8; Ludwig 2010, 88–89). Xenophon or his Socrates makes this silence "louder" by contriving to construct this part of his narrated dialogue, on the education of the overseers, so as to have it contain the highest concentration in the entire work of expletives that *profanely* invoke gods; these profane invocations are mainly by Ischomachus (XSD 170, 195). As for the psychological factors that Xenophon's Socrates means for us to deduce as driving the very pious Ischomachus to forget or to fail to introduce piety into his education of his overseers, we refer the reader back to our speculations about what might have been the reasons driving Ischomachus and his wife to forget piety in the selection and then in the education of their housekeeper (see also XSD 170). We also note that in the present discussion of moral education of overseers, the word for "justice" has appeared only in reference to punishment for servants, including the overseers (12.19).

Once again, the gentleman is presented by Socrates as insufficiently conscious of the importance and difficulty of nobly unselfish devotion as a factor in the virtues that he claims to instill or to cultivate (the wife of Ischomachus seems somewhat more perspicuous in this important regard: recall 7.37). This failure of self-consciousness is intimately related, we venture to surmise, to the tepidity or perhaps self-repression of the gentleman's eros.

## IN DILIGENCE

Socrates does not portray himself suggesting to the gentleman any better "tool" that could be used for "teaching" goodwill; but Socrates does present himself as now for the first time subtly taking the lead, becoming a kind of dialectical teacher of the gentleman in regard to the latter's teaching of virtue—or rather, in regard to the enormous *obstacles* to any teaching of virtue.

Socrates says that he next pointed out that even if, or assuming that, the gentleman were to succeed, as he claims, in imbuing his chief subordinates with *goodwill* toward himself—by gratifying the deeply natural goodwill toward *oneself* that each of those subordinates shares with pretty much all humanity—there is still needed in addition, on the subordinates' part, diligence or care (*epimeleia*[1]) in pursuing what they wish as good (for themselves); and such diligence, Socrates stressed, is lacking in "many" (12.8).

Once again Socrates depicts Ischomachus replying with an assertive or morale-boosting oath—"by Zeus!" and asserting that when he wanted to appoint such overseers, he taught them to be diligent (12.9); and once again, we hear how Socrates, now even more strongly, voiced his skeptical amazement (12.10): "How? (I said)—before the gods! For this, indeed I thought to be something *entirely* not teachable (*pantapasin ou didakton*)!"[2]

Once again Socrates reports the gentleman retreating, this time a bigger step back: "now it is not (he said), oh Socrates, possible to teach everyone, one after another, to be diligent."

Socrates then asked, with a somewhat surprising, laser-like, and aggressive insistence: "specify for me with complete clarity (*pantōs saphōs*) these" for *whom* it *is* possible (12.11)!

Socrates depicts Ischomachus as failing to do so. Instead, the gentleman began a list of those whom "*you* would *not* be able to make diligent"—"first," those lacking self-control in drinking wine.

But then Ischomachus offered no "second" item on this list. It seems that a brief silence ensued. For Socrates reports himself asking (12.12) if it was *only* those lacking self-control in this *one* respect, wine, who were incapable of becoming diligent (Socrates no longer spoke of being "taught" or "educated" in diligence)—or if there were not also some other types who were also incapable of diligence. After all, Ischomachus had seemed to start a listing, with his emphatic "first."

Swearing by Zeus, Ischomachus responded to this Socratic prompt by adding the set of those lacking self control as regards sleep.

There seems to have followed another brief silence. At any rate, Socrates presents himself as again having to push: "What then? (I said) Again, will *these alone* be incapable of being taught this diligence *by us*, or are there also others in addition to these?" (12.13).

What is Xenophon's Socrates provoking his audience to think about by these stuttering peculiarities of his narrated drama at this point? He was certainly making the gentleman into something of a rather droll spectacle, in his groping to answer Socratic questions about the most basic moral education of his chief and most trusted subordinates. And Socrates was discovering further dimensions of the gentleman's ignorance about his own moral-educative exercise of rule.

Socrates presents the gentleman as having finally gathered his thoughts sufficiently to respond with a major pronouncement (12.13): "To me at least it seems (said Ischomachus) that also those who are in a bad way erotically, as regards the things of Aphrodite, are incapable of being taught to be diligent about anything else" (in other words, the erotically infatuated are certainly diligent, but not about anything except their infatuation). And then Ischomachus added what might be taken as a startling and even somewhat poignant self-revelation: "for it is not easy to find a hope or a care more pleasant than the care for beloved boys; and when something needs to be done, it is not easy to find a punishment that outdoes in harshness that of being kept from those whom one erotically loves" (12.14). Perhaps Ischomachus is not (or in his younger days was not) as anerotic as he has appeared to be? Or: Is his disposition like that of the "cold king" Cyrus the Great[3]—restraining himself from what he experiences as a temptation whose dangerously blinding power he has noted in others, a blinding power that he maybe sometimes manipulates in others? That the latter of these two alternatives might be more likely seems suggested by what Socrates brings out in the immediate sequel. For Socrates says that he then asked Ischomachus whether those "erotically disposed toward *profit/gain*"[4] were also incapable of being educated in diligent care as regards field work—and Socrates has the gentleman replying, with a kind of relieved enthusiasm at the reminder:

"No, by Zeus! *They* are *very* easy to draw (*panu euagōgoi*[5]) into the diligence as regards these things! All that's needed is to show them that the diligence is profitable/gainful" (12.15). Ischomachus thus found himself able, finally, to give a sort of answer to Socrates's original, intensely pressing, question. The gentleman suggested that a sufficient (and perhaps necessary?) precondition of being "drawn" to diligence is erotically passionate love of profit or gain. This is in itself not an altogether implausible suggestion regarding human nature universally: consider Plato's *Hipparchus*. Could Socrates by this part of his narration be hinting at the essential role that passionate eros for one's own true improvement (one's truest "gain") plays in the hearts of those whom Socrates considers truly capable of diligence (diligence, that is, in exercising goodwill toward themselves)? But how does this apply to candidates for becoming a gentleman's slave overseers? What is the gain or profit in prospect for the overseers? Was Ischomachus suggesting that he needed to offer them substantial wages? Or a substantial share in his profits? Or had he somewhat thoughtlessly grasped at a straw, in order to answer Socrates's discomfiting questions? The gentleman as portrayed by Socrates at this moment in the dialogue seems oblivious to how problematic it might be for him to have someone as overseer who was erotically passionate about gaining a profit for himself. This impression is somewhat misleading, however, and will be in some considerable measure remedied soon.

Socrates at this point gently corrected, and tried to begin enlightening, Ischomachus. Socrates asked, "but as for the *others* (I said) [i.e., those *not* erotically disposed toward profit/gain], if *they* are self-controlled in the ways you bid them to be, and maintain measure in regard to being fond[6] of profit/gain, how do you teach *them* to become diligent in the ways you wish?" Socrates tacitly skipped to candidates from whose characters he dropped not only erotic love of profit but also good will toward the master. Evidently not having noticed these modifications, Ischomachus confidently replied: "Very simply (he said), oh Socrates! For when I see them exercising diligence, I both praise and try to honor them; and when they are careless, I try to say *and to do* whatever will *sting* them" (12.16). The words I have here italicized began to betray the fact that corporal punishment and its threat play a larger role in the gentleman's "educational" process than he cared at first, or maybe cares usually, to acknowledge—as now immediately became clearer. For Socrates responded by conspicuously turning away from any further explicit discussion of his challenging doubts as to whether it is possible to articulate qualifications that might render someone capable of being "educated" in diligence. Instead, he asked Ischomachus to clarify the qualifications of the one who is attempting to *carry out* such "education":

"is it possible for one who himself lacks diligence to make others diligent?" (12.17). The gentleman swore by Zeus that it was not possible and proceeded to draw a lovely analogy between a gentleman educator in diligence, and an educator in music, stressing the importance of the educator in each case setting "a beautiful example." But then the gentleman finally made evident the true, harsh lever by which he "educated in diligence"—and he thus clarified the meaning of the distinctive (harsh) "diligence" that must be exhibited by the master in his skilled educative activity.[7] The gentleman further betrayed the fact that his "educational" activity in bringing about what he called "the noble-and-good/gentlemanly things" situated him in close affinity with barbarian despotic rule, even over animals (12.18–20; XSD 169). As Socrates said in reply, "you *put into* (*parastēsēs*[8]) someone, and very strongly, this: that he must be diligent as regards the things *you* wish" (13.1).

## IN KNOWLEDGE OF THE ART OF FARMING

Socrates presents himself as next having asked, with apparent extreme naiveté: "when you have put into someone" diligence, then "will such a man be sufficient in overseeing, or is there something else that must be learned by him in addition?" Swearing by Zeus for emphasis, Ischomachus declared that of course the fellow needed to learn what ought to be done, and when, and how; and Ischomachus compared this needed knowledge with the knowledge of the art of medicine that is required to make even the most diligent curer into a doctor. Ischomachus thus spoke as if the knowledge needed by the overseers were rather complex, demanding, and even scientific; after all, the gentleman had introduced the theme of his education of his overseers by indicating that they needed to know (*epistasthai*) everything that he knows, as master of the farm (13.1–2; recall 12.4).

But the philosopher brushed past this required knowledge—the *intellectual* dimension of an overseer's education—as if he found the subject, of the *art* of farming, and education in that art, of little interest.[9] He asked, "so, if he learns also how the work needs to be done, is there still something else he needs in addition, or is this man now a perfected overseer (*apotetelesmenos epitropos*)?" (13.3).

## IN SKILLED RULE

Socrates presents Ischomachus having replied: "To *rule*, indeed (he said), I think it is necessary for him to learn—over the workers." To which Socrates rejoined: "So then (I said), you also educate the overseers to be capable of ruling?!" To this new Socratic expression of skeptical surprise at his educative claim, the now somewhat wary Ischomachus replied with circumspection: "I certainly try, at least." To which Socrates responded: "And how, indeed (I said)—before the gods!—do you educate in the[10] being *skilled* as rulers (*to archikous einai*) over humans?" Ischomachus's answer was rather defensive: "In a quite vulgar (*phaulōs*) way (he said), oh Socrates, so that probably you would laugh if you were to hear" (13.3–4). The gentleman obviously was aware that the sort of education in ruling that he teaches his slave overseers is held to rank far beneath the qualitatively higher sort of education in ruling (and being ruled) that is supposed to obtain among free republican citizens.

But Socrates professed to be in awe of the education Ischomachus claimed to provide his overseers: being able to educate "*skilled* rulers of humans" was no laughing matter for the philosopher who was in the act of founding political philosophy![11] Yet Socrates gave, as his reason for being so impressed, a characterization of "skilled rule of humans" that was rather unrepublican. He declared that he who "is able to make skilled rulers of humans" can "obviously teach skilled masters (*despotikous*) of humans," and whoever can do the latter can also make "skilled kings" (*basilikous*).[12]

This perspective suited well Ischomachus's self-admiring (see again the closing of chapter 21) conception of his quasi-divine educative rule over his overseers; and now, thus encouraged, he proceeded to deliver a preliminary elaboration of that conception (13.6–12). Skilled gentlemanly rule, he declared, rests on the recognition that the docility of a human being shares important characteristics with what is seen in the training of "the other animals," and in particular colts and especially puppies: for the latter are led, by rewards of needed pleasure, and by punishments of "trouble," to "do somersaults" and "to run around in circles."[13] To be sure, Ischomachus conceded, the human animal is superior by virtue of "judgment and tongue" and so "it is possible to make humans more obedient by a *logos* that shows them how is in their interest to obey"; still, "for slaves, what seems to be the beastly education, as seen in colt and puppy training, is very conducive to teaching obedience; by pleasing the desires of their stomach[14] you [sing.]"—Ischomachus assured Socrates—"would accomplish many things" (13.9). Ischomachus spoke as if he thought that the impecunious and perhaps overly high-minded Socrates had little or no experience in educating or ruling slaves, and Socrates in no way demurred from or belied this assessment (recall 2.3; cf. XSD 172).

Yet that a crucial dimension of skilled gentlemanly rule over slaves transcends the beastly education became clear when Ischomachus ascended to those "natures loving honor" among the slaves: "they," he said, "are spurred also by praise"; indeed, "some of the natures hunger for praise no less than the others do for food and drinks" (13.9; cf. *Hiero* 7.3). This obviously applied to those eligible to be overseers, in the gentleman's eyes. Xenophon provokes us to ask, does it not apply even or above all to the gentleman himself?—"It very much seems to me (he said), oh Socrates, that despondency/loss of hope (*athumia*) comes to be in the good, when they see the deeds done by themselves obtaining the same things for themselves as for those who neither toil nor are willing to run necessary risks" (13.11). In the gentleman's opinion, humans are not satisfied or even consoled by their virtue in and of itself, apart from deserved consequences.

At first Ischomachus spoke as if praise and honor were effective only with the elite minority; but then he went on to indicate that many or most humans can be, to varying degrees, thus governed, and he said that he taught the overseers—by praising them and reprimanding them, as well as by appealing to their "interest"—to employ (just as he does) praise and reprimand as a pervasive spiritual lever of rule over their underlings. In this context, as we've already seen, Ischomachus spoke of the importance of avoiding *athumia*, or the loss of *thumos* ("spiritedness"), in those who are "good," and also of the slaves' being "willing to run risks" (*kinduneuein ethelontas*) for him, as well as toiling for him (13.10–12). So: supporting if not confirming the Socratic thesis (13.5), the gentleman blurred what at first appeared his sharp distinction between skilled rule over most slaves and skilled rule over the few honor-lovers.

## IN A CERTAIN VIRTUE OF JUSTICE

Once again Socrates portrays himself as having next asked, again in apparent naiveté, if the goals of the education of the "perfected overseer" were now completed, or if something else were yet needed in addition (14.1). And once again Socrates has Ischomachus answering emphatically, swearing by Zeus, that indeed something else is very much needed: teaching the overseer "to keep away from the master's goods and not to steal!" (14.2). And once again Socrates reports himself expressing (though with considerably less emphatic skepticism than in the previous cases) amazement, while christening this an education in a *certain* "virtue of justice" (*tautēn tēn dikaiosunēn*)—with which designation Ischomachus readily agreed (14.3).

Looking back over Socrates's recounting of the unfolding curriculum of Ischomachus's education of his overseers, one gets the distinct impression that the gentleman had never before, prior to this Socratic questioning, laid out and surveyed in his own mind the four virtues that constitute the moral education which he claims and believes he gives his overseers. The four virtues mentioned remind one of the four cardinal virtues—with courage or manliness replaced, however, by good will toward the master,[15] and with moderation taking on the form of diligence, while prudence takes on the form of skill in ruling. The importance of justice, in the peculiar form of refraining from stealing from the master—under the threat, as it turns out, of imprisonment and even capital punishment (the gentleman's iron fist became more visible underneath the kid glove)—suggests a certain shakiness or limited reliability of the other three virtues of the "perfected overseers." Certainly the rule of (punitive) law suddenly ballooned to an enormous importance in the gentleman's account of his education of his overseers. Ischomachus now disclosed that he conceived of himself as a literally Draconian as well as Solonian lawgiver, who looked to the famous old Athenian lawgivers as models of the highest sort of lawgiver, one who sees his vocation as the inculcation, through his punitive laws, of "such a virtue of justice" (*dikaiosunēs tēs toiautēs*, 14.4) as prevents theft of the property one handles.

The gentleman conceded that he found "that not all readily heed this teaching" (14.3; see also 14.8): periodic, exemplary punishments are evidently needed.

But the fact that Ischomachus rules his slaves as a monarchical *lawgiver* accords with his understanding that he does not rule as a tyrant (see again 21.10–12).

The rule of law and tyrannical rule are so mutually exclusive in the Xenophontic-Socratic framework that in Xenophon's dialogue on tyranny at its potential best (*Hiero, or One Skilled in Tyranny*) Xenophon's wise Simonides refrains from ever mentioning law—and also "king," or "kingship" (*basileia*);[16] by the same token, tyranny is explicitly defined by the mature Socrates as "rule over the unwilling, and not according to laws, but however the ruler might wish," in contradistinction to kingship, which Socrates defines as "rule over human beings who are willing, and according to laws of the cities."[17]

One might well ask, however, whether the "willingness" of household slaves, even those belonging to a gentleman master, and hence the rule of law over such slaves, is not qualitatively different from the "willingness" of free citizens of the polis; is the "willingess" of such slaves not closer to the obedience of subjects under a wise tyrant? This question persists, though it may become less acute, when we take into consideration the fact that free citizens of a republic live bound by the chains of threatening and coercive or severely punitive criminal law, usually legislated by others in prior generations.[18] However that may be, this question does not appear to have troubled Ischomachus: he certainly saw no incongruity in adopting for his slaves the traditional Athenian (republican) criminal law governing theft. "To this extent he agrees with Socrates' view [expressed at 13.5] that there is no essential difference between despotic rule and rule over free men."[19] But Ischomachus was not satisfied with the republican criminal laws. While he saw approvingly that the great Draco and Solon wished to teach a certain virtue of justice by imposing punishments that "make unprofitable, for the unjust, shameful gain," Ischomachus made it clear that he saw this republican teaching as in need of the major supplement that can be found in "the skilled *kingly* laws." The latter, by also *rewarding* the just, so as to make it evident that "the just become more wealthy than the unjust," succeed in persuading "many even of those fond of gain" to "persevere in carefully not committing injustice" (14.5–7). Accordingly, the gentleman claimed (14.8–9) that he made his law-abiding overseers "rich."[20] More than that: "Those whom I recognize to be aroused to be just not only on account of acquiring more through the virtue of justice, but also on account of desiring to be praised by me, these I make use of even as free men—not only enriching them, but honoring them, as gentlemen/noble-and-good." And Ischomachus added a capital general point: "For it is this, in my opinion (he said), oh Socrates, that makes the difference between a real man fond of honor and a real man fond of profit—the willingness for the sake of praise and honor to toil at what is needed, and to run risks, and to refrain from shameful profit" (14.9–10; recall Ischomachus's teaching of his wife at 7.15–16 and 7.30). Yet—to repeat—courage or manliness (*andreia*) is conspicuously not a virtue in which Ischomachus educates his overseers; the freedom and the gentlemanliness that his lawful regime produces is more paternalistic, and much more profit-loving, than the freedom and gentlemanliness that is aimed at by the lawful regime of Sparta (see the *Regime of the Lacedaemonians*), or that is produced by the lawful regime of Xenophon's imaginary improvement on Sparta, the old Persia depicted in the *Education of Cyrus* (see also XSD 176). On the other hand, does not Ischomachus's household regime aim more unambiguously at gentlemanly freedom than does the democratic regime of Athens, under which gentlemen live in a somewhat embattled position (recall 11.21, and see the *Regime of the Athenians*)? And for a Socrates, might there not be a more hospitable place in Ischomachus's regime (living among Ischomachus's slaves or overseers) than there would be anywhere in the regime of Sparta or even of old Persia?[21] Taking this into account, or with a view to *both* what is good for the philosopher *and* what is good for the citizen, the Ischomachean gentlemanly regime might well appear a happy mean between Sparta and Athens. We may also note that in its virtuous paternalism the kingly regime of Ischomachus foreshadows somewhat the virtuous kingship that is articulated as the simply best political regime in Aristotle's *Politics* (bk. 3 end).

## SOCRATES'S SUMMARY REVIEW OF THE EDUCATION OF THE OVERSEERS

Socrates now (15.1) presents himself as having begun a transition from the theme of the education of the overseers to the theme of his own learning of the art of farming. He gave a synoptic summary of the curriculum that had been unfolded for the overseers, and then said, "no longer will I ask if something is needed in addition." Yet Socrates's formulation of the subjects of the education did not follow Ischomachus's formulations. Instead of saying, as had Ischomachus, that the latter "tried to educate" the overseer in "good will" (recall 12.5), Socrates now said: "you put it into (*empoiēsēs*) someone to wish the good things for you." Instead of saying, as had Ischomachus, that he "taught diligence" (recall 12.9–10; cf. 13.1), Socrates now said: "you put into the same person diligent care that the good things for you be accomplished." Instead of saying, as he had earlier, that the overseer "learns" (*mathē*—recall 13.3) how the work is to be done, Socrates now said: "you obtain the knowledge for him."[22] Instead of speaking, as he had earlier, about making the overseers "*skilled* at ruling" (*archikous*—recall 13.4–5), Socrates now said only: "you make him capable of ruling." Socrates thus quietly but clearly underlined the limitations of the gentleman as moral educator.

What is most amazing and thought provoking is that, instead of speaking of educating the overseer through law in a virtue of justice that would make him refrain from stealing his master's goods (recall 14), Socrates now asserted that the overseer educated by Ischomachus "is pleased for you in showing the fruits of the earth in the greatest abundance, even as you would be pleased for yourself." Socrates thus characterized the overseer educated by Ischomachus as animated by "the apparently much loftier justice which consists in entirely subordinating one's own prosperity to the prosperity of someone else" (XSD 178). Taking off from Ischomachus's declaration (14.9) that he honors as "gentlemen" the elite slaves whom he educates in justice by his praise, Socrates elevated such slaves to becoming nobler—that is, more selfless—in their dedication to the prosperity of the household and its king than is the gentleman-king himself! This is the first unambiguous introduction of self-transcending nobility in the entire work. What is Xenophon showing his Socrates to be up to here? Does Socrates not ironically prod young Xenophon, and us, to see that Ischomachus, as ruler of his household, does not ascend to such a lofty moral height?[23] Is that height not more accessible to a slave within his household? Are *enslaved* gentlemen then in a position to be morally superior to *free* gentleman? Or is Socrates hinting that there is something slav*ish* about such self-forgetting? What is the noble? Could Ischomachus answer these questions if he were asked by Socrates? Or do we have here again questions which the gentleman as such does not ask—but which Socrates presses his students to ask, and to answer?

CHAPTER SIX

# Teaching Socrates the Art of Farming

After Socrates's very peculiar and provocative summary of the curriculum of Ischomachus's education of his overseers, Socrates presents himself as having abruptly voiced a complaint about the gentleman's failure to elaborate the central item in his curriculum: "Ischomachus, do not leave out that part of the account that was rushed past, by us, in a most lazy fashion!" (15.1). This protest is comically "nervy." After all, it was Socrates himself who had led them to brush past any discussion of how the overseers were educated in the requisite knowledge of the art of farming (recall 13.2–3). No wonder Socrates reports Ischomachus as having expressed puzzlement as to what precisely Socrates might be complaining about. Socrates says he replied to the puzzlement by reminding Ischomachus of the latter's having said that "the greatest thing" (*megiston*)[1] would be for the overseers "to learn how each of the works should be done—and if not, no benefit of the diligence would come to be, if one did not know (*epistaito*) the things that need to be done, and how they need to be done" (15.2; cf. 13.2).[2]

At this point Socrates indicates that a somewhat nonplussed pause ensued on the part of Ischomachus (*entautha dē*), followed by his incredulous question: "is it the *art*, that now, oh Socrates, you are bidding me to teach—the one pertaining to farming?" Socrates presents Ischomachus as being familiar enough with the philosopher to find it astonishing that the latter should want to be taught the art of farming. In contrast, Socrates's earlier manifestation of *lack* of interest in the subject had not elicited from Ischomachus any sign of surprise.

Socrates says he responded in the affirmative: "because this is probably[3] (I said) what makes those knowing it wealthy, and those not knowing it live without resource, while toiling mightily" (15.3). Socrates spoke as if his interest in learning the art of farming might be not so much practical (aiming to take up farming himself) as quasi-theoretical or scientific—seeking to understand the knowledge that "probably" makes the decisive difference between prosperity or poverty for those who practice farming, however diligently they may labor. The philosopher ignored or left out of consideration not only the role of luck (*tuche*) but, what is much more, the crucial role of divine favor and the need to make sacrifices to win such favor.[4] We recall that Socrates has revealed, near the beginning of this work (2.16–18), that at some time in the past there occurred a rather profound change in his life activity, consisting of his undertaking an elaborate civic investigation caused by his "very great wonder" about why it is that "from the same works some are very much without resources, and some very wealthy"; and that the investigation led him to discover that the, or a, chief reason for success or failure is intrinsic to the knowledge or ignorance of the practitioners—though he immediately added a reference to the importance of divine providence as a crucial factor, in the case of Critobulus at any rate (while he ignored the power of chance or luck). It now appears that at the time he conversed with Ischomachus Socrates was inclined, at least, to see human knowledge of art as the decisive variable in determining success or failure—without need for crucial supplement from successful prayer and sacrifice to the divine.

However that may be, certainly Socrates presents Ischomachus as having failed to start to teach Socrates the art of farming, as requested. Instead Socrates portrays the gentleman as having launched into a paean to the art of farming—which he personified, indeed all but deified, and linked to the gods:[5] "how is the art not well-bred (*gennaion*) in its being most beneficial, and most pleasant to work at, and noblest, and most cherished by gods as well as humans—and yet in addition to these things, most easy to learn?!" For "we apply the term 'well-bred,'" he said, "to whatever animate things (*zōōn*) are noble and great and beneficial while being easy toward humans" (15.4).

Socrates presents himself as having been so put off by this reverentially personifying-deifying perspective on the art of farming that he immediately derailed Ischomachus's launch of this panegyric.[6] (Was Socrates's philosophic interest in the art of farming somehow antitheological?) Acting as if he had not heard a word that Ischomachus had just uttered, the philosopher gave a rather lengthy speech that began by going back and starting all over again his transition from the theme of the moral education of the overseers to the theme of his learning the art of farming: "I think I have learned well enough, Ischomachus, the following things you have said about what the overseer should be taught: . . ."

In this new iteration of the curriculum, however, Socrates gave a briefer summary, which was rather conciliatory in that it adhered to the way

Ischomachus had actually characterized the four moral constituents of his educative achievement: "I seem to have learned in what way you made the man good-willed toward you, as you asserted, and in what way diligent, and skilled at ruling, and just" (15.5). Then Socrates restated, but in gentler and clearer words, his complaint about the haste with which the intellectual component of the education had been treated (Socrates now reinserted the need to learn the *time when* to do various chores); and Socrates now gave a new, surprising basis to his dissatisfaction with the hasty treatment of learning the art of farming. Socrates reports himself as having spoken as if he himself might actually be planning to take up farming, immediately!—and farming now conceived as an eminently practical and complex art parallel to the art of medicine (15.6–9). Socrates recalls himself speaking as if he were viewing farming as a potential source of monetary profit for himself (see 16.9), rather than as something "most beneficial, and most pleasant to work at, and noblest" (that is, as Ischomachus had presented farming at 15.4; Ambler 1996, 128–29).

Socrates depicts Ischomachus as having replied by enunciating a strong assurance (calling on Socrates by name) that learning the art of farming is not an exhausting chore like the learning of the other arts, but is so simple that merely by observing and listening to farm workers "you would straightaway have the knowledge, so that you could even teach another if you should wish."[7] Going still further, Ischomachus declared: "I think it has quite escaped your notice that you" already "have much knowledge of it!" Then Ischomachus added a paean, not, this time, to a personified or deified art of farming, linked to the gods, but instead to the moral "characters" (*ēthē*) of the *humans* who practice the art, who are "most well-bred" (*gennaiotatous*) on account of their generous openness in sharing the "noblest" of their artful practices—in contrast to the way practitioners of the other arts jealously hide their most important artful knowledge (15.10–12).

Socrates quotes himself having replied that "*this* prelude is beautiful/noble, and not such as to turn the listener away from questioning!" (15.13). Socrates was no longer repulsed when Ischomachus delivered what we may characterize as a "humanistic" and demystified, even mundane, approach to farming as an art to be learned.

## EARTH'S COMPLEX NATURE, OR, HER DIVINE SIMPLICITY?

Socrates quotes himself as having seemed to have accepted Ischomachus's insistence that the art of farming is "easy" to learn; Socrates certainly urged Ischomachus to proceed on that basis to teach farming (15.13). Nevertheless, Socrates has Ischomachus starting off (16.1–2) as if he suspected that Socrates might be under the misleading influence of theoreticians or scientists, who analyze farming with "the greatest precision" while doing the least actual farm work, and who "claim that the one who is going to farm correctly ought to know first the nature (*phusin*) of the earth"—knowledge that "*they* say is very complicated" (*poikilōtaton*).[8]

The response Socrates reports himself having given fully confirmed any suspicions Ischomachus may have had. For even though Ischomachus began with the words, "Now first, Socrates, I want to demonstrate to you that the following that *they* say is *not* the case," Socrates defiantly replied, after having heard what "they" say: "Correctly indeed (I said) do *they* say *these* things!" For "he who does not know what the earth is capable of bearing will also not, I think, know what he ought to sow or what to plant!"[9]

Ischomachus rejoined by insisting that "it is possible to discern (*gnōnai*[10]) from" the fruits and trees on "someone else's land" (*gēs*, earth) what one's own land can and cannot bear. Ischomachus did not at first speak of a "neighbor's" land, and he never spoke of an "adjacent," or "next-door" neighbor; he seemed to be assuming that all the land in the country roundabout any given farm is pretty similar in capacity, except for that which is manifestly barren. Then he added: "and once, indeed, someone does discern, no longer is it advantageous to fight with divinity" (*theomachein*), or to go against what "the Earth is pleased to grow and nourish"; and "if, due to the laziness of those who have Her, She does not display Her capacity, it is often possible to learn (*puthesthai*) more truly about Her from a neighbor's place than from the human being who is the neighbor"—"for Earth lying waste nonetheless displays the nature of Herself," since if "She has the capacity to grow wild things beautifully, then, if tended, She will bring forth also the cultivated." On this theological basis, Ischomachus contended that "thus even those not very experienced in farming can nonetheless make distinguishing judgments about (*diagignōskein*) the nature of Earth" (16.3–5). Ischomachus thus expressed the conservative[11] outlook of traditionally pious Greek farmers,[12] who assume that knowledge of what divine Earth is pleased to grow—and what She would be displeased at having planted in Herself—is handed down and shared by each generation of the farmers in any given community, without any need for advice from theoreticians who have never wielded a hoe.

To this pronouncement of the gentlemanly view of what needs to be known about the soil, Socrates says he gave the following conciliatory but ambiguous reply: "But this (I said), Ischomachus, I think has now sufficiently restored confidence that it is not necessary to refrain from farming out of fear that I do not know the nature of Earth" (16.6).

Socrates added, however, a reason of his own for this confidence, a reason that was quite different from—and that subtly ridiculed—the pronouncement of Ischomachus:[13] "for also (I said) I just recollected the case of fishermen, who do their work at sea"; they don't hesitate to pass judgments praising the goodness and blaming the badness of the earth, by simply noting the coastal fields "as they scud past,"[14] without stopping to look or even slowing down, and their judgments mostly agree with what experienced farmers say—at least about the *good* land (16.7).[15]

Given this very, very low bar—by which even a sailor who rarely sets foot on land can aspire to be a "knower" of the agricultural capacities of the nature of the soil in its diversity—and spurred by Socrates's use of the verb for recollecting,[16] Ischomachus asked Socrates at what point he would like to start being *reminded* of his possession of *all* the knowledge needed for farming (16.8).

## PHILOSOPHIC PREPARATION OF FALLOW FOR SOWING

Socrates quotes himself as having given a remarkable response, to the effect that he thought he would be pleased to learn first that aspect of the farming art "belonging especially to a philosophic man."[17] This is one of the very rare occasions when Xenophon has Socrates speak of himself as philosophic. (Speaking in his own name, Xenophon never thus designates the master.[18]) Socrates reports that he proceeded to characterize the philosophic man, or himself as such a man, by specifying what it is that he would want to learn first about farming—namely: "how I might, if I should wish, by working earth, reap the *biggest* crops of barley and the *biggest* crops of wheat."[19]

We can be pretty sure that Socrates was not seriously planning to become a farmer. But as a philosopher, who was becoming the first *political* philosopher, he had as such achieved a perhaps unprecedentedly profound understanding of the vulnerabilities, practical and theoretical, involved in living the philosophic way of life; and he recognized the flux of fortune well enough to know that circumstances could arise in which he might need, and therefore would wish, to farm—and not merely for subsistence, but maybe even needing, and therefore wanting, to maximize his land's cereal crop yield (and thus his short-term cash income: Socrates did not mention any interest in farming grapes or figs or olives, or any other fruit trees—common Greek crops whose planting and cultivation required a much longer time to produce revenue; see chap. 19). We may surmise that if the philosopher were ever compelled to farm, he would not rest satisfied with the knowledge of the soil provided by Ischomachus's teaching, but would instead eagerly seek out scientific analyses of the natural capacities of the earth in its very complex variations.[20] (Consider the story handed down about the employment of meteorological science to bring about the wildly profitable economic enterprise of the first known philosopher, Thales: Aristotle, *Politics* 1259a6–20; Dorion 2013, 337.) Moreover, given what we learned from Socrates back in the first chapter, his characterization of the "philosophic" farmer here may also imply that under certain circumstances the Socratic-philosophic farmer might even need, and therefore aim, to maximize the *amount* of cultivated land he owned, and the *number* of workers he ruled, even outside his own city (recall 1.5). After all, what if a king or emperor, or the son of a king or emperor, were to become truly philosophic in the Socratic sense?[21] Is there not inherent in the philosophic life a very qualified, contingent, and strictly rational-prudent version of what we called back in chapter 2 the Cyrus-"vector"? We have to note that in the present passage Socrates once again, unlike the gentleman, did not limit the philosopher's conceivable maximization of crop yields to what can be achieved "by noble and just means" (recall 7.15, and more recently 14.9–10, in contrast to chap. 1).

Ischomachus, apparently quite unfazed by this sudden, lightning-like self-revelation of Socrates as a philosopher, began recollecting with and for Socrates as follows: "well, then, this indeed you know—that for the sowing, one needs to work at stirring up fallow" (16.10). Socrates replied without hesitation, "For I do know" (16.11). Ischomachus is presented by Socrates as having not used the most usual terms for ploughing (*aroō*) or digging up (*skaptō*) but instead a more general term that can mean a range of various sorts of stirring up;[22] what's more, Ischomachus is presented as having curiously altered the word for "fallow" (*neion*, feminine gender) by giving the word a spelling unprecedented in prior Greek literature: *neòn*—whose spelling happens to be identical, except for the accent (which would not have been marked in the original, pre-Hellenistic manuscripts), to the spelling of the common word for "youth," "young man" (*néos*, masculine).[23] Ischomachus's statement might therefore be read as: "well, then, this indeed you know—that for the sowing, one needs to work at stirring up a young man." This wordplay by our author Xenophon, immediately after putting in Socrates's mouth his sole explicit identification of himself as philosophic, points once again to the fact that this entire work is a drama of Socratic-philosophic education ("plowing" and "sowing") of the young, and first and foremost of Xenophon (and his kind).[24]

But of course the explicit and purportedly serious business at hand was depicting how Ischomachus helped Socrates to recollect his knowledge of how to work the earth for cereal crops. Through questioning, Ischomachus got Socrates to agree in rejecting winter as the time to "begin" plowing[25]—because, suggested the pupil Socrates, of the muddiness. Then Ischomachus got his pupil in the second place to agree on rejecting summer—because, suggested Socrates, the earth is hard for the yoked team to move.[26] Then, when Ischomachus suggested springtime as the likely correct time, Socrates agreed—because, he suggested, "the earth is especially movable/changeable at that time." The teacher Ischomachus decisively supplemented or indeed corrected this, by informing (not reminding) his pupil—addressing him by name—that the reason for beginning the plowing of the fallow ground in spring is also for the sake of thus providing the soil with herbal fertilizer by turning under the weeds before they have sprouted.[27] We note that Socrates had adduced what Aristotle would call a "material" cause or reason for spring plowing (a necessary bodily precondition), while Ischomachus adduced a "final" cause or reason (a goal or end).[28] Would Aristotle or Theophrastus, in reading this, have wondered whether Socrates is indicating that at this point in his life, when he was learning from Ischomachus, he was still too stuck in the limitations of pre-Socratic causal thinking (see also Plato, *Phaedo* 97–98)?

Ischomachus added that he thought Socrates "knows" in addition that "if the *neos* is going to be good, there is a need for it to be purged (*katharan*) of matter/wooden stuff (*hulē*)"—and "baked[29] as much as possible by the sun" (16.13). Socrates very emphatically agreed. When Ischomachus then asked if his philosopher-student "believed" there to be another way that this can be more effectively accomplished than if someone turned it over in midday in midsummer, Socrates ventured to assert that he "knew with precision" that this cannot be done better than by moving the earth *with the yoked team* as often as possible during the summer, nay, at midday in midsummer. In response to this, the teacher Ischomachus gently reined in his overly confident student by asking him "if humans" don't need to "make the *neon*" by digging in it *themselves*[30] and thus "making separate" the "matter/wooden stuff (*hulē*) from the earth." Socrates as a quick learner immediately incorporated with docility the corrective supplement (16.14–15). But Socrates failed to ask Ischomachus to give a reason for the superiority of humans over yoked oxen for the purgation, and Ischomachus failed to offer any reason. Instead Ischomachus then declared that Socrates could see that, as regards the *neon*, both of them held the same opinions. Socrates agreed that they were indeed of the same *opinion*, at least.[31] Knowledge is distinguished from opinion not least by including understanding of the cause or reason. But Socrates was evidently not going to insist on this distinction to his gentleman teacher.

## SOCRATIC SOWING, UNDER GOD

While Socrates thus presents himself as having been a pupil in need of some gentle corrective guidance from his teacher in "recollecting" the guiding purpose, and then the method, of working the fallow, the philosopher presents himself as having taken the lead prominently—and in theological terms—as the gentleman proceeded to guide him by questions through recollecting the *seasonal time at which* to do the sowing.

Ischomachus asked Socrates (17.1–2) if he "knew of any seasonal time other" than "that which all humans of the past and of the present, through making trial, know to be superior"—"for when autumnal time comes, all humans presumably look anxiously (*apoblepousin*) to the god, to see when, by wetting the earth, He will allow them to sow." Socrates replied at first matter-of-factly (not to say atheistically): "but all humans know not to sow voluntarily in dry land." Then immediately, however, the philosopher intensified the theological dimension of this universal human knowledge by adding that it was "clear that those sowing before being bidden[32] by the god wrestle with many punishments" (*pollais zēmiais*). Ischomachus's noncommittal response makes one wonder if he was not somewhat taken aback by this holier-than-thou response: "so then these things (said Ischomachus) *all us humans agree in knowing.*" Socrates chimed in with a theological reason: "Because, as regards the things that the god teaches (I said) *thus there comes to be thinking in agreement.*" Then the philosopher illustrated by adducing the divine teachings all humans have received to the effect that in winter it is better to wear thick clothing, if possible, and to burn fire, if there is wood (17.3).

The gentleman evinced no suspicion that Socrates might be blasphemously jesting about purported instruction from divinity. Ischomachus earnestly pointed out that there is, however, great disagreement over whether the sowing is best done at the start, or in the middle, or at the end of the rainy season. Socrates volunteered the theological reason for this great disagreement: "the god does not lead the year in an orderly fashion, but makes one year most beautiful for sowing at the start, and another year in the middle, and another year at the end" (17.4). When Ischomachus asked Socrates whether he considered it superior to pick out one of these three times— to gamble (if you will), or, instead, to spread the sowing over all three—Socrates did not take the opportunity to so much as hint that the proper response to this divine challenge might be prayer and/or consultation of auspices (contrast the Socratic teaching in *Memorabilia* 1.1.9 end); nor did Socrates refer to the possibility that he personally might receive special guidance from his *daimonion* if, as a farmer, he were to confront this challenge. Instead, our philosopher opted for the cautiously rationalist "spread of the bet"—and for this he was praised, as a good student, by the cautiously pious gentleman, who pointed out that Socrates had even anticipated his teacher on this crucial point (17.5–6). But: Had the gentleman recognized the profound theological implications that the philosopher had brought to the fore—in other words, the adumbration of what one may call the Socratic theology?[33]

Continuing to take the lead, our bright student for the first time in his education in the art of farming asked a question, and thereby set the next topic of instruction:[34] "in the casting of the seed, is there a complex art?" (17.7). It immediately transpired that Socrates asked this question not out of ignorance—he soon said he had observed sowers—but in order to bring out the fact that casting evenly, as is absolutely essential, is an art that requires so much dexterity, and thus long practice, that Socrates did not hesitate to compare it to *cithara*[35] playing. Sowing is certainly a skill that can *not* be learned with the ease that Ischomachus promised or boasted (one may wonder whether Ischomachus himself ever engages in casting seed with his own hand, as opposed to supervising sowers or the overseers of the sowers—11.16, XSD 195). Is the same not true of many aspects of farming (XSD 189)? Is the (true) art of farming in its epistemic complexity—including knowledge of the nature of earth (and of dung in relation to earth) in its diversity, and theological knowledge, and long experiential practice in casting seed, and similarly long practice in other manual farming skills—is this art truly so "easy" and thus "philanthropic" as the gentleman wished or hoped to believe (recall 15.4)? Does the gentleman farmer understand all that *truly* knowing the *true* art of farming would entail?

But Ischomachus was confident that he could help Socrates recollect the contrast between correct sowing in lighter soil as opposed to heavier. After Socrates established through questioning that by "lighter" was meant "weaker," and by "heavier" was meant "stronger," the philosopher professed a need to be taught, since he was uncertain which of the two following alternative analogies he should follow: (1) the analogy with the practices of diluting with more water the stronger wines, and assigning more burdens to stronger men and more responsibility to more capable men; *or*, (2) the analogy with the practices of giving more food to weaker draft animals, in order to make them become stronger (17.8–9). Socrates thus makes it very clear that he was problematizing sowing, by way of analogies. Chuckling, Ischomachus accused Socrates of kidding around with his introduction of the second analogy. The gentleman did concede, however, that weaker soil can be made stronger by a primary sowing aimed at providing herbal fertilizer, in place of absent dung fertilizer, for a crop to be sowed subsequently.[36] Nevertheless, swearing by Zeus for the first and only time in the section on farming (Zeus as the rain god of traditional belief is never referred to by name or explicitly, pace Meyer 1975 ad 17.4 and 20.11), and thus good-naturedly joining in the fun, the gentleman insisted that, as Socrates must agree, "all the weaker are to be assigned less to do." Socrates did not assent, however. (Socratic "sowing" may be more flexible than is Ischomachean.) Instead, Socrates abruptly asked another question that expressed his ignorance of the purpose of another related farming practice (17.8–11).

## THE OTHER MAIN TASKS OF CEREAL FARMING

What is the point (Socrates says he now asked) of sending in men working with hoes once the grain has sprouted? Ischomachus thereupon led Socrates by questions (17.12–14) to see the various purposes of the hoeing, and not least the need to cut out weeds—which Ischomachus compared to the useless drones in hives who rob the worker bees of the food that they have toiled to store. To this last, Socrates replied with a curse and then reflected "in his *thumos*" (*enthumoumai*) on the rhetorical power of good images (we are reminded again that Xenophon and his Socrates are acting as poet-teachers). Socrates confessed that the drone image had "infuriated him much more" than the simple statement on the weeds (which had, then, angered him against weeds to some extent). This episode of fury—at weeds—is one of only two occasions upon which the Xenophontic (or for that matter the Platonic) Socrates is ever depicted as becoming angry or indignant about *anything*—let alone as capable of being aroused to impassioned indignation by an image (17.14–15; see also *Symposium* 8.23–24). Socrates as narrator thus comically limns the place of *thumos* in his own "personal psychology."

Socrates portrays himself as having managed to calm down from his rage at the weeds enough to declare the likelihood that the next task in chronological order was *reaping* the grain, when it has reached maturity—and he asked Ischomachus to "teach what you have in regard to this." Socrates depicts Ischomachus as once again having proposed in reply that Socrates needed only to be *reminded* of his already "knowing" (*epistamenos*) reaping. More precisely, Ischomachus is portrayed as having challenged, in a spirit of jest, the legitimacy of Socrates's request to be taught, on the grounds that

Socrates already "had the very same knowledge in these matters" as did Ischomachus himself; and then the gentleman proceeded by means of interrogation to claim to "catch Socrates in the very act"[37] of being compelled to confess his possession of just such knowledge, contrary to his false pretension of ignorance (18.1–2). Socrates presents the gentleman as having here become somewhat infected, at least temporarily, with the philosopher's playful attitude toward his education in the art of farming. Socrates quotes himself confessing to the dereliction (*kinduneuō*—"I daresay": 18.3). Now what precisely would be the misdemeanor that Socrates presents himself as having been caught committing, red-handed, and as having confessed to? The misdemeanor is: pretending to be less knowledgeable than one in fact is—in a word, irony (*eirōneia*), one of the two extremes (the other being boastfulness, *alazoneia*) that Aristotle presents as the vices opposed to the virtuous, gentlemanly mean of truthfulness or candor. Aristotle adduces Socrates as his only example of the *eirōn*—the type of person characteristically engaging in this "refined" vice.[38]

After this remarakble arrest and confession, Socrates proposed investigating whether he also already knew (*epistamai*), without realizing it, *threshing*—the task that (as he already knew) comes next in time (18.3). Ischomachus proceeded to prove that Socrates did already know threshing. Or was this proven? Ischomachus declared at the conclusion of this interrogation: "so then as regards these matters (he said) you are not behind me in knowledgeable familiarity (*gignōskōn*)" (18.5). But does this "knowledgeable familiarity" constitute real knowledge (*epistēmē*), of the skill of threshing—knowledge of how to engage correctly in threshing? Was Socrates being truly educated in *any* of the practical skills required in farming? Is the gentleman as teacher being portrayed as a boaster (*alazōn*) who does not realize that he is a boaster—and is thus all the more risible?

Socrates reports that he declared that the next task they would need to perform would be purifying the harvested grain, by *winnowing*—which he did not ask to be taught, thus suggesting that by being "caught red-handed" he might have learned his lesson. Ischomachus proceeded again by interrogation to show Socrates that he already knew the skill of winnowing, to such an extent that he would be able "to teach someone else." Socrates's expletive ("by Zeus!") could be taken to express his delighted amazement at being made aware of his understanding of winnowing—or what he calls in conclusion the "knowing (*epistamenos*) that has escaped my notice" (18.6–9). But the expletive could also be a signal of the gently satirical drama about "knowing as recollecting" that Socrates is presenting here, featuring himself as chief performer. Certainly Socrates reports himself as having declared (with tongue planted firmly in cheek) that he had been thinking for a while that it may well have escaped his notice that he also has knowledge (*epistamenos*) of gold smelting, and of flute playing, and of artistic painting: for even as with farming, while he has never had any lessons in any of these, or ever practiced any of them, he has observed the practitioners. The gentleman replied by earnestly and complacently restating what had been his original, personifying or divinizing praise of the art of farming as "the most well-bred" because easiest to learn—the praise that had earlier left Socrates so cold (18.9–10; recall 16.4–13). Now, however, Socrates professed agreement with this praise, on the grounds of his being, as he now repeatedly declared, a "knower" (*epistamenos*), without having realized that he is a knower, of whatever pertains to *sowing* (18.10; recall 17.7–8; see XSD 192b).

## PLANTING TREES AND VINES

The preceding completed Socrates's education in that part of farming that he had said he would be pleased to learn first, as especially suitable for a philosophic man (16.9). Accordingly, while the turn to the planting of trees[39] was initiated by Socrates, it was not initiated by his asking to be *taught* (contrast 18.1, 3). Instead, what soon emerges is that Socrates aimed to use the discussion of planting[40] to execute a sly refutation, through questions, of Ischomachus's claim that the art of farming as a whole was knowable or learnable through recollection. Socrates "set up" Ischomachus by first asking an innocent-sounding question: "is it the case (I said) that the farming art includes also the planting of trees?" (19.1; planting had from the start been included in farming by Socrates—16.1; and in the next lines it becomes manifest that Socrates had witnessed many plantings). When Ischomachus of course answered in the affirmative, Socrates sprang his refutational question: "so how then (I said) would I know the matters pertaining to sowing but not know those pertaining to planting?!" When Ischomachus responded by urbanely expressing doubt as to Socrates's professed ignorance in respect to planting, the philosopher adduced, as overwhelming testimony to his ignorance, his lack of knowledge of the stages of planting, beginning with his ignorance of the kind of earth in which to plant each species.[41]

But Ischomachus firmly but patiently rose to the challenge of what he realized was Socrates's "testing of me."[42] Socrates proceeds to give us the amusing spectacle of himself having been forced by questioning to acknowledge, step by step—his answers punctuated by a veritable flurry of profanity, the most from him ever in this work[43]—that he was not inferior to Ischomachus (who was "said to be a terrific farmer," Socrates noted) in "knowledgeable familiarity" (*gignōskōn*) with planting, first of grapevines, then of fig trees and of "*all* the other fruit trees," and then of olive trees.[44] To repeat, the proof that Socrates was a knower in these matters was that Socrates had happened to see people planting vines and had also seen olive tree plantings along the roadsides—so, as Ischomachus conclusively asked, "therefore, seeing them (he said), with what about them would you not have knowledgeable familiarity" (*gignōskeis*), and "why would you reject the noble procedures for planting vines when it comes to the other sorts of planting?" Socrates wondered ("by Zeus!") why he had ever said earlier that he did not know (*epistamai*) how to plant—or why it seemed to him that he had nothing to say about how to plant (19.3–14).

Thus was Socrates confessedly refuted in his attempt at refuting the gentleman on the issue of the philosopher's knowledge and ignorance.

Reflecting on this amazing experience (and restraining himself from outward laughter), Socrates asked: "So then (I said), oh Ischomachus, is questioning teaching?" Then Socrates reports that he added: "for I am now learning in what way you questioned me about each thing: by drawing me through what I know, and showing things similar to these, you *persuaded* me, I think, that I *do* know the things that I did not believe I know" (*epistasthai*, 19.15).

This might well seem to be the most pregnant moment in the entire dialogue with Ischomachus. For it might appear that here Socrates got from the gentleman the inspirational guidance for that dialectical mode of philosophizing that became distinctive to Socrates as the founder of political philosophy.[45] Now if or since the source of Socratic refutational activity is the philosopher's having been taught by a perfect gentleman that interrogation is education, how could the refutational activity that is distinctive of Socrates possibly be corrupting of anyone?! This part of the *Economist* participates distinctively in Xenophon's "apology of Socrates." To be sure, there are some crucial differences between the interrogation, refutation, and thus education Socrates received from the gentleman and that which Socrates himself later deployed.[46]

A more troubling and truly serious lesson that may be delivered by this burlesque is the following. Socrates here would seem to show himself aware of a potential misapprehension that he must painstakingly guard against in judging the degree of his success in every attempted, serious dialectical-educative refutation. These serious refutations are aimed at producing shared *knowledge* through arriving at agreement via question and answer regarding opinions about the just and the noble.[47] Having achieved success in such teaching, Socrates then tests the interlocutor to confirm his hypothesis that the acquisition of such knowledge has profound consequences for the learner's religious experiences, and hence for "theology." The danger or limitation pointed to here is that the agreement arrived at, and above all its psychological aftermath, may be grounded in the interlocutor's merely being *persuaded* to agree that his original opinion has been refuted, merely being *persuaded* to agree with the conclusion, and, worst of all, therefore merely *exhibiting superficially* a psychological reaction that the interlocutor divines will conciliate and win the respect of Socrates—all without the interlocutor's adequate understanding of, without his having fully taken to heart, the refutation in each and every step and implication, and therefore without his actually experiencing in his very bones the psychological transformation for which Socrates is watching. So Socrates here indicates that he is well aware that he must as a dialectical teacher inspect with a warily critical eye the apparent successes and the apparent psychological outcomes of his dialectical refutations. Certainly Socrates here reports that at this concluding moment in his own education-by-being-interrogated (19.16) he was teased by Ischomachus with the prospect that by submitting to the gentleman's questioning he could also be "persuaded" that he knew how to test for genuine, as opposed to counterfeit, silver money[48]—and then "persuaded" that he knew how to play the flute, and then persuaded that he knew how to paint, and to engage successfully in other such fine arts. Socrates avowed that this was "probable," given that he had now been "persuaded" that he was a "knower" (*epistēmōn*) of how to farm. But Ischomachus no sooner held out this bait than he snatched it away. "This is not the case (he said), oh Socrates!" And Ischomachus restated his original praise of the Farming Art for Her radically distinctive or indeed unique "love of humanity" by which She is elevated far above all other arts.[49] Ischomachus concluded his teaching of the Art of Farming by illustrating how "She in many ways also teaches how one might most nobly employ Her." Oddly, however, the illustrations were not of lessons given by the Art but instead of lessons given by the Grape Vine (*ampelos*) in "Her" (*heautēn*) *natural* growth.[50] Socrates's narration contrives to have the gentleman's teaching on farming conclude by pointing to the truth that knowing any art depends on learning from nature.[51]

## DILIGENCE VS. KNOWLEDGE

The conclusion of his education in the art of farming prompted Socrates, as student, to ask a fundamental question (20.1): "Then how is it, oh Ischomachus, if the things that pertain to farming are thus so easy to learn, and everyone knows in a similar way what ought to be done," that "some live in abundance and have a surplus, while some can't provide even the necessities, but fall into debt besides?" This question recalls the philosopher's hopeful (and nontheistic, not to say atheistic) explicit premise for his whole education in farming: the likelihood that the art is "probably/perhaps what makes those having knowledge of it (*epistamenous autēn*) wealthy, and those not having such knowledge (*mē epistamenous*) live without resource, while toiling mightily" (recall 15.3). The question that Socrates now posed most obviously expressed simple puzzlement, but can we suppose that Socrates did not have in mind possible answers—and that he was not testing to see which one Ischomachus would deliver? Given the comical undertow that, we have repeatedly noted, especially pervades Socrates's recounting of his "education" by the gentleman in the art of farming, this question could be taken as conveying once again the soft-spoken challenge: Is what Ischomachus has been teaching really the *knowledge* that constitutes the *true* art of farming?[52] On the other hand, however, this question could be taken as a mildly plaintive expression of Socrates's loss of his hopefully philosophic premise for his education in farming. And if so: Must not divine providence, and human farmers' sacrificial worship as required to solicit divine favor, now be reintroduced as the (theological or pious) crux of farming?[53] Or: Does it turn out that a most important element in the true, scientific art of farming is the theology adumbrated by Socrates at 17.2–6? If so, the question becomes all the more pressing: What is the cogent basis for that Socratic theology? Is the basis found in the rest of the truly philosophic science of farming—as is most fully available to us in the later elaboration by Theophrastus?[54] Or: Does the truly philosophic science of farming depend upon a theological foundation established only by Socratic *political* philosophy—centered on *the* Socratic discourse now being delivered to Xenophon and his young friends, in very serious expectation of future observation of, and interaction with, *their reactions* to that discourse?

However this may be, the lengthy, nigh oratorical answer that Socrates quotes Ischomachus as having given makes the gentleman sound like something of a "convert" to the Socratic theology. For Ischomachus mentioned divine providence only in the following forms: attributing rain to "the god above," and attributing to Earth pleasure in Her being given fertilizer (20.11), and fairness in Her returning benefit for having been benefited by humans (20.14; recall 5.12), and, by Her making everything about Herself readily known and learned, fairness in testing and revealing who is "bad" and who is "good" among the humans who deal with Her (20.13–14).[55] Moreover, while divinizing Earth, Ischomachus never once even mentioned the "art of" farming[56] and no longer so much as hinted at personifying the art as a female divinity. Ischomachus thus steered clear of the sort of religious praise of the Farming Art to which Socrates had turned a cold shoulder at 15.4–5. Socrates presents the gentleman as if he had suddenly shifted from revering divinity in art to revering divinity in nature. Could it be that Xenophon, through his Socrates, here near the end of this work (i.e., in its most exposed part) indicates and promotes a "rhetorical project" that Xenophon adopts as a theological writer?

Still, the references to divinity were only incidental features of Ischomachus's forceful and richly illustrated homily on the decisive factor causing failure at farming: the lamentable lack of human diligence (*epimeleia*)—and not at all lack of knowledge (*epistēmē*—and Ischomachus treated as even less decisive the "seeming to have discovered something wise for the work": 20.5). Ischomachus's admonitory monologue took off from common opinion, or "the word that runs about" (*logou diatheontos*: 20.3). Revealing again his heart's preoccupations, the gentleman drew a parallel between farming and generalship: as in farming, what distinguishes those who are good and bad at generalship is diligence or the lack thereof; the knowledge component is easily possessed, by most private persons.[57] In the gentleman's version of the perspective of common opinion, as here reported by Socrates, knowledge (*epistēmē*) is certainly not the main constituent of excellence in these principal gentlemanly activities of war and of peace. In other words, Xenophon has his Socrates here make clear how contrary to respectable and common opinion is his provocatively paradoxical thesis equating virtue with knowledge.[58]

But Socrates portrays Ischomachus as having indicated or hinted at a more pointed (if implicit) criticism of the philosopher. For the gentleman suddenly broadened his field of vision beyond farming, to encompass the lack of diligence more universally, and declared to Socrates that "he who neither knows another money-making art, nor is willing to farm, evidently thinks to make a living by stealing or robbing or begging—or is totally irrational!" (20.15). Immediately after this quotation from the gentleman, Socrates for the first time, and for only a single sentence, switches to indirect discourse (in beginning to relate what Ischomachus said next, about the need for diligence in one's subordinate workers, and thus about the need to know how to rule in a way that instills diligence in subordinates). Socrates thus for a moment brings himself to the fore as narrator, more conspicuously than ever before—prodding his audience to ask and to reflect on the questions, "How does this Ischomachean declaration apply to Socrates? How, after all, *does* Socrates make his living? Does Socrates rule over any subordinate workers?" (XSD 100–105). One suspects that these not exactly admiring questions may have arisen in Ischomachus's mind.[59]

## THE PROGRESSIVE SPIRIT OF THE GENTLEMAN FARMER

Ischomachus, after completing his admonition on lack of diligence—whose destructive effects he highlighted in subordinate workers as well as in independent farmers (20.16–21)—is reported by Socrates as having ascended to what the gentleman manifestly regarded as a contrasting exemplar of truly diligent farming: his own father, who advised his son to buy land neglected by the carelessness or incapacity of its owners but who never allowed his son to buy land well worked by diligent farmers, on the grounds that such land was costly and allowed no "progressive improvement" (*epidosis*). For progressive improvement (Ischomachus said his father believed) is "what makes every possession and living thing delightful," and "nothing has more progressive improvement than land that becomes productive from having been idle" (20.23). Ischomachus thus suddenly revealed how deeply "progressive" or growth-oriented his gentlemanly spirit was, and how much he admired the perhaps even greater "progressiveness" of his father's gentlemanly spirit. It turns out that what energizes, what gives relish and vigor, to the gentlemanly life is the vivid consciousness of successfully loving to make one's possessions improved—and, simultaneously, to make them more beneficial to oneself:[60]

> and my father neither learned this from another, nor discovered it by worrying meditation (*merimnōn*),[61] but through love of farming (*philogeōrgian*)[62] and love of labor (*philoponian*), he said that he desired land such that he would have something to make, and would take pleasure in being benefited. For my father really was ([Ischomachus] said) by nature, oh Socrates, in my opinion, *the* greatest lover of farming (*philogeōrgotatos*) among the Athenians!

Ischomachus had first introduced his father as a practitioner and teacher of a "most effective form of *money making*" (20.22). He had further remarked that together with his father "we made many pieces of land worth many times their old value." And this devising of his father's, Ischomachus assured Socrates, "is so easy to learn that by hearing this now you will go away knowing it as well as I, and you will teach another, if you wish!" Ischomachus was a kind of proselytizer for his father's progressive money-making idea.[63] We are at first inclined to suppose that by this money-making idea, Ischomachus referred to the money that his father had made from the crops produced on the neglected lands that he had purchased, which he had then enjoyed improving and which he had thus made his cherished own (as the cherished products of his life's work as a gentleman farmer). But Socrates, evidently catching a whiff of something rather different, asked whether the father had retained as his own the lands that he loved to improve, or instead had sold them if he could find a high price. This provoked the reply: "And sold—by Zeus! (said Ischomachus); but, out of his love of his work (*philergian*) he immediately bought instead another, which had been neglected" (20.26—Ischomachus did not say that the selling price of, or profit from, the improved land needed to be high). Socrates submitted at length that this meant that the father was "by nature a lover of his work" or a "lover of farming" in the very same sense that sea merchants are lovers of the grain they work hard at importing with care (20.27–28). This provoked Ischomachus to exclaim: "Now you're poking fun (he said), Socrates!"[64] The magnanimously urbane Ischomachus did not take offense at what he evidently regarded as a merely playful teasing. Gentlemen farmers do not conceive of themselves, and are not conceived of by others, as engaging in merchandising, or as animated by mercenary love of their products (Pomeroy ad loc.).

Nevertheless, Ischomachus felt the need to add a mild apologetic: "I also believe those to be no less lovers of house building who sell the houses after having built them, and then build others." The perfect gentleman Ischomachus teetered on the verge of crossing the "sacred line" between: (a) the gentlemanly view of money, as a means or tool to be acquired only for the sake of, and within modest limits set by, nonmonetary ends achieved by engaging in enjoyably fulfilling gentlemanly activity; and (b) the businessman's view of money as something to be acquired lawfully but otherwise without limit, by buying and improving or creating and then selling, in a life-engrossing, endless increase of money or buying power until death.[65]

Socrates reports that he responded with a pithy statement that gave a semiserious but weighty ballast to what might have appeared his mere joshing witticism: "By Zeus! And to you (I said) I swear, Ischomachus, that I trust you: by nature all *believe* (*nomizein*)[66] that they love (*philein*) all these things from which they *believe* they would be benefited" (20.29). In his wavering, the gentleman—like most humans—does not really *know* what he loves. Unlike the gentleman, Socrates is animated by a clear-sighted love of gain of a kind that immunizes him against the confused "love" of the gentleman. Yet as we saw in what preceded (20.15), this immunization places Socrates under the shadow of suspicion of injustice in the eyes of the gentleman.

## THE LOFTINESS OF THE GENTLEMAN'S SKILLED RULE

At this point Socrates quotes himself—for the final time in this work—as having praised Ischomachus for the effectiveness with which his "argument as a whole" had persuaded Socrates of the "basic premise" (*hypothesis*) that "the skilled farming art is the easiest to learn of all" (21.1). In this congratulation Ischomachus seems to have sensed at least the shadow of an intellectual demotion of the farming art that is so central to the lifework of the gentleman. Certainly Socrates presents Ischomachus as having responded by vigorously reminding Socrates of, and stressing that he agreed with, what he presumed was the high intellectual regard in which Socrates held "skilled ruling"—as something "common to all the activities carried out through skilled farming, and skilled statesmanship, and skilled household management, and skilled conduct of war," and which, in its universality, requires a capacity for "knowledgeable judgment" (*gnōmē*), by which capacity some few are highly distinguished from others.[67] Ischomachus went on to deliver a quite grandiloquent[68] closing salute to the sublime spiritual and mental virtues of skilled (especially monarchic) leadership universally—including of course his own sort of gentlemanly household management of his large farm.[69]

Socrates's quotation of his emphatic affirmation of being persuaded by Ischomachus that farming makes the least demands on the intellect renders noteworthy (and quite amusing) Socrates's failure to report any response of his to the gentleman's impassioned case for the intellectual sublimity of skilled ruling over a farm.[70]

Ischomachus began to make his case (21.3) by invoking boatswains who, in their rule over the rowers of a trireme warship on an open sea voyage, are able to speak and to act in a way that "whets the souls of the humans to be willing to toil," so that they complete the trip rapidly, with sweat and mutual encouragement and admiration—in contrast to the failure of those boatswains who are "lacking in knowledgeable judgment" (*agnōmones*). By referring to the trireme rowers as "humans" rather than as navy men, and by saying nothing about the leadership of a trireme *in battle*, attended by the risk of death, maiming, and capture or enslavement (see *Memorabilia* 3.12.2), Socrates presents Ischomachus abstracting from the crucial difference between rule over rowers in a warship and rule in merchant ships over rowers who may be slaves or hired hands. This formulation thus skirts (and quietly indicates) a big problem in the gentleman's claim as to the commonality of the challenges and virtues of all sorts of rule.

The problem did not go away when the gentleman ascended to speak at greater length (21.4–6) about what differentiates good from bad "generals" (*stratēgōn*). He spoke first of the bad, whose "soldiers are unwilling to toil, or to run risks (*kinduneuein*), and, instead of obeying, pride themselves on their contrariety to their ruler, while not knowing (*epistamenous*) to be ashamed at shameful happenings." To these he contrasted "the divine and good, knowledgeable rulers" (*epistēmones archontes*—he ceased to speak of "generals"), who make these same followers (he did not say "soldiers"), together with others, have a proper sense of shame, so that they think it better to obey and, individually as well as in a team, pride themselves on obeying and toiling, not without hopeful spirits. The upshot is that, "even as a certain love of toil can come to be in private individuals" (*idiōtais*), so "in the whole army, under the good rulers, there comes to be both a love of toil and also a love of being honored through being seen doing something noble by the ruler." Ischomachus made no mention of running risks when speaking of what distinguishes the divinely good, knowledgeable rulers and their followers; this made smoother his transition to asseverating (21.7) that "*any* ruler to whom the followers are *thus* disposed—these become the rulers who are strong, indeed!" Swearing by Zeus (and thus adding force to a contestable claim), he demoted the importance for rulers of excelling over their soldiers in bodily fitness, in javelin throwing, in archery, and in ownership of the best horses, so that they are "foremost in running risks" (*prokinduneuōsin*) as they lead light-armed troops or cavalry into battle.[71] Finally, however, Ischomachus was impelled to spotlight a capacity that would seem rather sharply to distinguish skilled *military* rulers from skilled farm managers: their "ability to put into the soldiers [the thought] that they must be followed through fire and through every risk." Those who have *this* ability, Ischomachus declared (21.8), "one might justly call lofty-in-knowledgeable-judgment,"[72] and it is by "being knowledgeable (*gignōskontes*) in this that many follow them." Then he switched to the singular: "this is the one who might reasonably be said to advance with a strong hand—he whose knowledgeable judgment many hands are willing to serve; and great, in reality, is this man who is able to accomplish great things by knowledgeable judgment rather than by force (*rhōmē*)."

This last formulation smoothed the transition to farm management (21.9): "And thus also in private works, if the one in charge is an overseer or supervisor who is able to present laborers eager in spirit, intent, and persistent—these are the ones who accomplish good things—and make a big surplus!"

There is evident in this sermon of Ischomachus a tension between his awareness of the great respect due to the virtues of military leaders—given the risks that they must heroically meet and manage—and his more profound, if not quite openly defended, gentlemanly awareness that war is for the sake of peace and therefore the virtues of leadership in peace are superior to the virtues of leadership in war. But does the gentleman have a clear and coherent conception of the virtues and goals of leadership in peacetime?[73] Thus far, he has spoken only of the leadership exercised by supervisors and overseers, who are likely to be slaves (but we recall that Ischomachus conceived that he educated his overseers to be gentlemen: 14.9–10.)

Just as we are beginning to wonder where the gentleman *owner* of the farm (and of the slave laborers and overseers) fits into the picture as thus far drawn, Socrates has Ischomachus herald the entrance of the owner (21.10): "But when, oh Socrates! the Master (*despotos*) makes his appearance"—he who "is able to inflict the greatest harm on him who is bad among the workers, and give the greatest honor to him who is eager in spirit!" Well, if *then* the workers don't appear manifestly affected, "I would not admire him" (Ischomachus disdainfully declared, switching to the emphatic first person singular); but on the other hand, if "on seeing him, they are stirred, and ardor[74] is inspired in each of the workers, along with competitive love of victory in regard to one another, and love of excelling in honor," then, *this* master "I would affirm possesses something of the royal character!"[75] It was such ruling capacity, tested and revealed by the reaction of slave workers when their punishing and rewarding master appears on the scene, that Ischomachus proclaimed "is, in my opinion, *the* greatest thing, in *every* work where something is accomplished through human beings, including farming"; and he further declared, swearing by Zeus, that the acquisition of this royal ruling capacity requires "education" in the full sense—*paideia*—with the precondition of a "good nature." And not only that. This "greatest thing" requires finally (Ischomachus did not shrink from affirming, presumably on the basis of personal religious experience[76]) a sort of transfiguration into divinity (*theion genesthai*—21.11). "For," Ischomachus explained, "this—to rule over the willing—is not at all, in my opinion, on the whole a human good, but divine: they [the gods] clearly reserve it[77] for those who are truly initiated into the sacred mysteries of moderation!" (*tois alēthinōs sōphrosunē tetelesmenois*—cf. *Symposium* 1.10).[78] In contrast, "they [the gods] give tyrannizing over the unwilling, in my opinion, to those whom they hold to deserve living out their lives as Tantalus is said to in Hades:

spending all time fearing lest he will a second time die!" (21.12).[79] The gentleman conceived his divinely inspired, mystery-initiated, royal household management and rule to be at almost the opposite pole from the divinely damned, Hellishly insecure life of a tyrant (cf. 3.4 again and *Hiero* 10.4 again). Xenophon has his Socrates present the gentleman concluding his teaching of the philosopher in the *Economist* (*Oikonomikos*) with a peroration almost diametrically opposed to the peroration with which Xenophon has his poet Simonides conclude his teaching of the tyrant in *Hiero, or One Skilled in Tyranny* (*Tyrannikos*). Not the least of the polar opposites is Simonides's complete silence on the gods and on human piety or religious belief and religious experience (see OT chap. 7). There is, however, this important and thought-provoking lack of antistrophe in the formulation by the gentleman of the contrast between the kingly gentleman and the tyrant: whereas Ischomachus characterized the life of the tyrant as a "deserved" (*axious*) retributive punishment from the gods, he did not characterize the gentleman's royal, godlike life of rule as a deserved reward from the gods—*and* did *not* characterize the gentleman's life of rule and moderation as *intrinsically* "happy" or "blessed."[80] At the end, the gentleman spoke in such a way as to make his motivation for, and his expectation or hope from, ruling and moderation appear austerely noble—without mention of concern for either happiness or hopeful deserving. To be sure, his final words did evoke a vivid image of the afterlife, and of divine judgment in Hades. And we recall that Ischomachus began to relate his own activities by saying that he "served the gods" in order that they might "give happiness" (11.8). Moreover, the gentleman here at the end emphatically affirmed that he conceives and indeed experiences his masterly ruling as the human instantiation and reflection of the gods' rule, and the foremost character of the gentleman-owner as ruler is the fact that he "has the power to do the greatest harm to the bad one among the workers and to honor in the greatest way the one eager in spirit" (21.10; recall 13.11–12 and 14.9–10).

CHAPTER SEVEN

# Socrates Leading the Festivity of Gentlemen in the *Symposium*

Xenophon begins his most delightful and jovial writing in a playfully assumed, argumentative-defensive tone.[1] He speaks as if his earnest purpose in what follows is to defend the controversial proposition that not only the serious deeds of gentlemen but even their playful deeds are worth memorializing. As we soon see, this is a lampooning flattery of conventional gentlemen which serves to mask the chasm between them and the Socratics: in fact, it was only the chance and somewhat forced participation of the abnormal "gentlemen" Socrates and his followers that transfigured (not to say hijacked) this particular gentlemanly banquet, hosted by the ultrasophistic Callias, so as to make it the singular exception that is worth recounting (cf. Pellizer 1994, 180). To be sure, this means that a banquet hosted by an unusually sophisticated gentleman did afford an occasion for Socrates and his followers to express something of themselves such as they could never do in the context of the serious deeds of normal gentlemen.[2]

Xenophon claims to speak as an eyewitness[3]—but one who within the drama remains unseen and unheard (while making his authorial voice repeatedly audible, especially in the transitions: Bowen 1998, 18–19). This strange self-presentation is obviously calculated to provoke reflective wonderment.[4]

## THE SETTING

Xenophon reports the host Callias as having made quite clear the chief motivating reason why he extended a last minute invitation to the Socratics (1.4). Callias was on his way home to his dinner party when, on catching sight of the Socratics as a group, it occurred to him that they, being "men pure in their souls," and thus superior to military and political men,[5] could be very useful to him on this particular occasion—by providing refined adornment for the private pederastic-seductive gathering he was about to host in order to celebrate, impress, and woo his beloved "boy." The latter was Autolycus, the famously victorious young athlete,[6] who was being chaperoned by his father Lycon—an ominous presence, for this gentleman was in later years to become one of Socrates's three official accusers.

Socrates replied to this spur-of-the-moment invitation by protesting, in obviously ironic jest, against Callias's excessively overt presumption of his intellectual superiority, on account of his vast expenditures on sophist-tutors, over and against "us self-taught amateurs in philosophy" (*autourgous tinas tēs philosophias*—1.5). Callias responded by promising, with a hint of rueful envy, that he would also use the dinner party as an opportunity to display[7] much wisdom, that he had hitherto kept hidden, which would make him worthy of (finally?) being taken seriously by the Socratics (1.6).

Because of the peculiarly sophistic character of the gentleman-host of this private dinner party, Socrates had less need than in any other of Xenophon's presentations to veil his own character as a philosopher.

Callias's offer to display his hidden wisdom failed to elicit from Socrates an acceptance of the invitation. It was the followers of Socrates who, after first politely but repeatedly declining,[8] finally capitulated, on behalf of Socrates as well as themselves; they did so when they saw that by continuing to decline[9] they would offensively arouse the socially powerful Callias.[10] The Socratics, and not least Socrates himself, obviously had formed better plans for the evening than to spend it at the magnate's mansion helping him with his seduction.[11] But the followers of Socrates (if not Socrates himself) apparently felt that it would be imprudent to resist the pressure exerted by their very wealthy and prestigious host, who was evidently used to getting his way with social inferiors such as the Socratics.

Thus, at the outset Callias dominated.

## AUTOLYCUS: THE BEAUTIFUL POWER OF THE GOD OF LOVE

But Callias's planned festivities had difficulty getting underway, because he and his guests, including Socrates (to some extent), became dominated by a higher power. The company no sooner assembled in the dining hall than it fell under the enchantment of what Xenophon says immediate reflection would have held to be the "regal character by nature" of beauty, especially when it is exhibited in a youth suffused with "bashful reverence" (*aidous*) and moderation (1.8). "To begin with," this beauty of Autolycus[12] captivated the eyes of everyone (Xenophon stresses—so, the eyes of Socrates too) with a necessarily arresting force, like a light in a dark night (1.9). "Then," as they gazed, each and every one of them (Socrates too) was induced to undergo one or another of various spiritual effects. In some, divine possession by the god "moderate Eros" was evident: this was the case unmistakably in the lover, Callias—but also, it would seem, if to a much lesser degree, in those who assumed "more dignified postures" in addition to falling more silent. But there were certain others who, Xenophon indicates, only fell more silent. These would seem to be the ones Xenophon designates as "initiates into the mystery rites of this god." As such initiates, Socrates (and Xenophon), and maybe also Charmides, did not experience divine possession, and were soon able to look *away from* Autolycus, to the other onlookers; there they found something "worth contemplating" (unlike the beauty of Autolycus): namely, those others' manifestations of their awed religious experiences as they contemplated the beauty of the boy (1.10). Xenophon spurs us to watch, in what follows (and in his other Socratic writings), for indications of the character of, and the grounds for, the Socratics' "initiation into the mystery rites of this god"—an initiation that frees the initiate from divine "possession," while arousing his keen interest in contemplating the manifestations of divine "possession" in *others*, caused by *their* apparently inspired contemplation of erotic beauty.

## BREAKING THE SPELL OF DIVINE EROTIC BEAUTY

The company dined in a reverent silence—"as if by the command of someone superior," until the arrival of the jester Philippos (1.11–16). He introduced a rather inept version of the vulgar level of the Aristophanean spirit.[13] Philippos's jokes fell flat, but he finally managed through his shenanigans and lamentations[14] to liberate the guests (and especially Critobulus, who alone finally "guffawed") from awesome Eros to the point where they could be properly receptive to the elegant after-dinner musical entertainment.

This performance was produced by "some Syracusan guy" (*Surakosios tis anthrōpos*[15]) who prospered by traveling the world displaying in action his young and attractive, highly trained and skilled slave musicians and dancers.

Only after this complex spiritual succession—the company's powerful emotional and religious experiences evoked by erotic beauty, from which a (partial) liberation or relaxation was effected through vulgar comedy, giving way to refined delight at the instrumental music of lovely young performers—does Xenophon present Socrates as finding the atmosphere conducive to his beginning to try to take over and to direct the evening's play. From this point forward we witness a subtly comical and most instructive contest, as Socrates struggles, with mixed success, against a series of challenges to his efforts to make the evening enjoyable on his own terms (to the maximum extent possible). For while Socrates "in speeches dealt as he wished with all who conversed with him" (*Memorabilia* 1.2.14), the symposium is an affair of deeds as well as of speeches.

## LYCON: CIVIC VIRTUE AND SOCRATIC VIRTUE

Addressing Callias by name, Socrates started by politely flattering the "perfection" of the host's arrangements for their pleasure.[16] Socrates's manly oath—"by Zeus!"—anticipated, however, the little rebellion against Callias's luxurious plans that Socrates proceeded to stage. He did so through a speech which gave him occasion to express some jocosely extreme "manly" opinions, enforced by repeated manly oaths—"by Zeus!"—all of which succeeded in evoking a favorably bemused reception from Lycon. The latter's good-natured interrogation allowed Socrates to further impress the patriarch with the old-fashioned manliness of Socrates's stated educational views[17]—even inasmuch as those views encourage fathers to seek out others as exemplars of noble gentlemanliness to influence their sons.[18]

Unfortunately, this adroit rhetorical success of Socrates with the old guard was destabilized by a flurry of skeptical rejoinders from others in the sophisticated party (especially, one suspects, some who had heard Socrates speak skeptically on this topic on other occasions: cf. 4.1). Socrates appeared to stifle the untoward Socratic-skeptical discussion of the teachability, and hence the nature, of virtue by postponing such a dialogue with an appeal for attention to the commencement of the next performance by the Syracusan's lovely creatures (2.6–7).

In fact, however, Socrates (helped by Antisthenes[19]) used the subsequent series of increasingly impressive acts as the subject for drollery that indicated—in a manner instructive for his more alert students—something about his way of answering the subversive questions that had been tabled about virtue and its teachability. Socrates first made the private education of women, slave and free, into a comic allegory for education in civic virtue, centered on "courage" or "manliness" (*andreia*). Through this comic allegory, Socrates showed that he recognizes that civic manliness can display itself in actions that express daringly graceful self-control, deployed individually as well as through teamwork. But Socrates also indicated that he holds that this civic virtue is teachable by, and rooted in, a habituation that can in principle be well effected and employed by the sort of benevolently despotic regime or ruler of which the nameless "Syracusan" can be a farcical simulacrum.[20] (It will gradually transpire that this Syracusan's despotic regime is by no means loveless.) The quips made by Antisthenes and Philippos (at which no one laughed: 2.13–14) remind us that relatively free-wheeling, democratic Athens is deficient in such disciplined virtue and its teachers; but, when we reflect that this deficiency may be a necessary condition for the possibility of a party like the present one, we recognize that this defect of the Athenian democratic regime is not lamentable from every point of view.[21]

In responding to the censorious Antisthenes's taunting question about his failure as an educator of Xanthippe (2.10), Socrates in effect confessed that his inability to rule his temptestuous wife showed that he, in contrast to the "Syracusan," lacks the forcefulness needed to teach manly civic virtue, with its rootedness in a spiritedness (*thumos*) that is shared by horses and humans, male and female. Xenophon thus prompts in us readers the further wonder: To what degree is Socrates even capable of being taught, or of learning, manly and spirited civic virtue? How *does* Socrates participate in civic virtue—given that such virtue is a matter of serious, manly deeds more than speeches?

When next the slave boy performed a dance not requiring daring or teamwork, but deploying all parts of the body in graceful harmony that (Socrates stressed) enhanced the lad's beauty, Socrates responded by extending his playfully allegorical treatment of exercise in virtue (2.15–19). He first engaged in a sort of self-parody. He told the Syracusan that he would enjoy learning from him such dance postures as the boy exhibited. ("Socrates had not expressed a desire to be taught the dangerous act of the dancing girl, i.e., manliness"—XS 148.) When asked the reason for his desire to learn the boy's dancing postures, Socrates declared his intention to use the postures in his own dancing, "by Zeus!" At this, "all, indeed, laughed" (while Socrates kept a straight face, of course—2.17). "The contrast between the effect of Socrates's statement and that of Philippos' jest could not have been greater: Socrates is much better at making people of some refinement laugh than any professional jester" (XS 147–48; see also Halliwell 2008, 147–51).

Continuing to hold the audience in his hand as comedian, Socrates explained "with a very straight face" that and why he engages in his singular "dancing" (2.17–19). He thus "strips" and "exercises in the nude" (*gumnazomenos, apoduesthai*) not for its own sake, nor for display, nor for the edification or benefit of others, but as a self-taught, strictly solitary activity, through which he promotes his health and enhances his pleasures and develops his all around supple strength (while admittedly making an effort to diminish his specific lack of fitness—"a bit of a belly"[22]). Socrates made it clear that he does not teach, or even usually disclose, his private, nude "exercise."[23] But, together with Charmides, he also let it be seen that at least one of his youthful companions has been able to discover this astonishing, private and solitary, Socratic activity and has gotten Socrates to explain it, and has then gone off to approximate it in solitude, within the limits of the youth's ability to "learn" or to "know." (I believe that the figure of Charmides is here meant to begin to evoke, as a kind of avatar, the figure of Xenophon in his youth.)

While Socrates thus evinced playful eagerness to learn from the Syracusan some additions to his own "dancing," Socrates gave no sign that he had any taste for the "Syracusan's" career of using his knowledge of various sorts of gymnastic and dance to create shows of virtue that impress a wide-ranging audience, in many cities, and thus gain profit and repute—as well as respect from a few of the wise, such as Socrates. As Strauss points out (XS 178), a clue to the signification of this nameless Syracusan is the fact that according to Xenophon in his *Hellenica* (3.1.2), a "Syracusan" is the author of a book that is indistinguishable from the crowd-pleasing *Anabasis*. This "Syracusan guy," we venture to surmise, is a comic avatar of Xenophon's authorial genius, presented as if, or on the playful assumption that, it had not suffered Socratic "corruption."[24]

## SOCRATES STRIVES TO MAINTAIN THE UPPER HAND

In crude response to the subtle Socratic humor, Philippos managed finally to outdo Socrates in mirthful success with the gathering, by presenting a mindlessly slapstick parody of the dancing that Socrates had appreciatively made the vehicle for his thought-provoking jests. Philippos thus promoted a hilarity that conduced to thirst for increased wine drinking.[25] The party moved in a conventional direction.[26] Socrates accepted this development because in the present company he evidently found desirable for himself, as well as for the others, the inebriation that, in his words, puts to sleep the soul's pains and awakens its thoughts of friendliness. Still, Socrates sought (without complete success) to put a brake on Philippos's oenophiliac influence, so as to maintain the possibility of (playfully subtle) conversation and judgment (2.24–27).

Gradual inebriation by wine is one thing; *sexual* "drunkenness" (cf. 8.21) is something else. When, shortly afterward, Charmides was so Xenophontic (see *Memorabila* 1.3.8–13) as to react to the next musical performance by expressing an incipient aphrodisiac intoxication, induced by the Syracusan's beautiful slave-singers, Socrates took stronger action. Appealing first to the company's gentlemanly self-esteem, and then to Callias's promise "to display his wisdom," Socrates managed to lead the party back on the track of a playfulness involving thought.[27] Yet we soon see (4.8–9 and 4.10 beg.; see also 4.52 and 6.1) that Socrates had to continue to contend with Charmides's roguish erotic proclivity, directed in part toward the kissable Niceratus, and seconded by Critobulus (not to mention Xenophon, who as author is the creator of all this erotic trouble for Socrates).

This was not the only headwind Socrates encountered in his effort to pilot the symposium. When Callias agreed to fulfill the promise he had made to display his wisdom (*sophian* 3.3, recall 1.6) on the condition that each of the others bring forward "whatever each of you *knows that is good*," Socrates ventured to speak for everyone with a precision that raised the stakes and made more likely mutually instructive self-disclosure: "but no one will gainsay you by not saying what each holds that he *knows that is worth/deserves the most*" (*pleistou axion epistasthai*). Callias responded by proceeding to tell about "that of which I am *most proud*" (3.4), soon equating this with what is most beneficial (3.5)—and Socrates seemed to acquiesce in this dilution of his own proposal (3.7–10; though see 4.6). On these last, unintellectual terms (pride and benefit, instead of knowledge), Lycon and even the blushing Autolycus could participate—with the result that the latter again became temporarily the cynosure (3.12–13). But after Socrates had helped briefly to spotlight and to gratify these guests of honor, he suddenly "Socratized" the party by imputing to the company a commitment that each had supposedly made to "demonstrate"[28] that that of which he is proud is in fact "worth much" (*pollou axia*—4.1). Lycon and Autolycus obviously did not have a place in this Socratic trial of wits. Accordingly, they now receded into the background.

## CALLIAS VINDICATES HIS CLAIM TO SUPERIOR WISDOM

Leading off, Callias proclaimed his superiority to the Socratics in respect to that with which the latter appear most preoccupied: "during the time in which I hear you puzzling over what the just is, I am making humans just!" (4.1; the Socratics may well appear to be all talk, talk, talk about justice, with too little evidence of teaching people to be more just, or even more law-abiding: see Plato's *Cleitophon*, and compare *Memorabilia* 4.4.5–10 and

1.4.1). When Antisthenes, the risibly contentious Socratic doppelganger, attempted (predictably[29]) a "refutation" of this aggressive claim, Callias vindicated his boast, in part by deftly deploying an outrageous sophism—and then by having the nerve to address Antisthenes as "Oh sophist!" (4.2–4). Yet Socrates validated this comically dubious victory, sealing the defeat of his own acolyte (4.5). Why?

We may surmise that Socrates must have appreciated Callias's needed expansion—the addition of economic incentives—of the previous indication by Socrates of the basis of education in civic virtue (see *Economist* 13.6–12). And Socrates must have good-naturedly relished Callias's satiric mimicking of two of Socrates's famous refutational theses: on the one hand, the contention that virtue is rooted in motivating knowledge of what is truly good for the virtuous (4.2); and, on the other hand, the insistence that the dedicated practitioner of an art, including especially the arts of teaching justice (3.5) and of prophecy (4.5), is as such concerned with the good, not of himself but of those whom his art serves (4.4).

But through the juxtaposition of these two famous Platonic and Socratic theses, in this context, Xenophon has his Socrates point to the grave implicit question or puzzle that was apparently unrecognized by Callias: What is the good for oneself that a wisely virtuous person reaps by the practice of any art, and in particular the art of teaching justice? This question was here made more acute by the fact that Socrates was the only speaker other than Callias who had emphatically declared that what he prides himself upon is the possession of an art (3.5 and 3.10).

Socrates at this point indicated one possible kind of answer to this question by adducing the example of the art that is most intimately connected with devotion to the gods—prophecy (4.5).

A very different answer to this question was suggested by what Socrates had said earlier (3.10) about the money he might be able to make from practicing the pimping art (*mastropeia*) on which he claimed to pride himself. The latter reminds us of what we have learned from the *Economist* is Socrates's philosophic love of gain. But—Xenophon provokes us to wonder—what is the true and serious gain that Socrates reaps from his practice of the art of pimping?

The reason that this question of the gain that accrues to the practititoner of an art does not trouble Callias seems to be that he looks down on what he regards as the plebian, utilitarian justice that his art teaches to *others*; he himself does not need the recompense that such justice entails; his is the high-minded perspective of a gentlemanly *noblesse oblige* that transcends justice as understood and conveyed by his didactic art (4.3: this generosity of Callias provides a foothold for Socrates's later exhortation of him to a more erotic dedication to civic leadership, and thus to a richer justice).

## NICERATUS: THE SIDEKICK OF CALLIAS

In this *noblesse oblige* the wealthy Callias was joined by the next speaker, the amiable, handsome, wealthy, and amusingly fatuous Niceratus.[30] He "was (apart from Autolykos and Lycon) Callias's only original guest" (Bowen 1998 ad 3.5)—and thus gives us a glimpse of what the (conventional) symposium's conversations and speeches would have been like without the Socratics present. Niceratus sportively[31] demonstrated the vast personal, political, and military betterment that his somewhat sybaritic (and thus un-Socratic: 4.8) version of recitations of Homer would bestow on those who "associated with" him—if, that is, they "paid court to" him (4.6).

## CRITOBULUS: THE SENSUALLY BEAUTIFUL SOCRATIC

Niceratus's Socratic counterpart, the amiable, handsome, and wealthy Critobulus, now claimed his turn to justify his pride—in his own beauty (4.9). Responding to Socrates's earlier skeptical question as to whether Critobulus could claim that his beauty enables him "to make us better" (3.7), the young man contended that personal beauty like his attracts to its serene and more than royal possessors extraordinary devotion and service, endowing its devotees with "every virtue." On one hand, "we who are beautiful" deservedly take pride in the fact that we effortlessly obtain for ourselves the good things for which others must toil, or run risks, or persuade. On the other hand, as one of the beauties who "draws humans to *every* virtue," Critobulus claimed that he could justly think better of himself than can Callias, who can claim only to make others "more just" (4.13–15). Still, though he specified other virtues, Critobulus could not quite bring himself (in the presence of Socrates) to mention wisdom as a virtue that beauty inspires in its lovers (XS 155). The virtues that Critobulus spoke of were the generous, sacrificial, risky, and self-restraining. So virtue, as Critobulus presented it, culiminates in selfless devotional service, even enslavement, to the beautiful, as to that which is highest. And while Critobulus claimed to pride himself on being beautiful, what obviously most passionately moved and consumed him was his experience of being, in his own turn, virtuously devoted to the beautiful Kleinias. His speech prompts wonder at a well-known phenomenon: Can we figure out why it is that even the regally beautiful person, the high object and beneficiary of others' devotion, is so drawn to becoming virtuously devoted to someone else who is beautiful? How and why is even the beautiful needy—of the beautiful?

We get a clue to the answer if we duly note that Xenophon has his Critobulus's playful praise of beauty remain within the pious limits appropriate to conventional gentlemanly good taste.[32] Critobulus did not include in his lighthearted speech any reference to the awesomely serious, religious experience of the beauty seen in Autolycus: the religious experience that he, along with the other gentlemen, underwent only a short while before, at the start of the evening. When Critobulus specified "every virtue" that beauty such as his own inspires, he was not so hubristic as to include piety in this jesting. Apart from his casual swearing "by all the gods," Critobulus broke his silence on the immortals, and verged on inappropriate speech, only in a concluding afterthought: after defiantly addressing Socrates by name, he was thus apparently reminded of the need to defend beauty against the telling criticism that it swiftly fades,[33] and in a mildly desperate reach, he adduced the significance of elderly beauty as displayed in the august civic worship of Athena; this, he submitted, supplies evidence that the beauty of worshippers of the goddess endures—at least into old age.

What is most notable in Socrates's elaborate response to this speech of Critobulus is the reason Socrates gave for his burlesque horror at Critobulus's kissing of the latter's beloved boy Kleinias (4.25–26). Socrates spoke of something which went unnoticed in the speech of Critobulus: this "terrible fuel of erotic love" contains, Socrates insisted, an "insatiability," linked with "certain sweet hopes." Socrates added a comment that indicated that he was thinking of the spiritual, and not merely the carnal, implications of kissing. "It is for this reason," Socrates then went on to declare, "that one who is to be capable of sound or moderate mind must abstain from kisses of those in bloom."

Yet Hermogenes's complaint here (4.23) was obviously not groundless: it was evident that Socrates, despite his jeremiads, "overlooks" Critobulus's passion for Kleinias with indulgent amusement—much as he allows Critobulus to drag him to rural comedies (recall *Economist* 3.7).

Charmides was moved to interject himself to pose a different challenge to the master (4.27), having obviously pondered with a certain skepticism the "frightening away from beauties" that Charmides characterized Socrates as having addressed to "us who are friends." Charmides relied on, and revealed, more of his intimate observations of Socrates's actual behavior. Charmides teasingly asked if the deeds of Socrates—his actual intimacy with the beautiful Critobulus—accorded with his words. The specific example

Charmides adduced could plausibly have been accounted for by Socrates as an illustration of the degree to which his own hard-won wisdom, and consequent self-control, has immunized him, as the wise philosopher, against the dangerous consequences of the erotic temptations away from which he reasonably warns his less mature, more susceptible followers. Was it not some such response that Charmides hoped to elicit—an indication that erotic infatuation is not quite so permanently dangerous a thing as Socrates proclaims it to be? If so, Charmides was disappointed. What Socrates confessed to, no doubt with some comic exaggeration, was a rather long-lasting wound that his "heart" had suffered as a result of his having only momentarily lowered his guard, even in a mild self-indulgence of *eros*. Socrates emphatically refused to acknowledge any complete immunity to becoming infected in some degree by the "sweet hopes" implicit in *eros*. This would suggest that the passionate nature of even the strongest, most rational soul never becomes entirely invulnerable to the "wounds" of *eros*. And this might explain why Socrates permitted himself, with someone like the lighthearted and clever but rather shallow Critobulus, a kind of sexually flirtatious outlet that, for the sake of clear-headed and deeper, simpler friendship, he did not allow himself with his more promising (more truly beautiful) young intimates such as Charmides. Certainly Xenophon explicitly underlines that Socrates and Charmides had been mingling seriousness with their joking: Charmides's challenge or complaint was partly serious, and received a partly serious response.[34]

## CHARMIDES: THE POLITICALLY RESTLESS SOCRATIC

The fact that Charmides had now brought himself to the fore made it easy for Callias to call upon him to speak next—falsely claiming that it was Charmides's turn to speak, when in fact it was the turn of Antisthenes (4.29). Was the wealthy Callias especially curious to hear how Charmides would turn the catastrophe of his recent impoverishment into a boast?

When Charmides had first announced his poverty as a source of his pride, Socrates had endorsed the boast, and had offered a cue as to what the young man could or should present as the grounds: indigence can be said to conduce to a more unenvied, hence more carefree, more unguarded private life (3.9). The ironic speech Charmides now proceeded to give did follow this cue inasmuch as he stressed that his becoming poor had provided him the freedom to come and go as he wished—and above all to consort with Socrates without any longer being reviled, or even paid attention, when doing so.

But Charmides insisted on situating this newfound freedom, and his entire experience of poverty and wealth, in its crucial *political* context—which he limned as follows. In democratic Athens, so long as he was rich, Charmides experienced being the exploited, anxious, and threatened "slave" of the regime, but when he became poor, he shared in the regime, "like a [poor] tyrant" (except, of course, that he remained the associate of Socrates). Charmides's closing words, and his response to Callias's question, indicated his openness to an improvement in the economic and political situation of himself (and of his friends?—see *Memorabilia* 3.7 end).

In his material desires, Charmides appears to stand somewhere between Critobulus and Socrates (cf. *Economist* 2.2–13). But the youthful Charmides sounds somewhat more ambitious, less averse to risk, less troubled by being envied, than either. "Charmides, in contradistinction to the first three speakers, does not claim to make human beings better." He "enjoys being together with Socrates" (XS 158).

Xenophon depicts Socrates as having said, in response to Charmides's speech, not a word, of either praise or blame (see *Memorabila* 3.7, esp. 3.7.5–7)—in striking contrast to Socrates's favorable response to Charmides's original boast (at 3.9). Xenophon presents Socrates as having cut off further discussion of Charmides's remarks, and as having avoided taking his place in turn as speaker next after Charmides; Socrates instead spoke up (4.34) to hand the floor to Antisthenes (who had been skipped by Callias's intervention). In the sequel, Xenophon presents his Socrates as having contrived, with some help from Charmides, to distance his own speech as far as possible in time from that of Charmides. As we learn from the *Hellenica*, Charmides in a few years was to become part of the regime of the Thirty, and was appointed one of the Ten who administered Piraeus, under whose harsh rule Autolycus met his death in 404–3 BC, after a famous act of defiance to a Spartan occupier. Xenophon quietly indicates a major reason why Lycon later became one of the official accusers of Socrates.[35] We note that we are now at the center of the work as a whole—where the weakest or most vulerable part of a speech or writing ought to be situated (*Memorabilia* 3.1.11).

## ANTISTHENES: THE MORALISTIC SOCRATIC

Antisthenes responded to Socrates's invitation no doubt as Socrates had hoped—in a way that overlaid the hint of politically ambitious restlessness in the previous speech of Charmides. Antisthenes delivered an edifying oration exalting the materially impoverished *and politically unambitious*

Socratic way of life. Antisthenes made it clear that he recognized asceticism to be only the exterior of the Socratic life. At that life's core, he emphasized, are vast spiritual riches and pleasures, which are generously shared with all who are capable of enjoying them. Yet what those spiritual riches and pleasures are, Antisthenes did not—probably because he could not—indicate.[36]

## HERMOGENES: THE PIOUS SOCRATIC

"Someone"[37] called upon Hermogenes to speak next, in the sixth place, even though he had originally been last in the order. Originally, this sixth place belonged to Socrates; now Socrates will be the one to speak last. Xenophon thus indicates that he means to make Hermogenes and Socrates appear in some sense interchangeable, to the extent possible (XS 163). Hermogenes's greatest role in Xenophon's writings is to be the medium through whose refraction we hear Socrates's "apology to the jurors" and, what is more, what Socrates was intending in that reputation-defining rhetorical action. Here in the *Symposium*, Hermogenes's speech, together with Socrates's response (the combination of which, Xenophon stresses, was "spoken seriously"), repaired a massive lacuna in Antisthenes's previous portrait of how the Socratic way of life appears. For Antisthenes, whose peculiarly limited *eros* is focused on what he perceives to be Socrates's ascetic external being, had been silent about Socrates's piety or concern for divinity.[38] Hermogenes's speech corrected this falsification of the Socratic image and thereby circumscribed a major dimension of the "spiritual riches" of Socrates that Antisthenes was unable to specify. Socrates is in truth passionately concerned to gain, to confirm, and to maintain knowledge of divinity, as the key to knowledge of "the beings" (*ta onta*). Antisthenes fails to see how much the distinctive asceticism of Socrates—along with his appeal to his *daimonion*—is a product of this passion. As for Hermogenes, the profundity of his piety is expressed in his indicating that the knowability of *ta onta*[39] for the gods (4.47) entails the unknowability of *ta onta* for humans: Hermogenes cannot answer a question as to the "what is" (*ti esti*) but only a question as to the "what seems to me" (*to moi dokoun*—6.1).

Hermogenes testified to experiencing the presence of nameless gods who generously care for him and whose attributes (especially *their* knowledge of *ta onta* and of the future) may be gathered from "barbarian" as well as Greek belief. He further testified that these gods communicate with him through personal revelations—by "messenger voices" while he is awake, by dreams in his sleep, and by omens through birds (4.47–48).

Socrates responded: "Well, there is nothing incredible in these things" (4.49; cf. Plato, *Apology* 33c4–8). Socrates had only one question, which brought out a very important fact that Hermogenes had not made clear on his own. Hermogenes has the gods as his friends,[40] who never cease to watch over him day and night, *because* he "serves" them (cf. Plato, *Euthyphro* 12d5ff.). We may surmise that Hermogenes had not thought to mention this because, as we later hear, he is consumed by his erotic love of gentlemanliness (8.3).

## FORESHADOWING THE FIRST PART OF THE INDICTMENT OF SOCRATES

Philippos kept his seventh speaking place (4.50), which had been given him by Lycon (3.11)—who, according to the original order, would have had to speak next, to defend with a speech his pride in his son. This unseemly challenge (Danzig 2017, 138) was warded off by the urbanely, irrepressibly, erotic Charmides, who drew in the Syracusan as a substitute, gaily daring him to speak in praise of his slave boy (whose beauty Charmides had earlier confessed to finding sexually very attractive—3.1). The Syracusan replied by expressing his alarm at the "plotting to corrupt the youth" that he perceived afoot—impugning by implication the whole Socratic crew (4.51–52; recall 4.18).

Xenophon has the Syracusan express in comic form one of the accusations that Lycon will eventually make in a deadly earnest indictment on behalf of the city.

Socrates responded with a good-natured, bantering interrogation revealing that the accusation expressed jealous possessiveness more than concern for the youth's true welfare.[41] But the unhypocritical Syracusan candidly pointed out that his erotic possessiveness also serves a purpose that Socrates could surely understand: the Syracusan needs obedient "puppets" for his shows that win for him and for his puppets ample sustenance from "thoughtless" popular audiences—in which thoughtless audiences he takes pride, as the objects of his showman's exploitative manipulation.[42]

## SOCRATIC "PIMPING" AND "PROCURING"

This prompted Callias to recall (4.56) that Socrates too had claimed that he "deserved to take pride in an art that is disreputable"; Callias asked for Socrates's justification. (Socrates's art of "pimping" here comes to sight as akin to the Syracusan's showmanship, and, as Socrates now proceeds to explain what he means by "pimping," the kinship between the two appears more vivid: both are aimed at exploitatively manipulating audiences—of differing sizes.)

Socrates replied to Callias by launching a self-parody of his notorious dialectics.[43] He proposed that they all come to "an agreement on what sort of works belong to the pimp," and to this end he asked the company to answer his questions without reserve, so that they would know how many matters they agreed upon: "'do you agree' (he said)?—'Certainly,' (they said)," and then Xenophon intrudes himself to say: "once they replied 'certainly,' they all answered this for the rest." Socrates proceeded to establish that all agreed on "the work of a *good* pimp": namely, making and teaching the female or male who was being pimped to be attractive, not least through speeches (rhetoric), to those with whom there would be intercourse. But then Socrates asked which would be the "better" pimp: one who only makes his clients attractive to a *single* individual, or one who makes them attractive "*also* to many" (*kai pollois*). "Here, indeed," Xenophon says, "they split" (*eschisthēsan*). Some answered: "it is obvious, that it is this latter one, who [does so] to most." Others answered: "Certainly" (4.59). Those who, by this latter, were simply going along without thinking were not "splitting." Those who "split" must have been respondents who "did not wish to state the unpopular alternative" (XS 164).

Socrates proceeded as if there had been no split and pushed the "*popular*" version of the good pimp a step further. He asked whether the "*perfectly* good pimp" wouldn't be one who displayed clients who were attractive to *the city as a whole*, and when this elicited emphatically expressed agreement ("by Zeus!"), Socrates asked if such a pimp wouldn't therefore justly be proud of the art and justly receive handsome pay; when this too garnered unanimous agreement, Socrates declared that the art, thus popularly conceived, belonged to "Antisthenes here" (whose inadvertent practice of this art we have already witnessed).[44] Socrates thus buried his own version of the art of pimping (4.60–61).

When Antisthenes expressed irritated bewilderment—"To me (he said) you are turning over, oh Socrates, the art?!"[45]—the master replied, "Yes by Zeus! For I see you very much practicing also the art that follows upon this one: . . . procuring" (*proagōgeia*—4.61). The severe Antisthenes was not in the least amused (4.62). To mollify his offended disciple Socrates adduced examples of the "procuring" that he saw Antisthenes had already accomplished. These examples suggest that Socratic "procuring" involves employing private rhetoric that brings together private individuals (including Socrates) who are strangers—for their mutual, private, educational, and sometimes monetary benefit (4.64; Morrison 1994, 198–99, 200–201). Socrates did not deny that he too practices such private "procuring," even on his own behalf, and he soon was to allow his allied "pimping" or "self-pimping" to reappear (see 5.1 and 8.5, as well as Plato, *Theaetetus* 151b).

Was Antisthenes more than a stopgap candidate for someone who would effectively practice, on behalf of the Socratics, the popular and civic "pimping" that also makes persons pleasing to the many and to the city as a whole? Given Socrates's own abdication of this latter art, the Socratic circle seems to have been in want of a good, self-conscious practitioner. Did not Xenophon eventually fill this need (together with Plato)?—a need that appeared more urgent in light of the popular reputation Socrates had acquired, as indicated in the recent production of Aristophanes's *Clouds*, which was soon to be deployed against Socrates by the understandably provoked Syracusan.[46]

## SOCRATIC BEAUTY

Callias called next for the beauty contest (5.1), to which Socrates had earlier challenged Critobulus. Originally, Critobulus had playfully proposed to match his own erotic *physical* beauty against Socrates's *wisdom*—the philosopher's *spiritual* beauty, one might well say. It was Socrates who had insisted on substituting a contest over sheer physical, sexually attractive beauty (4.18–19), and now, it was Socrates who insured that on these terms his defeat would be risibly decisive. With Critobulus's cooperation, Socrates thus presented his understanding of (his) spiritual beauty, and its relation to erotic physical beauty, under the mask of self-mockery—which he and Xenophon made more significant by turning it into a proleptic parody of Socrates's deadly courtroom quarrel before the city's judges (Danzig 2017, 144). Socrates, after calling himself "The Pimp," summoned Critobulus to a forensic cross-examination (5.1–2). The judges and jurors—the pretty slave boy and slave girl—voted "by secret ballot" (with pebbles in some kind of urn[47]) to determine what the loser "must suffer or pay."[48] When the urn was poured out, "all the votes" vindicated the claim made by Critobulus on behalf of his (and Autolycus's) erotic beauty. Socrates protested that bribes had "corrupted both jurors and judges."[49] The failure of Socrates as "pimp" (in his own terms) was plain.

Socrates was of course not earnestly trying to compete on the level of physical beauty. Not only Critobulus, but Xenophon and Socrates himself declare that Socrates's looks are as ugly as a donkey's, or the ugliest Silenus's

(4.19, 5.7). But as Critobulus showed he was well aware, Socrates does seriously consider himself more beautiful than Critobulus in respect to the spiritual dimensions of a beauty that is pleasing to reason. The principle of that beauty Critobulus, out of his familiarity with Socrates, articulated as follows: the beautiful is that which is well constructed by art with a view to the work for which we acquire each implement, or well endowed by nature with a view to what we truly need. Perhaps because this principle implies a harsh ugliness in nature (*Apology* 27), Socrates was not able to defend it publicly, even here in play, without conspicuously blurring the distinction between the natural and the artful: Socrates had to introduce an appeal to divine design as well as to divine generation. On this basis, Socrates got Critobulus ("testifying" for the city) to make a sort of bow to the Socratic principle, even while on the way to defeating it by popular acclaim.

## FORESHADOWING THE MOST SERIOUS PART OF THE CITY'S INDICTMENT OF SOCRATES

The jolly conviviality which Socrates had brought about, on his terms, was not all-inclusive. In the first place, imbibing had made Hermogenes not more jovial but now conspicuously[50] saturnine—especially as a consequence, we may surmise, of his dismay at his master's willingness to treat divinity, and beauty and love as associated with divinity, in such a jocular manner. Hermogenes had stressed, shortly before, his absolute dedication to avoiding all but piously auspicious speech in regard to the gods.[51] Yet when questioned by Socrates, the well-disposed Hermogenes articulated his complaint about Socrates's speech in a good-natured and harmless fashion, speaking only of Socrates's monopolizing loquacity. In response, Socrates humbly confessed to *this* fault, and to being thereby refuted by Hermogenes. Socrates was thus able to cajole his grave friend into partaking a bit in the party spirit. Socrates went so far as to suggest that Hermogenes should adorn his speech with some of the graceful charms taught to the slave girl by the Syracusan (6.1–5). This comment recalled the admiration Socrates earlier expressed for the Syracusan's didactic abilities.

In the immediate context, however, the comment evidently brought to a head the "envy" (6.6) felt by the Syracusan on account of Socrates's transformation of the gentleman's play through his monopolizing speeches. Socrates's wit had displaced awed appreciation for the astounding feats of virtue and beauty produced by the Syracusan. The popularly pleasing artistic skill which the Syracusan embodies naturally begins by being hostile to Socrates, even or especially to Socrates's successful, refined playfulness.

The Syracusan did not of course express his true complaint but instead sought to pin back Socrates's ears by playing the nasty card provided by the popular view of Socrates as the godless "thinker"—the view that was given its most laughable (and therefore least harmful) version in Aristophanes's *Clouds*.[52] The Syracusan thus inadvertently helps us to see why Xenophon wants his Socrates to appear so close to and approved by the very pious Hermogenes. Once again, as when the Syracusan earlier took the place of Lycon, the Syracusan introduced one of the two mortal charges that the city will eventually bring against Socrates, and once again the Syracusan bespoke a jealous envy that in part animates (and to a degree contradicts) the "official" accusations (6.6–8). The jealous envy here expressed is not paternal or popular but artistic (the Syracusan does have something in common with Aristophanes).

The two complainers, Hermogenes and the Syracusan, represent comically two sides of the city's most serious charge against Socrates (not believing in the gods that the city believes in). Xenophon speaks of the two as having constituted a *single* "disturbance due to wine" (6.10 end), and he interweaves their complaints: Hermogenes was most truly upset by Socrates's insufficiently pious reverence but openly complained only of his monopolizing loquacity; the Syracusan was truly envious of Socrates's monopolizing loquacity but openly introduced popular doubts about the philosopher's piety.

The pugnacious Antisthenes responded to the threat (6.8–10) by attempting to fight fire with fire, enlisting the nasty power of popular comedy, in the person of the hired jester, to mount a reviling counteroffensive against the Syracusan who had invoked the *Clouds*; but the urbane Socrates, speaking with notable firmness, absolutely prohibited any such counter-"reviling." The deficiency of Antisthenes as a "procurer" became clearer, even as did Socrates's wish to conciliate the Syracusan. It is hard to imagine that the latter was without some gratitude to Socrates for reining in Antisthenes and Philippos—just as it is hard to imagine that Socrates was not earlier aware that he was provoking the Syracusan's envy (and thus attention) by stealing the show.

## SOCRATES BECOMES THE TEACHER OF THE "SYRACUSAN"

Socrates completed his conciliation with the Syracusan in the moments that followed. The joking and drinking had now proceeded to a point where the company began to become raucous (7.1). Socrates was able to impose some order by leading everyone in a song,[53] which allowed the stage to be set for another feat by the Syracusan's creatures. At this point, Socrates confessed to the Syracusan that he himself was indeed a "thinker" and had been devoting some constructively critical thought to the Syracusan's choice of themes. Socrates taught the Syracusan that his displays of youthful human virtuosity, while perhaps wondrous, and in some cases providing a certain pleasure, were ill suited to achieve the refined gentlemanly approval that the Syracusan most wanted in the present circumstances (7.2–5). Socrates made it clear that he was not denigrating the Syracusan's preoccupation with his human "wonders" and their display; Socrates even drew a sympathetic comparison with the very different sorts of readily available natural "wonders" with which he himself (as "thinker," as philosopher of nature or as natural scientist) is preoccupied—wonders that Socrates indicated are even more unsuited to a gentlemanly symposium. (Socrates and the Syracusan are akin in that they are not in their element among the gentlemen at play, and both need, in greatly differing degree, to obscure their wisdom in such a setting.) Socrates advised the Syracusan to substitute, for his planned but inappropriate human marvels, dancing figures in which would be portrayed or "written" (*graphontai*) gracefully refined and thus attractive feminine divinities—including those (Naiad) Nymphs who Socrates had earlier said generated beauties that somehow resembled him (7.5; recall 5.7). The presentation of divinity of this type (recall 1.10: Socrates of course did not suggest that Zeus or Dionysus or other such Olympian gods be presented) would seem to provide a gentlemanly middle ground, hospitable to both Socrates and the Syracusan, in between (and perhaps adumbrating) the Socratic study of nature and the Syracusan's knowledge of (subtheoretical) human virtuosity.

Swearing by Zeus, the Syracusan gratefully agreed that Socrates had spoken "beautifully" (he did not say "correctly," or even "well"); brimming with inspiration, he then promised that he would prepare a performance that would indeed please the company (7.5).

## SOCRATES'S ORATORICAL PRESENTATION OF HIS POLITICAL PHILOSOPHIZING

Xenophon next puts before us his Socrates delivering an oration exhorting Callias to the erotic love that issues in dedication to civic leadership. The elocution began (8.1) by in a sense returning to the opening scene (Huss 1999, 393)—reminding the company of "the presence among us of Eros," of Whom "we are all votaries." Socrates expressed his knowledge of the divinity by a most thought-provoking and pithy characterization: Eros, Socrates declares, is "a great *Daimon* [cf. 8.5], and equal in age to the gods who are always coming into being, though youngest in shape; and in greatness extending over all things, while yet being equal in extent to the human soul."

Socrates's initial blanket claim, that "all of us are votaries of this god," was rendered complicated by his subsequent enumeration of the highly diverse ways in which various individuals in the party partook of *eros* ("only Lykon and Philippos are not given romances of some sort here"—Bowen 1998 ad loc.). Speaking of himself, Socrates declared that he was not able to speak of any period of time during which he was not ceaselessly in love with someone or something (*erōn tinos diatelō*, 8.2). But of course it was the love exhibited by the host Callias, for Autolycus, that Socrates put in the (most flattering) spotlight (8.7–11). Addressing Callias, Socrates proclaimed that "the cause" of his love affair's being known far and wide was the renown of the couple's fathers along with their own personal fame.[54] Socrates said that his admiration for the nature of Callias had been now enhanced by seeing that Callias's love was for a youth who displayed to everyone strength and endurance and manliness and moderation, rather than luxurious softness. Callias thus seemed, Socrates averred, to be in the grip of the love that is likely inspired by the "Heavenly Aphrodite"—who sends down upon us the love of the soul, and of friendship, and noble deeds—in contrast to the carnal love that is likely inspired by the "Wholly Popular Aphrodite." Yet the "evidence" Socrates offered for this ascription to Callias of the Heavenly Aphrodite was only the "gentlemanliness" of the beloved boy and the fact that he saw Callias inviting the boy's father to the couple's "intercourse." What is more surprising and disturbing, Socrates confessed his ignorance as to whether there really are two distinct Aphrodites—as is suggested by traditional worship.

Socrates was interrupted by the piously earnest Hermogenes, who could not hold back from gushing congratulation of Socrates for simultaneously "gratifying" (i.e., flattering) and "educating" his errant brother Callias (8.12). If it is comically doubtful how much this speech of Socrates succeeded in elevating the *eros* of Callias, there is no doubt that it succeeded in the important task of reinforcing Hermogenes's admiration for Socrates. What's more, we see that by the end of the speech Socrates had won the (only slightly qualified) admiration of Lycon (9.1)[55] and had stirred young Autolycus (8.42).

Acknowledging Hermogenes's encouragement, Socrates became still more homiletic. He first said that he wished to testify to Callias that the love which is enamored of the soul is "much stronger" (*polu kreittōn*) than that which is enamored of the body. The premise of this testimony was again (as in Socrates's speech on pimping—Huss ad loc.) taken from the present company's shared, conventional, gentlemanly opinion: "we all know," affirmed Socrates, that "there is no intercourse worth mentioning without friendship (*philia*)"[56]—which "is called a private and voluntary compulsion" when it arises in "those who admire character."

Now "even when both cherish[57] [one another] mutually," the body's bloom, and hence friendship (inasmuch as it is based on love of the body), "swiftly fade." But the soul continues "increasingly deserving of being loved" so long as it progresses toward greater practical wisdom.

Moreover, in carnal love there is surfeit with "the boy," while this is less so in the "friendship for the soul," on account of the chastity involved—which, "contrary to what one might suppose," fulfills our prayer to Aphrodite that She make us more seductively graced by Her in words and deeds (8.12–15).

Socrates's paean to spiritual vs. physical love culminated in his declaring that "there is no need of a speech" to the effect that the beloved will be admired and cherished by one whose soul is flourishing with a reverent and well born disposition, and a bodily form befitting the free, and who has the capacity of being a friendly-minded leader right away among those his own age (8.16 beg.). Thus, for a moment, Socrates verged on evoking the model of a chaste passion between young men rather close in age, whose love may metamorphose into a lifelong friendship. Before the shadow thus cast on Callias's love for Autolycus could become too obvious, Socrates smoothly shifted gears.

Returning to the conventionally pederastic framework, Socrates declared (8.16 end): "I will teach in addition" that "such a lover" is likely to be cherished reciprocally by "the boy."[58] But Socrates's argument consisted at first (*prōton*) of rhetorical questions suggesting only that "the boy" could feel for his high-minded pederast no "hatred"[59] at least.

Then, however, Socrates slipped back to speaking unconventionally—as if it could be assumed that the sort of "friendly love" that he was celebrating is completely mutual (*koinon to phileisthai*—8.18 beg.). He proceeded to ask anaphorically whether there must not follow from such a friendship a series of nine "aphroditically seductive" consequences, at the center of which list was "taking pleasure together in noble deeds." The result, Socrates concluded, is that such a couple "live out their lives into old age erotically loving [no longer one another but rather] the friendship,[60] and using it."

Then, gliding back yet again to conventional pederasty, Socrates painted in lurid colors the reasons for doubting that an older man's physical erotic passion would ever lead "the boy" to reciprocate, with any friendship whatsoever (8.19–22).

Having thus made his (richly complex and highly ambiguous) case for the greater "strength" of spiritual as opposed to carnal love, Socrates announced that he would show that "the intercourse, for one who admires the body rather than the soul," is "lacking in freedom/liberality" (*aneleutheros*—8.22). But now, abruptly and without warning, Socrates's model of spiritual love became that between an older *teacher* and a younger *student*,[61] in which the student "justly *honors*" his teacher, who has "educated him in the things he ought to say and to do." (What animates a wise teacher, according to Socrates, appears to be not so much a desire to be loved as a desire to be honored: see also *Apology* 5 and *Memorabilia* 4.8.7.) In the light of this new model, of affectionate friendship between older teacher and younger student, Socrates for a moment spoke with such disgusted vehemence in condemnation of a teacher's "excitedly reaching for" (*oregomenos*) a student's body—and pleading like a "beggar" for "a kiss or some other such groping" (*psēlaphēmatos*)[62]—that the philosopher had to apologize, adducing as his excuse the effects of the wine on him, along with "the Eros that is ever dwelling with me," which "goads to unbridled speech against the Eros that is its wrestling antagonist" (*antipalon*). Socrates here testified that he never ceased to experience the presence within him of divinity, or quasi-divinity, in the form of Eros (the total silence in this work on the *daimonion* of Socrates may be explained by the fact that the *daimonion* is only another term for his *eros*—see Plato's *Theages*). Socrates's higher indwelling *Eros* is evidently not alone and never ceases wrestling against a lower, indwelling physical lust. This is the sole occasion in the Socratic writings of Xenophon or of Plato where Socrates is depicted as confessing, and not altogether jestingly, that he is propelled and overcome by a tinge of anger or *thumos* (recall *Economist* 17.14–15). Socrates thus seemed to betray the fact that his own liberal or free desire, as a teacher, to enjoy the appropriate honor from students whom he affectionately forms, and whose judgment he respects, is inevitably shadowed by a longing that is slavish. But this was not Socrates's last word.

For he proceeded to draw the contrast between the two loves in very different terms. The initial and strong surface impression was of a further denigration of carnal love in contrast to spiritual. But on closer inspection Socrates's new simile proves to be much more ambiguous, thought-provoking, and then, as we catch on, decisively revealing. We hear of "one who turns his intelligence [*nous*] to the form [*eidos*]" and who as such seems to Socrates "to resemble a renter of land"—"not concerned with how it will become worth more" but with "how he himself will reap the most fruits from it" (*hopōs autos hoti pleista hōraia karpōsetai*). On the other hand, there is "the one aiming at friendship instead," who as such "resembles one who has acquired his own farmland as *private property*": "bringing from everywhere whatever he can, he makes the beloved worth more." Now it is a question which of these is more "liberal" or "free": the one who works to improve another, out of devoted *possessiveness*, or the one who works to reap the most fruits for his own intelligence from another's form (*eidos*)—*without possessive* devotion (and without what we remember "is called a private and voluntary compulsion"—8.13). No doubt Socrates's primary aim in deploying this simile was to exhort Callias (and Autolycus) to a spiritual, rather than carnal, love affair. But Xenophon has his Socrates by this simile also afford us a glimpse of a distinguishing characteristic of some, at least, of Socratic teaching friendships. We may surmise that Socrates's own educative *eros* included, in some cases, the highest version of the "renter's" mentality. And I venture the further surmise that what Socrates's *nous* had to gain from his "rental" of the "form" (*eidos*) of some of his beloved students was decisive empirical evidence bearing on the question "*quid sit deus*"—as regards the divinity that we all seem to encounter, in one way or another, when we open ourselves to the experience of *eros*.

Socrates concluded the nonmythic portion of his exhortation to Callias by declaring (in an echo of Critobulus) that "the greatest good" for "one who seeks to make out of his boy a good friend" is that he is thereby "himself compelled to train in virtue." (This is a good that is of course superfluous for a man who is already truly virtuous.)

Socrates next said that for the benefit of Callias he also desired to make the case for spiritual love on "mythological" grounds. And here Socrates allowed myth to provide a glimpse of a crucial aspect of the target of erotic-spiritual hope. For the philosopher now spoke of the achievement or gift of human immortality. He declared that the divine Father of gods and men bestows a deathless life, with Him in heaven, on those mortals whom He loves and honors for their souls—but not on those after whose bodies He lusts.

Yet Socrates did not speak of this with all the gravity that one might wish. For he asserted that Zeus loved Ganymede for his soul and not for his body—which Socrates claimed to prove by adducing and interpreting some invented etymology, along with counterfeit Homeric texts.[63]

Socrates further claimed that the famed love affairs of the heroic demigods are celebrated not because they slept together but solely because they emulated and inspired one another's greatest and noblest deeds.

Descending to "the noble deeds in our own time," Socrates continued to speak mythically—and with amusing tendentiousness, especially about Spartan pederasty.

I believe the serious point of these mythic *jeux d'esprit* was to indicate that human spiritual purity is not maintained or maintainable by the gentlemanliness that the city and the civic tradition emulate, but only by the radically different gentlemanliness visible in Socrates.[64]

Socrates concluded with a peroration addressed most emphatically to Callias (8.37–40): given the love of honor that obviously drives Autolycus, if you want to win the youth, you need to discover what it was that Themistocles knew, what Pericles knew, the manner in which Solon "philosophized" so as to legislate the strongest laws for the city, and what the Spartans train at. Your family background, your high priestly office (ministering to the civic gods led by Bacchus/Dionysus), your shapely and strong body, all make you eligible to be chosen as the leader of Athens. Socrates thus exhorted the luxurious and "philosophy"-loving Callias, who hitherto has looked down on politicians (recall 1.4), to the emphatically *political* "philosophizing" that prepares for civic leadership.[65]

This concluding part of the oration, Socrates confessed, might seem too serious for a drinking party, but it is not to be wondered at: for "I never cease to be a fellow lover, with the city, of those who are good by nature and who are zealous, with love of honor, for virtue." As Callias recognized, Socrates here put into practice his "pimping" art—and not only for Callias: he left the strong impression that, contrary to the impression left by Aristophanes, exhortation of younger men to erotic civic leadership within the Hellenic tradition was the authentic expression of Socrates's own philosophizing and erotic passion. Certainly Socrates affirmed that he and the city love the same distinguished, erotic, and ambitious young men (Bartlett 1996, 181). We can be sure that two such young men among those present, Charmides and Xenophon, thoroughly appreciated this oratorical performance.

## XENOPHON'S ART OF SOCRATIC PORTRAITURE

Xenophon as artist delicately makes his presence felt by creating the coincidence that the young Autolycus now had to leave on his exercise walk: this was highly fortunate, since the performance of simulated gods that the Syracusan had designed, in reacting to Socrates's advice, turned out to be suited only for men of marriageable age (Ollier 1972 ad loc.). The Syracusan substituted, for the representation of gracefully beautiful feminine deities that Socrates had recommended, a highly sensuous drama that evoked and exalted the lawful and pious expression of the most naturally harmonious erotic passion—the heterosexual version of that physical passion that Socrates in his speech was meanwhile contemning as "drunkenness" inspired by "the vulgar Aphrodite" (see 8.21).[66] The Syracusan succeeded in breaking up the evening by erotically exciting most of the audience—not, like Socrates, to thought-provoking erotic laughter, let alone to nobly erotic civic ambition, but rather—to following Dionysus into the immortalizing sensuality of connubial bliss (Bartlett 1996, 185). And there was suddenly revealed what Socrates had presumably divined from the outset: the seam of love that knits together the wonderfully agile cooperative "virtue" of the "puppets" educated by the Syracusan. The latter's closing spectacle spoke to, and made to shine forth, that primary power of civilized and civilizing *eros*, the heterosexual pillar of civic life, from which the evening, dominated by Socrates, had largely abstracted. The performance directed by the Syracusan was thus a successful rival, but also a kind of clarifying complement, to Socrates's whole performance. In this way was Xenophon's work on love made complete, as an artistic whole. The art of Xenophon makes Socratic love luminescent against the backdrop of lawfully Dionysian love.

By drawing attention at the outset to his attendance at the symposium, and then turning himself into a kind of ghostly (not to say divine) presence, Xenophon prods us to bear in mind his authorial omnipresence. Then, through the figure of the "Syracusan," Xenophon shows us the "raw material," so to speak, out of which his Socratic education made him the consummate artistic author that he became. And especially in the *Symposium*, taken as a whole, Xenophon allows us to see that his artistic vocation culminated in the illumination of the nature of Socrates by way of portraying him in his relation to a richly instructive range of contrasting sub-Socratic human types.

CHAPTER EIGHT

# Deliberate Defiance in the *Apology*

Xenophon states the purpose of his *Apology of Socrates to the Jurors* at the outset: "to recall (*memnēsthai*) also how, when he was summoned to the judicial proceeding," Socrates "*deliberated* about his defense and end of life" (#1).[1] This short work will grant us access to the inner, strategic thinking that dictated, in the shadow of death, the character of the speech and of the demeanor of Socrates before the jurors. Xenophon explains that he needs to provide such an unusually intrusive recollection and disclosure because of a massively perplexing, and potentially disgraceful, feature of Socrates's conduct at the trial: his offensive *megalēgoria* ("big talk," "arrant public boastfulness").[2] "Others have" already "written about" the trial, Xenophon says, and "all" of them have "encountered his *megalēgoria*"—"by which it is also clear," Xenophon adds, "that Socrates really did speak in this way." (Xenophon writes as if, without this prior written testimony from others, the reports of the *megalēgoria* of Socrates at the trial could scarcely be credited. At the same time, Xenophon begins to let us see that he himself was not a witness to the trial.) But these writings of others have failed to "make it quite clear that" Socrates "at that time held death to be preferable to life for himself, so that the *megalēgoria* appears to be rather imprudent of him (*aphronestera autou*)." Xenophon aims to defend Socrates's reputation for prudence or practical wisdom—*phronesis*—by showing how, contrary to what one might at first suppose, his offensive boastfulness at the trial was dictated by a careful deliberation, whose cornerstone was the judgment that, at the time, death was preferable to life.

## THE PUZZLE AS TO THE PURPOSE OF SOCRATES'S OFFENSIVE BOASTFULNESS

Xenophon's wording in the preceding quotation—"preferable for himself"—may convey the initial impression that a, or the, chief concern of Socrates in his deliberation was his own immediate self-interest (so Ollier 1972, 96). Accordingly, we soon hear Socrates quoted giving, as his principal explicit reason for preferring death to life, his thus avoiding the otherwise likely onset of the ills of old age (#6); and Socrates is quoted as welcoming the idea of being executed by hemlock poison because it is "the death that has been judged by those in charge of this business to be the easiest" (see also #32)—instead of "ending life pained by sickness or by old age, where there converge all the harsh things bereft of cheer" (#7–8).

Yet Socrates is reported to have immediately added that this mode of dying is also "least troublesome to friends, and productive in them of the greatest longing." So, in judging what was best for himself, the philosopher included the welfare of his friends as well as their love for him (or his being loved and missed by them). And shortly before this, Socrates made it clear that in judging what is best for himself there bulked large the consideration as to whether or not he could continue to enjoy "knowing that I have lived my entire life piously and justly" (#5).

But if his far-from-selfish calculation of what was, at the time, best for himself along with others made the aged philosopher welcome the prospect of death by hemlock poison, and hence made his rather suicidal "big talk" not imprudent, the question remains: What deliberation made such offensively boastful speech positively prudent and advisable? What was the purpose, or thinking, of Socrates, such that "his boastful speech fitted his thinking (*dianoia*)" (#2)?

Initially the reader may suppose (and Xenophon allows, and to some extent even encourages, careless readers to draw the conclusion—see esp. #32) that our author is contending that Socrates engaged in the offensive boastfulness as the best way to goad the jury to impose on him the relatively painless death of hemlock poisoning, this liberating him from the troubles of old age.[3] But an assiduous and thoughtful reading of the *Apology* as a whole shows the error of such a simplistic reading of what Xenophon means to teach as the purpose and hence deliberation of Socrates.

To begin with, while Socrates is quoted as concluding his account of the preferableness of death to life, for himself at his age, by declaring his intention to engage in "big talk," he is *not* reported as saying that the *purpose* of the "big talk" was to provoke the jury to condemn him to death. Socrates reportedly spoke of the latter as a likely outcome *incidental to* his deliberate choice to engage in boastful speech.[4]

Moreover, if Xenophon considered that all that was required, in order for the reader to understand the purpose and deliberation behind the boastful speech, was knowing that the aged Socrates had decided that death was at the time preferable to continued living, then the work ought to end in sec. 8 or 9—or ought to skip then to sec. 32. For by sec. 8 or 9 Xenophon has completed the demonstration that Socrates had decided on the timely preferableness of death—and Xenophon has done this by presenting the "proclamation" (*exangeile*—#2) of Hermogenes, reporting his conversation with Socrates to this effect. Why does Xenophon go on, to devote most of his *Apology* to Hermogenes's further "proclamation" of excerpts from the defense speech of Socrates, and also excerpts from what Socrates said *after* being convicted, which illustrate the arrogantly boastful speech—especially since Xenophon says that this aspect of the speech has already been shown in and through the writings of others? How are these excerpts from the speech needed in order to help us to understand fully Socrates's purpose and thus his preceding deliberation? And why, in giving the excerpts, does Xenophon continue to rely solely on the testimony of Hermogenes? We have, in fact, indubitable evidence that Xenophon could, without giving any quotations from the defense speech, and without relying solely on Hermogenes, demonstrate that Socrates at the time of his trial preferred death to life: this is precisely what Xenophon does in the last chapter of his *Memorabilia*. There we find reported the same conversation of Socrates that is reported in the *Apology*—but, in the *Memorabilia* version, it is reported as being at least in part a conversation that Socrates had "with Hermogenes *and with the others*" (*Memorabilia* 4.8.10). The two distinct versions of the conversation are replete with more or less subtle, but important, and richly thought-provoking, differences. The most remarkable variation is the utter absence, in the *Memorabilia* version, of any mention or hint of Socrates having decided, after deliberation, to talk in a boastful or arrogant manner at his trial. What's more, in the *Memorabilia*, Xenophon praises in his own name the defense speech of Socrates, without giving any hint that it contained "big talk" (4.8.1 end). So: Xenophon can, without referring to the boastful character of the defense speech, explain that and why Socrates decided that he welcomed the death penalty. This suggests that the latter decision does not in itself entail the deliberation by which Socrates decided that he needed to engage in boastful speech.

To be sure, Xenophon declares in his own name the judgment that the "big talk," by arousing envy, made the jurors more inclined to vote to *convict*

Socrates (#32—*katapsēphisasthai*). Xenophon does not say, however, that the "big talk" is what led to the *death* penalty (see also #23). And such irritating talk was not the sole, or even the most efficient, means to obtaining the death sentence—as becomes evident when we attend to the twofold sequence in the trial procedure. In section 23, speaking in his own name and not by way of Hermogenes, Xenophon makes it clear that the jury in Athens first decided the guilt or innocence of the accused; then, if the finding was guilt, the jury decided in a *second* vote, after further speeches and a second collective deliberation, the penalty—by *choosing between* the penalty proposed by the accusers in the formal indictment and an alternative penalty proposed by the convicted defendant. In the case of Socrates, the accusers in the formal indictment specified the death penalty. Now this means that all Socrates had to do, in order to bring upon himself the death penalty, was to bring about the first vote, of "guilty" (and he could achieve this by refusing to say much of anything in his defense), while letting the jury believe that he would subsequently do the thing normally done by those convicted, namely, propose a reasonably stiff counterpenalty. Even as it was, the jurors in voting Socrates guilty[5] would have presumed that he would offer to undergo the penalty of banishment,[6] or of some substantial fine financed by his friends and supporters. The jurors and accusers must have been astonished when—as Xenophon stresses, speaking in his own name—it transpired that Socrates offered no counterproposal at all (#23), and that hence their vote to convict entailed, in the upshot, capital punishment!

The boastful talk in the defense speech, and what's more, the *continuation* of boastful talk in which we hear Socrates engaging *after* he refused to offer a counterproposal, and had *already* been condemned to death (#24–26), were simply not necessary as means to achieving the death penalty. The "big talk" at the trial, before and after the death penalty, was, at most, one of several possible courses of action that would have contributed to securing the death penalty.

What then are we to understand to have been the Socratic purpose, and consequently the Socratic deliberation, that led to the strategy of boastful speech?

Xenophon provides a crucial clue immediately after reproducing portions of Socrates's oration illustrating the "big talk," as it was remembered by Hermogenes. Xenophon suddenly ceases to report upon the trial by way of citing the testimony of Hermogenes and instead steps forward to speak in his own name, employing the first person singular. He stresses (#22–23) that in this work he is being very selective—that he has omitted a great deal of what was said in defense of Socrates, not only by Socrates himself but by the friends who also spoke in his behalf. Xenophon then explains what guides his selection—and thereby indicates the purpose of Socrates that animated the deliberation that this work is meant to help us see: "for me, it has sufficed to make clear that, on one hand, at that time[7] Socrates made it his goal above all else[8] to appear neither to be impious as regards gods nor unjust as regards human beings; and on the other hand, that he did not think he ought to hold out against dying,[9] but believed that then was even an opportune time for him to die." Xenophon thus sets before us the challenge of puzzling out, from the other clues he provides in this work, what deliberation led Socrates to the conclusion that arrogant boastfulness was the best means by which a philosopher like himself, in his fraught circumstances, could project the image of *being neither irreverent nor unjust*.[10] The suggestion is paradoxical, if only because the boasting obviously did not, and was not intended to, win the hearts of the jury. How can talk that infuriates the jury, goading them to vote him guilty, make him appear pious and just?

## HERMOGENES AS A KEY TO THE *APOLOGY*

Who was it above all others, and what sort of a person, before whom Socrates intended to appear neither impious nor unjust by "talking big"? We need not look far. Xenophon has done everything in his power to spotlight one member of the audience at the trial: Hermogenes. The *Apology* presents Socrates as he appeared to, and was remembered by, Hermogenes. Xenophon keeps this fact squarely before us, by couching most of the work in the awkward phraseology of "he said that Socrates said . . . and said that he said," and so forth. In effect, Xenophon lets us see that if we are to comprehend Socrates's purpose in "talking big," we need to understand how that boastful talk, and its prelude and aftermath, struck Hermogenes in particular, and we need, above all, to understand why the impression made on Hermogenes was so important to Socrates: "Hermogenes, the son of Hipponicus, however, was a comrade of his and proclaimed (*exēggeile*) about him such things as make it clear that his boastful speech fitted his thinking" (#2). Socrates intended to make an impression primarily upon Hermogenes (and others akin to Hermogenes) and then, through Hermogenes's "proclamation," upon still others; Xenophon's written *Apology* vastly amplifies that "proclamation," and its audience, down through the ages.

### WHAT HERMOGENES EMBODIES

What kind of man, then, is Hermogenes? The other three Socratic writings of Xenophon show that he is a figure of some importance in the Socratic circle. In the *Memorabilia* (2.10.3), Socrates is quoted recommending Hermogenes as a most effective helper and executor, in the following terms:

> Hermogenes is not wanting in judgment, and he would be ashamed if after being benefited by you he failed to benefit you in return. Indeed, one who serves voluntarily, whose mind is benevolently disposed, who is steadfast and capable of doing what he is bid, and who is not only capable of doing what he is bid but also has the power to be useful on his own initiative both in exercising foresight and in deliberating beforehand, is, I believe, equal in value to many servants.

In the *Symposium*, as we have seen, Hermogenes is one of the principal speakers. Hermogenes is present not because he was originally invited by Callias, but only because he was with Socrates when, at the last minute, Callias ran into Socrates and invited the latter, along with those in his company. Near the beginning of Socrates's long speech on love in the *Symposium*, when Socrates lightheartedly surveys some of the company, we find a vivid, if somewhat tongue-in-cheek, sketch of Hermogenes's personality:

> And as for Hermogenes, who among us doesn't know that, whatever gentlemanliness [*kalok'agathia*] may be, he is melting away with erotic love of it? Don't you see how serious are his brows, how steady his eye, how measured his speeches, how gentle his voice, how cheerful his character? And although he associates with the most august gods as friends, don't you see that he doesn't feel contempt for us human beings? (8.3)

Hermogenes comes to sight here as a man of profound moral seriousness and pride, whose genial sense of his own dignity is enhanced by a belief in a very special, personal, or even intimate relationship with the gods—not necessarily all the gods, but surely "the most august." Hermogenes is further characterized as having a kind of love affair with gentlemanliness. As the immediate context shows, love here is *eros*, the passionate longing for, the devotion to, someone or something beyond oneself. Hermogenes longs for the gentlemanliness he does not wholly possess. Indeed, Socrates's words—"gentlemanliness, whatever it may be"—suggest that Hermogenes, like Socrates himself, does not regard as unambiguous or without puzzle the meaning of "whatever may be gentlemanliness." In this respect Hermogenes is to be contrasted with Lycon, who is also a prominent figure at this drinking party and who later becomes one of Socrates's three formal accusers. Lycon has no love or erotic longing for gentlemanliness because he "knows" he is a gentleman. What he ardently longs for is that his son, Autolycus, may grow up to become as perfect a gentleman as his father (*Symposium* 2.4–7, 3.12–13, 9.1). What could it be that has distanced Hermogenes from such confidence in conventional gentlemanliness? Is it not likely to be at least in part the influence of Socrates, with his interrogation of conventional gentlemanliness? But what led or attracted Hermogenes to fall under the influence of Socrates? And how does Hermogenes's distance from conventional gentlemanliness go together with his immense pride and his sense of closeness to the most august gods?

It comes as something of an illuminating surprise to note that Hermogenes is the brother of Callias! They are both sons—but Callias is the sole heir—of the very wealthy Hipponicus. From his father, Callias has inherited not only vast riches[11] but one of the most respectable lineages in Athens. Socrates says near the end of his speech on love, addressing Callias: "For the greatest things belong to you: you are of a good ancestry [*eupatridēs*], a priest of the gods of Erechtheus's descent, gods who led the army under Iacchus against the Barbarian, and now in the festival you make an appearance as priest that is more impressive than your ancestors" (*Symposium* 8.40). As is abundantly clear from the *Symposium* (1.4, 4.62), as well as from Plato, Callias has made use of his rank and wealth to become *the* patron of the sophists and to make his home into a kind of salon where the intellectually most respected find hospitality (see also Plato's *Protagoras*; *Cratylus* 391b-c; *Apology of Socrates* 20a). Callias is, in a word, the splendid pinnacle of Athenian upperclass society. It should perhaps come as no surprise that he also became a man of very dubious morals, around whom scandal swirled (see Andocides, *On the Mysteries*).

It was into this prestigious and luxurious world that Hermogenes was born and from which—for reasons we do not know—he was cut off.[12] His extraordinary pride, we may surmise, is fueled by his understandable reaction against what he feels to be the unjustly marginalized position to which civic and family convention have relegated him.[13] Similarly, his idiosyncratic piety can be understood as a manifestation of his lofty refusal to accept the conventional estimation of his religious stature, among gods and men, especially in contrast to that of his brother, the high priest by convention. The unorthodox character of Hermogenes's piety is brought into sharp relief earlier in the *Symposium*. At Socrates's urging, a playful contest is held in which a number of those present give speeches displaying that on which they most pride themselves. When it is the turn of Hermogenes to state what will be the subject of his speech, we read the following exchange:

> "And you, Hermogenes," said Niceratus, "upon what do you pride yourself most of all?"
>
> And he said, "The virtue and power of my friends and that, being of this sort, they are concerned with me."
>
> At this point everyone turned toward him, and many asked in unison whether he would make clear to them who these were. He said that he would not begrudge doing so. (3.14)

The company obviously find it almost comically incredible that poor old Hermogenes should claim to have any powerful friends. Well, these powerful friends of his turn out to be certain "omniscient" and "omnipotent" gods, common to Greeks and barbarians alike, whom Hermogenes refrains from naming, and who signal the future to Hermogenes through voices and dreams and the flight of birds (#13 and 48; cf. Plato's *Cratylus*, esp. 397c–d). After Hermogenes's brief speech on these unnamed gods and their care for him, which Xenophon says is the only wholly serious speech in the *Symposium*, Socrates initiates an exchange that Xenophon treats as part of this "seriously spoken logos":

> "Well, there is nothing incredible in these things. Yet I for my part would gladly learn how it is that you tend to them and thus have them as friends."—"By Zeus!" said Hermogenes, "Even very inexpensively! For I praise them but spend no money, and from what they give me I always offer up something, and I speak in pious fashion as much as I can, and in matters in which I have invoked them as witnesses I never voluntarily lie."—"By Zeus!" said Socrates, "If you, being of this sort, have them as friends, then the gods too, it is likely, are pleased by gentlemanliness!" (*Symposium* 4.49; see also *Memorabilia* 1.3.3)

Socrates and Hermogenes have in common a proud passion for gentlemanliness conceived as free of the need for riches, and as linked to a claim to a distinctly intimate relationship with unconventional divinity.

## The Strategic Importance of Hermogenes

The picture of Hermogenes emerging from this varied presentation is that of a gentleman of the greatest high-mindedness, who has had many of the benefits of an aristocratic upbringing but whose circumstances, especially economic, have induced him to take his proud distance from, and even to hold in some disdain, much of what is held to be conventionally respectable in terms of family and religion. But no one could possibly suspect him of indecency, sedition, or impiety. He stands apart, in a kind of quiet moral aloofness. I venture to suggest that Xenophon wants to teach us that individuals of this kind, with this sort of status, when properly cultivated, can become shields and defenders of, and (what is more) crucial spokesmen for, the Socratic philosopher—especially when "the chips are down," when the philosopher is embattled or subject to persecution.

In the eyes and in the reports of men such as Hermogenes, the Socratic philosopher, even or especially when he is in religious and civic disfavor, can appear as a heroic kindred spirit. Socrates's frugal self-sufficiency, along with his propensity to question or to voice wonderment at the customary notions of gentlemanliness and of education for gentlemanliness, harmonize with Hermogenes's own independence and reservations in these matters. More importantly, the unorthodox piety of a Socrates—specifically, his combination of avowed ignorance or cautious inquiry about the gods, together with his claim to possess an idiosyncratic, private, divine guide (*daimonion*) by which he receives special guidance for himself and his friends—strikes a deeply sympathetic chord in a man like Hermogenes. The fact that Socrates's heterodoxy, and especially his *daimonion*, eventually led him into conflict with the powers that be does not necessarily come as a shock to Hermogenes. Moreover, Hermogenes is aware of the injustice that is all-too-endemic in Athenian-democratic courtrooms, and he is therefore eager at first to prompt Socrates to devise a defense that will enable him to escape conviction—"by any means necessary" (#4 and 8). Hermogenes knows Socrates to be a great talker, while he himself is capable neither of eloquence nor of quick-witted argument (Plato, *Cratylus* 408b). From Hermogenes's noteworthy refutation of Socrates in the *Symposium* (6.3), it would appear that on occasion he can be disapproving of what he views as Socratic loquaciousness. Yet in Socrates's courtroom oration Hermogenes heard, and recalls, and proclaims to others, an awesomely articulate defense of their shared, marginal, but fiercely proud position in society (cf. Pucci 64). It seems altogether likely that Hermogenes was far from being displeased that circumstances at the time of the trial allowed Socrates finally to throw caution to the winds and to speak his mind. Xenophon makes it clear that Hermogenes retained a vivid memory of at least substantial parts of what Socrates said—before, during, and after the trial—and "proclaimed" this to anyone who would listen. Once we understand Hermogenes, we begin to realize that the account Xenophon provides by way of such a man's memory is one that Xenophon wants us to see is bound to be somewhat filtered, and thus distorted or exaggerated in key respects.

Yet Xenophon insists that the world listen to how Socrates appeared at the time of his trial to Hermogenes; Xenophon wants the world to think of Socrates ending his days in close association with Hermogenes, and to recognize Hermogenes as Socrates's friend and spokesman or transmitter. To begin to see better the reasons for this, consider in the first place the *reputation* that surrounds a man such as Hermogenes. No one sees a threat in Hermogenes, despite or even because of his unorthodox religious views, and if the belief in his harmlessness is tinged with a bit of contempt, that is no bar to the general opinion that Hermogenes, with all his oddness, is a man of unquestionable probity and piety. Hermogenes is the perfect witness for Xenophon to appeal to when he rebuts those who accuse Socrates of lying about the existence of his guiding *daimonion* (*Memorabilia* 4.8). To the public, a man like Hermogenes is almost the polar opposite of a man like Alcibiades. When Xenophon seeks to refute those who adduce Critias and Alcibiades as evidence that Socrates corrupted young Athenian citizens, Xenophon crowns his counterargument with a list of seven counterexamples of those who "consorted with him not in order to become popular public leaders or skillful in the courtroom, but in order to become gentlemen . . . not one of whom either in his youth or in his later years did anything wrong or incurred accusation": Hermogenes is at the center of the list (*Memorabilia* 1.2.48). How could someone who is the bosom comrade of a man such as Hermogenes be justly suspected of impiety or corruption—even or precisely if he, like Hermogenes, claims an idiosyncratic relationship with divinity? Hermogenes and men of his sort are living proof that proud, even assertive, unorthodoxy as regards the divinities, and as regards education in gentlemanliness, is by no means a necessary sign of corruption. By associating himself and his reputation with a man known to be like Hermogenes, the philosopher secures protection for himself and his students. And by leaving behind a man such as Hermogenes as his outspoken defender, the philosopher—with the help of his student Xenophon—continues, postmortem, to gain important protection for his educational enterprise, for his surviving and his future followers.

What's more, the offensive "big talk" of Socrates that a Hermogenes relishes and memorializes can secure more than protection; it can win respect, among a certain specific and crucial portion of future citizenries. For there will always be a few proud, more or less nonconformist, republicans or monarchists who share something of the spirit and taste of Hermogenes. These are spirited individuals who, upon hearing or reading the report of Hermogenes, can join him in admiring the Socratic exhibition of indomitably outspoken independence (see Pucci ad #15). These are citizens who, even if they are unlikely ever to become followers of Socrates, can be led by Hermogenes to see in the philosopher a greatness of soul and a pride for which they feel a kinship and a respect or even a certain reverence. Thus precisely the provocatively boastful speech that goads the citizens en masse to kill Socrates may, in years to come, attract a few hearers and readers who will take a strong stand defending other outrageously proud and independent, religiously unorthodox or dissident, philosophers.[14]

Last but not least, Hermogenes's depiction of the philosopher as a man of vauntingly proud independence may awaken the admiration of spirited, nonconformist *young* people with philosophic potential. Xenophon's Hermogenes is thus also the carrier of a message of seduction to souls considerably superior to his own.

We do not exaggerate too much if we characterize Hermogenes as an "evangelist" of Socrates: the verb Xenophon chooses—*exangelō*—to designate the reporting of Hermogenes, and thus the bulk of the *Apology*, has the root from which our words "angel" and "evangelist" derive, and the same word appears a bit later in the *Apology* (#13) as the verb Socrates uses for his transmissions to his friends of counsels he receives for them from divinity.[15]

We cannot overlook, however, the peculiar difficulties or dangers that a man of Hermogenes's type poses, and which Xenophon shows Socrates trying gently to alleviate. However sound the judgment of such a man may be, he is constitutionally liable to an assertion of his dignity and independence that may become imprudent. In the particular case of Hermogenes, the political risk is lessened by his limited abilities as a speaker. Nevertheless, the example of public arrogance with which Socrates closes his life could prove a dangerous precedent for Hermogenes and his type—were it not for the fact that Socrates goes to great lengths to stress, to and through Hermogenes, the prudential precondition for his outspokenness: namely, his confidence, corroborated by the divine sign, that for his own good, at his advanced age, death had become preferable to continued life. With a view to the educative effect on Hermogenes and others like him, there is a deep appropriateness in Socrates's somewhat incongruent mixture of quasi-heroic boastful display with hardheaded, self-interested calculation. This is of a piece with what Xenophon shows more generally: Socrates striving to inculcate, in noble acquaintances whose tendencies to headstrong or imprudent pride need tempering, the need to modulate one's austere dignity by circumspect attention to one's security and one's mundane needs (see bk. 2 of the *Memorabilia*, chaps. 7–end). Socrates's famous *daimonion*, and thereby his conspicuously idiosyncratic piety, bespeak a life guided by a divine inspiration that is attentive to, rather than sacrificing of, personal security (see #5, 8, and 33). As for Hermogenes's other, less dangerous proclivities—his heavy moralism, "his complete lack of understanding of what irony is or requires" (XS 172), his tendency to withdraw into an unphilanthropic isolation—the *Symposium* reveals, with Xenophon's characteristic deftness, the manner in which Socrates sought to correct these vices and make of Hermogenes a more convivial and useful member of society.[16]

We must finally stress that the usefulness and importance of Hermogenes as a spokesman for Socrates is fully actualized, not through any efforts of Socrates himself but through the rhetorical genius of Xenophon. For, taken by himself, Hermogenes is too minor a figure to attract great future respect or repute for Socrates. Hermogenes's report of Socrates is immortalized not because it is by Hermogenes but because it is by Xenophon—a man whose noble exploits in war, and whose educative writings in peace, established him as a figure bound to attract the respect and even the awe of future generations of proud gentlemen. The strategy of making Hermogenes the transmitter of a major aspect of the Socratic legacy is part of the grander and more complex Xenophontic-Socratic rhetorical strategy.

## Hermogenes as Apt Conduit for Socrates's Self-Disclosure

We have still to uncover the deepest and most significant role played by Hermogenes as transmitter of recollections of Socrates. By means of the report he attributes to Hermogenes, Xenophon provides otherwise unavailable glimpses of crucial dimensions of Socrates's self-understanding and self-esteem—dimensions that in any other context it would be imprudent to make so plain.[17] The *Apology* affords a context that is relatively safe, because of its brevity and because the testimony of Hermogenes is likely to be disregarded or downplayed by most readers (especially given what "has been written" about the trial "by others," above all Plato).

Xenophon's three other Socratic writings avoid the self-exalting "big talk" that is memorably gratifying or attractive to Hermogenes (and to readers who share something of the latter's taste). On its face, this might seem to imply that the other three Socratic writings are far more reliable or accurate. But that this conclusion is too hasty becomes apparent as soon as we recognize that the other three Socratic writings exaggerate in the opposite direction, by indulging in the gracefully urbane and harmless vice of untrue self-deprecation (irony or *eirōneia*).[18] The other Socratic writings of Xenophon mute or veil Socrates's sense of superiority to his fellow men. This implies that the truth about the Xenophontic Socrates's self-understanding lies somewhere between the impression given by the *Apology* and the impression given by Xenophon's three other Socratic writings. We therefore need to read the *Apology* as a major counterbalance. What's more, since irony also characterizes, pervasively, the Socratic writings of *Plato*, they too are in need of this counterbalance provided by Xenophon's *Apology*. In short, we would be well advised to allow the *Apology*'s recollection of Socrates a weight out of all proportion to its brevity and lack of certain superficial charms. As regards the latter, we have to add that Socrates's *megalēgoria* overlaps with *alazoneia*, the chief characteristic of Aristophanean comedy.[19]

## WHAT THE REPORT OF THE PRETRIAL CONVERSATION WITH HERMOGENES REVEALS

If we are to profit as we should from the *Apology*, we need first and foremost to scrutinize the contrasts between the *Apology*'s and the *Memorabilia*'s versions of the Socratic conversation that took place prior to the trial. To repeat: in the *Memorabilia* there is no hint of the "big talk" that pervades the *Apology*. The more we ponder the contrasts, the more we will recognize how Xenophon has contrived to make even this part of the *Apology* play a key role in what we have called the "counterbalancing" function of the work.

### Socrates's Whole Life as His Defense

According to both versions, Hermogenes said that he initiated the conversation with Socrates after he had witnessed the latter "conversing about everything except the trial."

The *Apology* (#3)—which unlike the *Memorabilia* employs direct discourse—has Hermogenes recollecting that he asked: "Shouldn't you be considering, Socrates, also how you will make your defense?" And then recollecting that Socrates answered: "Don't I seem to you to have gone through life attending to the making of a defense?" Hermogenes reports that when he then asked in puzzlement, "How?" Socrates answered: "In that I have been all along doing nothing unjust: which I believe to be the noblest[20] attention to the making of a defense."

The *Memorabilia* (4.8.4; see also 4.4 and 4.8.11)—which is devoted to displaying the justice of Socrates—gives a version of this last which is much more edifying (XS 136). Socrates is reported as having "said that he all along was doing nothing except investigating the just things and the unjust things, doing the just things and refraining from the unjust things." This paraphrase, in contrast to the direct quotation of Socrates in the *Apology*, suggests that Socrates claimed that he had philosophized throughout his life about nothing except justice and that he had neglected no duties of just citizenship. The *Apology*, in remarkable contrast, "excludes everything political in the life of Socrates" (Pucci 8—who goes on to say, "this discrepancy between the two works is significant and shows how the *Apology* is carefully constructed and how it is thought as an autonomous work").

## The Relations between Socrates and His God(s)

When Hermogenes, evidently dissatisfied, proceeded to remind Socrates that the Athenian courts are often misled by courtroom orations into "*killing*" those who have done nothing unjust, while they often release the unjust who by their orations manage to arouse pity or favor, the *Apology* reports (#4) that Socrates confessed, swearing by Zeus, that he had *twice*[21] already been opposed by his *daimonion* as he himself was undertaking to give thought to his defense speech (a bit later, Socrates asserts that "the gods" protested in opposition when he, together with his friends, were starting to plan a speech that would seek to employ "every sort of means of acquittal"—#8[22]). When Hermogenes expressed his amazement at this, Socrates responded by taking Hermogenes's astonishment to be provoked not by Socrates's disobedience to the *daimonion* (Socrates evidently did not think this would seem unusual to Hermogenes) but by the *daimonion*'s opposition to Socrates planning a speech that might by hook or by crook avoid conviction and death; and so Socrates launched into his explanation of the decisive reasons he had discovered why it was a good time for him to die, saying: "Do you believe it to be amazing if it is *also* the god's opinion that it is better for me to die now?"

In striking contrast to the preceding, the more pious *Memorabilia* version gives no hint that Socrates stubbornly persisted, in defiance of "the god's" first prohibition, in planning a tricky defense speech. And in the less boastful, more humble *Memorabilia* version, Socrates is reported as having asked, in response to Hermogenes's expression of astoundment: "Are you amazed if it is the god's opinion that it is better for me to die now?"

The *Memorabilia* thus gives the impression that Socrates *first obeyed* "the god's" prohibition and *then* figured out the god's reasons that made the commandment rationally good (Socrates employed reason as handmaid to irresistibly commanding revelation). In other words, the *Memorabilia* has no suggestion that Socrates's obedience to the god was *contingent* on the philosopher's *first* deducing by and for himself the sound reasons for the behavior commanded by the revealed prohibition (XS 137).

The *Apology*, in contrast, reveals that the philosopher did not always obey his *daimonion* and in this key instance (as in all others?) refused to do so *until* he had *himself* deduced, by his own independent reasoning, the rational benefit of what "the god" had twice commanded—and that Socrates then imputed the reasoning, that he had by himself deduced, to "the god" as well (revelation was made a handmaid to reason).

## Socrates on the Relation between the Pleasant and the Good

Socrates began to articulate the reasons for thinking his death was timely by asking, according to the *Apology* version (#5), "Don't you know that until now I would never concede to anyone among humans that he has lived a better life than mine?" The reason immediately given was that the life of Socrates had contained what is "most pleasant." These words provoke the reader to wonder: To what extent did Socrates judge the goodness and worth of a life by its enjoyment of pleasure? This wonder is further instigated by the striking fact that "the *Apology* speaks only of the *easy* character of Socrates's death; the *Memorabilia* speaks only of its *noble* character" (XS 138; my italics). This wonder is still further aroused by the *Apology*'s version (#6) of Socrates's formulation of the evil that he foresees if he advances further into old age and declines: "If I perceive myself becoming worse and I find fault with myself, how would I continue to live *pleasantly*?"

In contrast, the nobler formulations reported in the *Memorabilia* have Socrates clearly distinguishing the pleasure of life from its goodness and subordinating the former to the latter (see also ibid. 4.8.11). After specifying ways he is likely to decline in old age, Socrates is quoted as saying, "By not perceiving these things, life would not be worth living, but perceiving them, how would it not necessarily be living worse, *and also* more unpleasantly?" (*Memorabilia* 4.8.8). And Socrates's formulation of the superiority of his life was: "Don't you know that until this time I would never concede to anyone among humans that he has lived either a better, or a more pleasant, life than mine?" For "I think they live best who best attend to their becoming the best possible; and they live most pleasantly who especially perceive that they are becoming best" (*Memorabilia* 4.8.6). This suggests that what is humanly best is progress in excellence or virtue—and for Socrates, that would be progress, above all, in wisdom or in understanding of the nature of things. Such progress is not itself the greatest pleasure (mortal wisdom or knowledge may always be alloyed with some pain), but it is accompanied by *awareness of* one's progress in wisdom, as the greatest good, and that awareness is a very great, or *the* greatest, pleasure for humans.

The *Apology* version (#5) adds a major supplement, by its report of what Socrates said next: he defined the greatest pleasure, whose enjoyment made his life second to no other human's, as a kind of "knowing" (*ēidein*), namely, the *knowing* that his "*entire* life" had been "lived piously and justly" (he did not say "nobly")—which resulted in "my strongly *admiring* myself" (*ischurōs agamenos emauton*) and "finding" in "those who associated with me" the same recognition (*tauta hēuriskon kai tous emoi sungignomenous gignōskontas peri emou*). Self-admiration, together with finding out that respected associates join in recognizing one as admirable, adds a further major dimension to the pleasure of the Socratic-philosophic life, beyond the pleasure of awareness of progress in wisdom.[23] And Socrates's formulation suggests that the *most* solid and admirable part of his philosophic life was his self-consciousness of his *perfected* knowledge of piety and justice, both of which were enacted *throughout* his *entire* life.

## Socrates's Moral Satisfaction with His Entire Life

As noted above, Xenophon reformulates this last remark in the *Memorabilia* (4.8.6)—where no big talk is allowed—in more humble terms: "they live most pleasantly who especially *perceive* that they are *becoming best*, as I have *perceived* in my own case." Perceiving one's ongoing improvement entails awareness of room for improvement. But according to the *Apology* version, Socrates now *knows* that he has *never* been deficient, *never* in need of improvement, as regards piety and justice. How is this conceivable?[24] Does he not mean that the perfection he eventually achieved in his *knowledge* of piety and justice vindicated *all* his behavior in his entire previous moral life? Certainly, in the *Apology* as a whole, Socrates never speaks as if there were any period in his life that he finds morally imperfect or morally immature. This despite the fact that, as Socrates admits in the *Economist* (6.13–17, 11.1–6), there was a time in his life, as a mature philosopher, when he had little or no idea what his fellow citizens meant by "the noble," or what a gentleman's way of life was and, what is more, had no wish to inquire or to find out. Whereas the mature, transformed, Socrates's relentless interrogation concerning the *kalon* is a, even the, major theme of the *Economist*, *Symposium*, and *Memorabilia* (see similarly Plato, *Phaedo* 100, 538c-d; *Apology* 21d), the word barely appears in Xenophon's *Apology* (#3, 26, and 29).[25] Xenophon's *Apology* does not refer to, and hence offers no explanation for, Socrates's Aristophanean infamy as having once been devoted to religiously and morally dubious natural scientific investigations; not a word is said to refute the rumored charges—repeated elsewhere in Xenophon—that Socrates was a "thinker of the things in the heavens," of the "most useless things," such as "the distance between fleas' feet."[26] The *Apology* ignores what is sometimes called the "Socratic turn," or the metamorphosis from the "pre-Socratic" ("Aristophanean") Socrates to the Socrates who initiated political philosophy.[27] By the same token, in the *Apology* there is no reference to Socrates having become, rather late in life, a husband and father, who looked to Aspasia as educator of wives.[28] The *Apology* thus masks, for more uninformed readers, a very grave question about the piety of Socrates.[29] At the same time, it instigates more knowledgeable readers to wonder: Was Socrates, at the time of his death, maybe not so different as is elsewhere claimed from the freethinking philosopher of nature whom Aristophanes blew up into comic proportions?[30]

## Socrates's Self-Admiration

In the *Memorabilia* version (4.8.7) Socrates is quoted as proceeding to add that his continuously joyful recognition of his steady improvement has in part resulted from and depended upon his "encountering other humans, and comparatively contemplating myself," and also from his noting that his friends (*philoi*) have continuously agreed with his judgment of himself—and this last "not because they love me" (Socrates hastens to add) "but because they too think that by being together with me *they* are becoming better."

In the *Apology's* rendition (#5), Socrates is reported to have said only that, "while strongly admiring myself, I found that also those associating with me recognized the same things about me." This formulation, in contrast to that in the *Memorabilia*, suggests that the philosopher's deeply gratifying self-admiration was not very dependent on comparing himself with others; and also that it was not very dependent upon, though it was ratified and supplemented by, the enjoyable admiration he received from others (not necessarily friends—XS 137) who associated with him. Accordingly, whereas in the *Memorabilia* version (4.8.8) Socrates is reported listing, as one of the ills of old age he foresees he will suffer if his life is prolonged, "becoming worse than those in comparison to whom I was better," in the *Apology* version (#6) he makes no reference to being troubled by such a prospect.

Here again, we may surmise that Xenophon wants us to excogitate the truth as lying in between, and as somehow synthesizing, the two versions. We note in this regard that while in the *Memorabilia* version, unlike in the *Apology* version, Socrates is reported as having made emphatic reference to his friends and their love for him as well as their deriving benefit from associating with him, it was not their love, nor their being benefited, but their confirming his estimation that he was steadily progressing in what is best, that he said contributed substantially to making his own life most pleasant.

## The Close of the Conversation

Here we find the most stark and sustained contrast between the two versions of what is the last dialogue of Socrates recorded in Xenophon.

In the *Memorabilia* (4.8.9–10), Xenophon has Socrates insisting that his dying as a victim of injustice is not shameful but will bring him posthumous public fame (as a kind of martyr).

In the *Apology*, however, Hermogenes quotes Socrates declaring his opinion that "the god," by getting him to stop his planning of a speech that would have secured acquittal, was "probably out of goodwill arranging" for him the private benefits of dying not only at the right *time*, for himself, but in a *manner* (hemlock poison) that would be the least painful for himself and, for his friends, the least troublesome and the most conducive to their mourning him and missing him (#7–8). At this point Socrates is quoted declaring to Hermogenes his intention to "talk big"—"displaying as many noble things as I believe I have obtained both from gods and from humans, and the opinion I hold about myself" (#9). So, in the *Apology* version too, Socrates is concerned with his public persona and future fame—but as a triumphantly just and justified "winner," not as a martyr, not as a victim or "loser."

## WHAT THE REPORT OF THE DEFENSE SPEECH REVEALS

In order to catch on to what Xenophon means to disclose through his Hermogenes's report of the defense speech itself, we need also to compare, meticulously, this reported "big talk" of Socrates, as he rebuts the twofold official indictment, with Xenophon's own, rather ironic, rebuttal of the twofold indictment, elaborated in the first two chapters of his *Memorabilia*.

The official indictment as Hermogenes recalled it (#10) is subtly but importantly different from the formulation by Xenophon at the outset of the *Memorabilia*: in the *Apology* version ascribed to Hermogenes, the indictment charged that Socrates does "not believe in [worship—*nomizoi*] the gods whom the city believes in [worships] but carries in (*eispheroi*) strange or novel (*kaina*) divine things (*daimonia*); and he corrupts the young." As Patch observes (in Bartlett 1996, ad loc., following XS 129–30): in contrast with the *Memorabilia*, "the corruption charge is here less clearly distinguished as a separate, second charge."

This prepares us for the most remarkable overall contrast between the defense of Socrates against the official charges that Xenophon gives in the *Memorabilia* and the defense quoted from Socrates himself in the *Apology*. In the *Memorabilia* Xenophon shrewdly draws attention away from the graver, more widely believed[31] charge of impiety, by devoting three times more space to refuting the less widely believed, less dangerous, charge of "corrupting the young"—a charge that Xenophon makes still less dangerous by failing even to entertain the possibility that the imputed corruption consisted in teaching impiety, or doubts about the gods of the city: the *Memorabilia* keeps the charge of corrupting the young widely separate from the charge of impiety. In the *Apology*, Socrates is quoted as brazenly doing the reverse. Socrates devotes three times as much space to refuting the impiety charge and transforms that refutation into a vaunting of his own divinely celebrated virtues; then, Socrates makes the refutation of the charge of corrupting the young grow out of the vaunting of his own virtues, thus making his refutation of the corruption charge into merely a kind of appendix to the refutation of the impiety charge. What's more, Socrates dares to give as the leading example of what it would mean to corrupt a young person: "to make someone impious from having been pious" (#19).

## The Rebuttal of the Charge of Impiety

Socrates is quoted by Hermogenes as beginning his rebuttal in a way that anticipates Xenophon's own lawyerly trick of seizing on a major ambiguity in the wording of the indictment (*Memorabilia* 1.1.2). The verb *nomizō*, when applied to humans in their posture toward divinities, can mean either "*believing in*" or "*honoring, worshipping*, according to lawful custom."[32] The *Apology* quotes Socrates rejoining as if the latter were the intended meaning of the accusation—which Socrates is then able to dismiss as preposterous, given that "others who happened along, and Meletus himself, if he wished, could have witnessed me sacrificing in the public festivals and on the popular altars" (#11). Prefiguring Xenophon's *Memorabilia*, Socrates is reported to have said not a word in response to the accusation that was doubtless uppermost in the intention of the prosecutors and in the minds of the jury: that Socrates did *not believe* in the gods in whom the citizenry *believes* (the gods in whose civic ritual worship he conspicuously, but perhaps disingenuously, joined).[33] But in the *Memorabilia*, Xenophon at least adds that Socrates *did* "believe in [some sort of] gods"; *and* that he manifestly sacrificed not only on public occasions, but also privately, at home; *and* that he plainly made use of conventional divination (*Memorabilia* 1.1.5). In the *Apology*, Socrates is reported as having asserted none of these things (cf. XS 130).

In the *Apology*, after having in this manner rebutted the charge of not "worshipping/believing in" the gods of the city, Socrates is quoted as proceeding to respond to the charge of carrying in strange or new *daimonia* (#12–13). Here again we find initially an anticipation of Xenophon's mode of rebuttal in the *Memorabilia* (1.1.3–4): Socrates is reported as assuming that this accusation refers to his famous claim to be guided by a singular divine monitor, and he is quoted insisting that this entails nothing unconventional—just as Xenophon insists in the *Memorabilia*. But whereas the latter speaks only of Socrates's "*daimonion*," Socrates in the *Apology* is quoted proclaiming that he was guided by "a voice of a god," or "of *the* god."[34] And whereas the *Memorabilia* assimilates what Socrates experienced only to rather ordinary forms of divination, Socrates in the *Apology* has the nerve to parallel his personal religious experiences also to that of the priestess who delivers from Apollo the Delphic oracles, the most authoritative divine revelations in Greece! No wonder that, as Hermogenes reported, "on hearing these things, the jurors raised a clamor—some disbelieving the things said, some envying them" (#14; as Pucci notes, ad loc., "the inferences about the motives for the judges' behaviour are Hermogenes'").

After this point, the quoted report of Socrates's defense speech diverges very, very widely from Xenophon's defense in the *Memorabilia*.

According to Hermogenes, Socrates defiantly responded to the crowd's clamor by saying: "Come on, listen also to other things, so that those of you who wish to can disbelieve still more that I have been honored by *daimonia*!" (plural; #15). Socrates then launched into his tale of the extraordinary public honor he claimed to have received from the Delphic oracle. He dared to contend that the oracle had proclaimed, in response to a question put to it by Chaerephon, before a crowd of witnesses, that "no human was more free/liberal (*eleutheriōteron*),[35] nor more just, nor more sensibly moderate (*sōphronesteron*)" than Socrates. When "the jurors, as was to be expected,[36] upon hearing these things, made an even greater clamor" (they obviously found the tale outrageously incredible and hubristic), Socrates is reported to have added fuel to their fire by conceding, with heavy irony, that his divine honors had indeed been outdone by those accorded to Lycurgus, whom the oracle likened to a god: "I was not likened to a god, but was merely judged superior by far[37] to humans." Then Socrates immediately upped the ante further by calling on the jurors to adopt what we have seen was earlier disclosed to be Socrates's own critical posture toward the truth of divine revelations: "but nevertheless, don't you merely trust by faith in the god, but scrutinize one by one each of the things the god says!" (#15). Socrates proceeded to ask an anaphoric series of didactic questions, treating the assembly of jurors a bit like a classroom and leading the students through a series of reflections on the nature of the divinely honored virtues of the great Socrates. By putting himself, as divinely celebrated, in juxtaposition with Lycurgus, Socrates pointed off to the contrast between his (philosophic) versions of the virtues in question and the (civic) versions of the same, which were ascribed to the divine man reputed by Greeks to be the greatest lawgiver of all time.

Socrates first (#16) contended for the truth of his being unrivalled in freedom or liberality (*eleutheria*). He did so by adducing his liberation, through self-mastery, from his physical appetites ("who do you know less enslaved to bodily desires?") and from any need to accept either gifts or pay. Socrates made no reference to the fraternal *civic* liberty of republican citizens, that is, the meaning of liberty upon which Lycurgus focused (*Regime of the Lacedaemonians* 7.2; also 8.2, 11.3, and 12.5), nor did Socrates refer to the liberality of civic largesse that marks the perfect gentlemen Ischomachus (*Economist* 2.9 and 11.9). We further note that the distinctive Socratic virtue of "freedom" or "liberality," unlike the versions of the virtue seen in Lycurgus and Ischomachus, would seem realizable in almost any kind of civilized regime, republican or *non*republican—like Hiero's tyranny.[38]

Proceeding next to the demonstration of his unsurpassed *justice* (#16 cont.), Socrates asked: "Whom could you reasonably believe to be more just than he who is so in harmony with what he has that he needs in addition nothing that belongs to anyone else?" Socrates's "justice" would seem to be simply another facet of what he previously designated his freedom or liberality: his superior independence from the needs and fears that prompt men to compete with (but also to help) one another. A few sentences later Socrates gives a shocking (Vander Waerdt 1993, 31) illustration of what this superiority means concretely. Near the end of the Peloponnesian War, during the siege whose sufferings prefigured the grim defeat of Athens by Sparta (see *Hellenica* 2.2), "the others pitied themselves, while I went on with no greater difficulty than when the city was especially happy" (#18; this "must have been particularly galling to his listeners"—XS 132). Socrates does not say that his justice consists in law-abidingness, or in helping others.[39] And he does not, in what follows, identify his helping others (especially through education) with his justice (XS 132).

It is a gentleman of the type of Hermogenes who is especially open to admiring such radical self-sufficiency and self-mastery as the central pillar of virtue or excellence. That this radical independence of Socrates was by no means without benefit to others was made clear, Hermogenes reported, as Socrates went on to vindicate his unsurpassed "wisdom" (#16 cont.: *sophon*—which Socrates had the nerve to substitute for the oracle's less exalted "sensibly moderate"[40]). Socrates here identified wisdom with prudence (or lifelong seeking and learning of whatever good he could), and he highlighted evidence that the best sort of people believed that they accrued benefit from Socrates's prudent pursuit of (his own) good. Socrates adduced as testimony how "many of the citizens aiming at virtue, and also how many of the foreigners, chose me, above all others, with whom to associate" and that "I am asked by not a single person to return benefits, but many confess to owing me" (#17). After adding that "while others provide for themselves expensive enjoyments from the market, I contrive from my soul, without expense, more pleasant things for myself," Socrates returned momentarily to the justice of the matter: he asked how—if the preceding could not be refuted—it would not be "just" for him to be praised by gods as well as humans (#18).

At this point, Socrates is reported to have switched, abruptly, to the second charge, of corrupting the young. If we pause to look back over what has preceded, we become aware that the entire defense speech, as reported here, has in an important sense not two, but three, parts: the answer to the charge of impiety has segued insensibly (by way of the tale of the Delphic oracle's pronouncement) into a second and longest central section,[41] whose theme is the vindication of the distinctive moral virtues of Socrates as announced and blessed by the oracle—and as centered on his self-mastery and achievement of his own good.

## The Rebuttal of the Charge of Corrupting the Young

Socrates is reported to have addressed the second charge ad hominem: "And nevertheless you, Meletus, assert that I, by doing such things, corrupt the young?!" (#19). Socrates then commandeered the definition of "corrupting the young," or the identification of who are meant by "corrupters of the young": "And surely we know who are the corrupters of the young!" He specified this knowledge by posing a series of six challenges to his accuser Meletus: "say, if you know anyone having become, through me, from pious, impious; or from moderate, hubristic; or from practicing a good regimen to extravagance; or from being like a measured drinker to a drunk; or from a lover of toil to a softy—or subject to any other wicked pleasure!" It would obviously have been foolhardy of Meletus to incur the risk of a suit for slander by adducing any such corrupted individuals.

But Meletus was hardly left speechless. He shrewdly declared (invoking father Zeus in an oath) that he knew of people whom Socrates "has[42] persuaded"to obey him, as opposed to their own parents!

Socrates had to confess the truth of this charge.[43] What's more, Socrates did not contain but rather enlarged the damage when he went on to say that this charge was valid as regards "education, at least"; for Socrates proceeded to claim that with respect to the education that he held to be "the greatest good for human beings," he was reasonably judged by the young to be preeminently best—while he indicated at the same time that his practical wisdom as the superior educator differed not only from the doctor's wisdom about health but from the forms of prudence preeminently honored by "*you* Athenians" in "*your*" political life. But the portion of the speech reported by Hermogenes concluded with Socrates asking Meletus, rhetorically, if he did not think it "amazing" for him to be prosecuting a man for a capital crime on account of his being judged by some to be the best at what is the greatest good for humans, education (#20–21).

## AFTER THE TRIAL

We have already discussed the passage, immediately following the quotation of the defense speech, in which Xenophon steps forward in the first-person singular and explains the basis for his selection from all that was said at the trial (#22–23). We now add that this passage ends with Xenophon's one and only record of a statement made by Socrates in the days after the trial: to give additional evidence that Socrates believed his death to be timely, Xenophon reports that "when his comrades wished to steal him away," Socrates "would not go along, but even seemed to make a joke of" their plan, by "asking if they knew of some territory outside of Attica inaccessible to death" (#23—Xenophon does not report Socrates gravely pointing out that the escape his comrades had planned would have constituted a serious violation of the law). There is no conspicuous *megalēgoria* in this vignette; as Gray (1989, 139) intelligently observes, commenting on this and subsequent sections not attributed to Hermogenes, "Xenophon appears to use this section to suggest that Socrates had indeed adopted the unpleasant trait of *megalēgoria* only as a deliberate expedient for the trial, and that it was not his natural way with his friends." There is also no parallel to this section in the *Memorabilia*, and so we have here, in the quip about the omnipresence of death, the singular report of the final statement by Socrates in the writings of Xenophon. This gently mocking chastisement of his friends for their failure to face up to the grim inescapability of death appears to be the subtle signature, or last testament, of Xenophon's Socrates.

## AT THE TRIAL, AFTER THE VERDICT

However that may be, Xenophon certainly does provide a report, from Hermogenes, of things Socrates said at the trial after he had been judged guilty and had refused to offer a counterpenalty. In his final words to the jury, Socrates is quoted as having remained relentless in his *megalēgoria*—and, indeed, as having in some respects escalated his deliberate offensiveness.[44] He cast in the face of the jurors an accusation of the "great impiety and injustice," knowingly committed, by those who had suborned (literally, "instructed") the "perjured" witnesses who testified against him and by those witnesses who were thus "persuaded" (#24).[45]

Hermogenes reported Socrates as having then asked, rhetorically, why he should think any the less of himself than before he was convicted, since he had not been refuted in his denial of the charges; and now we hear new versions of his refutations—first of the charge of impiety: "I manifestly never, in place of Zeus and Hera and the gods with these, either sacrificed to strange/novel divine things (*kainois*[46] *daimosin*) or swore by or named[47] other gods" (#24). These words make explicit that the gods at issue in the indictment were the Olympian gods; Socrates thus made more conspicuous his refusal to address the question of whether or not he "believes in" those Olympian gods. As regards the second charge, however, the report has Socrates seeming to have softened his stance. He asked, rhetorically, how he could have corrupted the young when he was habituating them to endurance and frugality. He no longer mentioned the possibility that he had previously put in the foreground: that the accusation of corruption referred primarily to his making the young "impious" (#25; recall #19).

But what thus at first appeared to be a toning down of the *megalēgoria* turned out to be the inlet to a further, rather wry, provocation. For Socrates then had the gall to speak as if the death penalty had been directly intended all along by the jurors (who had voted only to convict him, prior to his springing on them the trick of refusing to follow customary procedure and name a lesser counterpenalty). He listed four crimes for which he said the established penalty is execution—temple robbery, breaking and entering, kidnapping for enslavement, and treason—and pointed out that not even the prosecutors had said he had committed any of these, making it "amazing how it could ever have appeared to you that some deed had been done by me deserving of the death penalty!" (#25). In contrast to Xenophon's parallel statement in the *Memorabilia* (1.2.62), Socrates is not quoted here (from Hermogenes) as having claimed to be speaking in accord with the laws of Athens; and Socrates is not reported to have mentioned—i.e., he did not deny—three capital crimes in Athenian law that Xenophon lists when *he* is protesting, in the *Memorabilia*, the innocence of Socrates: stealing in general (*kleptōn*) and, more specifically, theft of clothing (*lōpodutōn*—a crime which is repeatedly charged against Socrates by Aristophanes in *Clouds* 179 and 1498) and purse cutting (*ballantiotomōn*). Socrates here is also not quoted denying (as Xenophon does, speaking in his own name in the *Memorabilia*) that he was the cause for the city of a war going badly or of faction (consider the career of Alcibiades, and *Memorabilia* 1.2.9–11; XS 134).

Socrates then declared to the jury (according to Hermogenes) that he also ought not to think less of himself because he was dying unjustly—that, on the contrary, "the shame of this is not on me but on those who passed the sentence" (#26). We see that Socrates was confronting, and confuting, the very common tendency to think that unjustly dying (or otherwise suffering), without being avenged, is ignominious—a sign of weakness, of being a "loser," or even of a lack of divine favor.[48]

In his own parallel report in the *Memorabilia* (4.8.9–10), Xenophon quotes Socrates speaking to this effect not in public, to the jurors, after the conviction, but only in private, to Hermogenes and others, *prior* to the trial. Moreover, in the *Memorabilia* Xenophon has Socrates asking, much less assertively (and indeed almost plaintively): "Why is it shameful for me, if others are incapable of recognizing or doing just things by me?" Then Xenophon in the *Memorabilia* quotes Socrates saying that he has seen that the repute of men of the past is not the same for those who have done injustice and for those who have suffered it; and then, that he "knew" that he too "would draw the attention of humans and that if" he "died now, it would be an attention that was different from that given to those who killed him." Xenophon does not have Socrates going so far as to say that the fame of victims of injustice is superior to that of their oppressors, nor that his own fame will be so. After all, the fact of the matter is, "*public* opinion" does not reliably honor victims, as opposed to perpetrators, of injustice. Yet *decent* opinion ardently longs and strives for such (often neglected) memorializing. This signals that the intrinsic benefit of justice, as the supreme moral virtue of the soul, is not evident enough to decent opinion for such opinion not to be anguished by the failure of justice and injustice to be supported by extrinsic sanctions—at the least, by lasting and superior honor or fame.

Now in the *Apology*, Hermogenes reports Socrates using his big talk to assuage such anguish, at least as regards his own case. Socrates is quoted boldly proclaiming his being "consoled" (*paramutheitai*) by assimilating his fate and future fame to that of the demigod-hero Palamedes (descended from Zeus), who is glorified (Socrates rather preposterously claims) by "much more beautiful hymns" than those glorifying his murderer, the demigod-hero Odysseus.[49] Socrates is thus reported as having deployed his "big talk" in asserting everlasting sanctions for justice and injustice, primarily in his own and Palamedes's cases. We have to note, however, that Socrates of course could not deny that the murderer Odysseus is also glorified in song, if by much less beautiful hymns (Socrates claims), and Socrates did not go so far as to say that the "much more beautiful" songs about Palamedes are all about that hero's victimhood—as opposed to his fabled great deeds, inventions, and discoveries (including of numbers and of the alphabet). On close inspection, we see that in point of fact, what Socrates is reported predicting that he will be memorialized for, in the future, is the *same* as what has been testified about him in the *past* (*hypo tou parelēluthotos chronou*)—i.e., *before* his victimhood: that is, his having never done injustice to anyone or made anyone more wicked, but instead having benefited those who engaged in dialogues with him by teaching them whatever good he could, without charge. The intrinsic benefit and joy of this latter activity does not provoke any anguished longing for compensatory glory.

Accordingly, Xenophon in the *Apology* declares in his own name, no longer through Hermogenes, that "having said these things, very much in agreement with the things said [before], he departed, beaming in his eyes and demeanor and stride" (#27).

But: Socrates perceived that those "following"[50] him were of a totally different disposition—weeping! So the philosopher was moved to try to buck up these "followers" by making explicit, for once, the austere resignation whose ceaseless presence in his heart was and is an inescapable ingredient in the philosopher's (therefore necessarily qualified) happiness: "What's this?! You're weeping *now*?! Have you not long known that from the very moment when I came into being the death sentence was pronounced on me by nature?!" Socrates then conceded that "if it is the case that I am perishing before (*proapollumai*) good things have ceased flowing, then I and my well-wishers ought to be pained," "but, if it is the case that I am bringing life to an end (*kataluō ton bion*) when harsh things are to be expected, then I think that you all ought to be of cheerful spirit, on the assumption that I fare well" (#27). Socrates thus declared to others what he had previously disclosed only to Hermogenes. Yet, looking closer, we see that in these comforting words Socrates did not actually declare that "good things had ceased flowing" into his life (and how could that be simply true?), nor did he go quite so far as to say that *he himself* ought to be of cheerful spirit (*euthumēteon*) if it were the case that he was bringing his life to an end when harsh things were to be expected. A bit later, Xenophon, speaking in his own name, partially repairs this (#33): he says that Socrates "showed the strength of his soul," in that "when he recognized that death was superior for him to continued living, then, even as he did not hold out against the other good things, so he was not soft in the face of death, but cheerfully (*hilarōs*) both accepted it and paid the debt (*epetelesato*)."

## "SO IT IS SAID"

The framework of the *Apology* now becomes fundamentally altered. Xenophon ceases to quote from or to rely on Hermogenes. Instead, our author speaks in his own name and relies, for information about what Socrates did and said at the trial, on anonymous reports—on what "is said." In Xenophon, this expression—"is said" (*legetai*)—often gives a subtly ironic indication of more or less questionable reliability.[51] And we now hear of two instances in which Socrates conducted himself in a manner absolutely unprecedented and unmatched in all the Socratic writings of Xenophon (and, for that matter, in the Socratic writings of Plato). Xenophon compels his thoughtful readers to wonder: at the termination of the trial, did Socrates become momentarily overcome by ordinary passions which he in his previous life had transcended? Or, is our author playfully promoting rumors that portray Socrates as resembling a conventionally proud or great-souled man more than Socrates ever really did, or could? (Does Xenophon here playfully push the line of Hermogenes to an extreme even beyond Hermogenes?) Certain it is that these last reported events make vivid, by way of contrast, Socrates's having previously always transcended the passions he now "is said" to have exhibited.

In the first place, Socrates "is said" to have responded to a passionate lamentation uttered by one of his devoted followers—who declared that what was hardest to bear was the injustice of Socrates's death—with a gently ridiculing joke accompanied by a smile or a laugh (#28; the Greek word is ambiguous). "This is the only occasion when the Xenophontic Socrates is explicitly said to have smiled or laughed," even though in the other Socratic writings "he jests not infrequently, not to say always" (XS 140 and 159); there were doubtless very many occasions when Socrates found comical or laughable other people's, and his followers', expressions of impassioned moral opinions, but we do not anywhere else hear any suggestion of Socrates "letting himself go," in that outburst of overconfident triumph or liberation that is human laughter at its core, and which signals a temporary, explosive quest and hope for a mighty change in or forgetfulness of one's limited human condition (see Plato, *Republic* 388e).

In the second place, Socrates "is said" to have taken a somewhat manly revenge on his enemy Anytus, the leading prosecutor (#29; XS 140; Pucci ad loc.). As Anytus walked past, Socrates "is said" to have recalled for his listeners how he had incurred the bitter enmity of Anytus by criticizing the slavish vulgarity of the latter's education of his son; then Socrates "is said" to have told his listeners that Anytus in his "glorying" (*kudros*)[52] was "depraved" (*mochthēros*), since he did not know "that the one of us who is the victor is he who has done the more advantageous and nobler things for all time." But report has it that Socrates did not stop with this. Assimilating himself to those who Homer claimed obtain the power to prophesy at the time of their deaths, Socrates "is said" to have claimed oracular powers allowing him to predict that the son of his enemy Anytus, "through having nothing serious to care for, would fall victim to some shameful desire and advance far in wickedness" (#30).[53]

Xenophon, taking up the baton of the Socratic revenge, proclaims to the world in his own name that "the young man did indeed take such pleasure in wine that he did not stop drinking night or day, and finally became worthless to his city, to his loved ones, and to himself"; and, "as for Anytus, on account of the base education of his son, and on account of his own stupidity, he has happened upon a bad reputation even after he has died" (#31).

However it may be with Socrates, there can be no doubt that our indubitably manly author, through this writing, did in fact exact a lasting revenge from Anytus. Xenophon brings the work to a close with a final eulogy of Socrates, highlighting the master's wisdom and his being "most well born" (*gennaiotēta*).[54] But neither here nor anywhere else does Xenophon ever ascribe manliness (*andreia*) to Socrates. Xenophon's last, somewhat wryly envious words are: "if one of those striving for virtue has associated with somebody more helpful than Socrates, I believe that one to be the real man (*andra*) worthy-of-being-deemed-most-blessed."[55]

APPENDIX

# Preliminary Observations on the Contrasts and Complementarities between Xenophon's and Plato's Presentations of Socrates

Taking a synoptic comparative view of the place that Socrates occupies in each of the two thinkers' oeuvres, we observe that in Plato's dialogues Socrates is the unrivaled, central figure (especially if we recognize that the Athenian Stranger in the *Laws* is a "reincarnated" Socrates and that Timaeus and the Eleatic Stranger are in large part foils to Socrates). Plato's Socrates is explicitly identified, and identifies himself, as a "philosopher" or as "philosophizing." What's more, we find Socrates presented as praising and exhorting to the philosophic life as the best life—above all in the *Republic*, where Socrates contends that the rule of philosophers would be the solution to mankind's political problems.

In Xenophon's Socratic writings, in contrast, there is no explicit exhortation to philosophizing, nor is there ever any praise of the philosopher or of the philosophic life. No hopes for mankind from the rule of philosophers are ever held out. Indeed the very words for "philosopher" and "philosophizing" hardly ever occur. In Xenophon's oeuvre Socrates has a rival cynosure: Cyrus, the hero of a fictional saga (the *Education of Cyrus*) of the most successful ruler plausibly imaginable. Cyrus the Great as political exemplar is portrayed by Xenophon as utterly unenlightened, nay, untouched, by philosophy or philosophers. Outshone but not diminished by the epic of the great Cyrus are more historical (but not altogether unfictive) portraits of a number of impressive smaller-scale rulers, led by Xenophon himself (in his *Anabasis*) and including most notably the younger Cyrus, Hiero, and Agesilaus. To a much greater extent than Plato, Xenophon places Socrates and his way of life (and the kindred wise poet Simonides and his way of life) in contraposition with the character and way of life of the outstanding political ruler—while spotlighting himself, Xenophon, as the unique and fascinating amalgam: "the Socratic prince" (see Buzzetti 2014). Anticipating Cicero,

Xenophon makes nuch clearer than does Plato that participation in political rule continues to hold substantial attraction for a genuinely Socratic-philosophic thinker.

But in Xenophon's writings, the opposition between Socrates and political leaders (including above all Xenophon himself) becomes sharpened when we see that Socrates is never said by anyone to possess the virtue of courage or manliness (*andreia*) and is never credited with any military experience. Plato, contrarily, has interlocutors repeatedly highlight the military virtues and achievements of Socrates—which are not left unnoticed by the Platonic Socrates himself, in Plato's (but not in Xenophon's) *Apology of Socrates*.

Xenophon makes the deficiencies of Socrates as a ruler comically visible in his accounts of the master's confessed inability to rule his own wife, either as regards her relations with himself or as regards her relations with their son Lamprocles. In Plato, Socrates's wife and children are barely mentioned, and Socrates's relations with them play no significant role.

The underlining of Socrates's self-conscious lack of ability, and of ambition, to rule seems to free Xenophon, however, to give clearer indications than does Plato that Socrates was a diligent and most effective teacher of, and sometime eloquent exhorter to, *others'* practically skillful engagement in civic rule—chiefly in Athens (e.g., Pericles the Younger, Critias, Alcibiades, Charmides, Callias) but also (implicitly) in educating Xenophon for his successful leadership in Asia. In other words, Xenophon makes clear that Socrates was a supreme expert in knowing how to rule, without ever being enabled or inclined to put that knowledge into practice himself. Plato gives indication of Socrates's expertise as a knower and teacher of political rule only in more indirect ways—perhaps most extensively by the teaching and the drama, in the *Laws*, of the Athenian Stranger (the "reincarnated" Socrates).

Plato depicts Socrates as a kind of political thinker and political teacher most obviously and massively when, in the *Republic*, Socrates elaborates a seemingly naive, preposterously impractical, utopia. The Platonic Socrates is thus presented as envisioning, experimentally, how grotesquely the philosophic life would have to be trammelled, and civil life reconstructed—most notably as regards divinity and the family—in order to make possible a *forcing* of the "coincidence" of a version of the "philosopher" with the "king" or supreme political ruler.

Xenophon's Socrates engages in no such revealing (failed) thought experiment. Xenophon's best regime is elaborated by the author himself, in his novelistic, but far from preposterous, portrait of Cyrus the Great. In this depiction by Xenophon of the best regime and best civic education, mathematical and astronomical and metaphysical education play no role, and musical education is barely visible; in Plato's *Republic*, in contrast, while the warrior philosopher kings receive no specific education in politics or rule, they are extensively educated in music, theology, mathematics, astronomy, metaphysics, and a version of dialectics. And as Aristotle observes (*Politics* 1265a4), Plato's "Socrates" (= Athenian Stranger, according to Aristotle) brings the regime of the *Laws* "little by little around toward that other," of the *Republic*—this is most obviously the case with the introduction of the Nocturnal Council and its studies of cosmology, astronomy, and theology (and this process is taken still further in the *Epinomis*, which has come down to us as the Platonic sequel to the *Laws*).

As part of the Platonic Socrates's construction of his imaginative thought experiment in the *Republic*, he lays out a rather tendentious but richly heuristic tripartite account of the soul, in which *thumos* ("spiritedness") holds a high place, mediating between desire below and reason above; this account is ratified by Plato's Timaeus in the course of the latter's visionary explanation (before an audience including Socrates) of the origin of the universe. Xenophon's Socrates gives no such schematic or cosmic accounts of the soul and its "three parts," but his corpus as a whole makes even more evident than does Plato how *animalistic* is *thumos*—while underlining the centrality of *thumos* in civic virtue and manliness, and its all but total absence from or invisibility in the psychology of Socrates himself.

In Plato, a critique of the rule of law in the name of a philosophically conceived science of statesmanship is delivered by the Eleatic Stranger in the *Statesman*, with Socrates listening, in (perhaps disapproving) silence. The Platonic Socrates's own most notable statement on law is his presentation in the *Crito* of the personified Laws of Athens elaborating arguments showing why Socrates (and all others) must always obey the laws, even at the cost of one's very life.

In Xenophon a critique of law is delivered explicitly only by the young scamp Alcibiades (in the *Memorabilia*), but tacitly if more comprehensively by the poet Simonides when trying to enlighten the tyrant Hiero in the dialogue named after the latter. Going well beyond Plato, Xenophon not only stresses the law-abidingness of Socrates but also exhibits Socrates insisting on the identification of the lawful with the just (most notably in his quite comical refutation of the sophist Hippias in the *Memorabilia*).

Xenophon in his *Economist* and *Symposium* incorporates himself as a silent observer and student of Socratic conversations that he explicitly claims to have recollected and recorded almost verbatim. In his *Memorabilia* he also often indicates how he personally was affected by such witnessing; above all, he indicates that he monitored (and learned from) Socrates's problematizing of the noble or beautiful (*kalon*) and the just in a series of brief but incisive dialogues. In his *Anabasis* as well as his *Memorabilia* Xenophon depicts himself as the sole or chief interlocutor in brief, quite comical, dialogues with Socrates that do not end in agreement. Xenophon thus makes us witnesses to memorable moments in his own education or conversion (or "corruption") by Socrates—an education and conversion that certainly did not lead Xenophon to become simply an imitator of the way of life of the master, whom he nonetheless obviously admired more than himself, or any other man. Xenophon also discloses that a major dimension of his experience of being educated by Socrates was participation in reading groups of Socrates and his beloved friends studying the treasures left behind in great old books (*Memorabilia* 1.6.14). Xenophon subtly but explicitly salutes Plato as his superior fellow student of Socrates (*Memorabilia* 3.6). Otherwise, however, despite declaring in the *Memorabilia* that Socrates was dedicated to making his companions expert dialecticians, and despite creating vivid references in the *Memorabilia* (by Hippias) and in the *Symposium* (by Callias) to Socrates's and his students' well-known preoccupation with rendering interlocutors perplexed about justice, there are in Xenophon practically no exhibitions of Socrates engaging in dialectical refutations of *promising* or even semipromising youths, especially as regards their opinions of justice. But the impish Xenophon does tease and provoke his readers by unfolding, at some length, Socrates's refutational conversion of the opinions about justice held by a quite *un*promising youth, Euthydemus.

In sharp contrast, Plato in his Socratic writings never refers to his own education by Socrates, nor to any conversation that he ever had with Socrates—indeed, Plato never claims to have been personally present at any conversation of Socrates. The only time Plato ever portrays himself in proximity to Socrates is as a spotlighted member of the audience in the *Apology of Socrates*, offering to pay a substantial fine on behalf of the master, apparently somewhat against the latter's wish or intention. Plato never discloses that a major part of Socrates's teaching consisted in his leading groups engaged in studying and discovering the treasures in old books. Plato never shows Socrates teaching his young intimates how he learned about the noble by questioning and listening to a perfect gentleman (the nearest Platonic approaches to such a very touchy and pregnant scenario are the conversations in the *Laches* and in the opening pages of the *Laws*, as well as the brief interrogation and refutation of Cephalus in the opening of the *Republic*). Instead, to a much greater extent than Xenophon, Plato stages Socrates refuting *un*gentlemanly opinions about the just and the noble, expressed and defended by sophistic interlocutors (most notably, Thrasymachus, Gorgias,

Polus, Callicles, Protagoras, Meno, Hippias, and Critias). Yet Plato does also depict Socrates engaged in pretty elaborate refutations of the moral opinions of a number of more or less promising younger men (e.g., Alcibiades, Polemarchus, young Kleinias, Charmides, Theages, Lysis, Menexenus, Protarchus, and Agathon). And Plato's *Apology* has Socrates providing, especially through his tale of his reaction to the Delphic oracle, an illuminating glimpse of the theologico-political core of what distinguishes and animates Socratic dialectical-refutational philosophizing.

Plato does not make it as evident as does Xenophon—most dramatically in the latter's account of Socrates's painstaking conversion of Euthydemus—how necessary or important it was for Socrates to exercise successfully his refutational testing and converting on *un*promising youths and interlocutors. In Plato, this dimension of the Socratic project is visible in the Eleatic Stranger's implied critique, in the *Sophist*, of Socrates's choice of often unpromising interlocutors; it is also glimpsed in Socrates's refutation of Cephalus in the opening pages of the *Republic*, and most vividly in the Athenian Stranger's Socratic refutation of Kleinias and Megillus in the opening pages of the *Laws*.

Connected to the preceding contrast is the fact that Plato never so clearly discloses, as does Xenophon quite boldly and explicitly, that Socrates disposed of a cohort of "hunting dogs" among his followers, who were assigned the task of spreading wide "nets" throughout Athens to capture various sorts of "prey" for Socrates in the execution of his refutational project.

Plato dares repeatedly to bring to the fore the Socratic critique of retributive justice by way of the thesis that virtue is knowledge and vice is ignorance; in Xenophon, this quasi-signature of the Platonic Socrates is not at all emphasized—though it is briefly if obliquely spotlighted, and in crucial respects clarified, in various passages (see esp. *Memorabilia* 1.2.18–24).

Both Plato and Xenophon highlight the momentous transformation that marks Socrates's biography: his midlife "turn" from being a "pre-Socratic" philosopher, focused on studying the nature of the whole, to becoming the founder of political philosophy as the study of "the human things," opinions as to the just and the noble, through refutational dialogue. Xenophon in his *Economist* suggests that Socrates underwent this turn as a consequence of having been instructively chastized by Aristophanes's comic critique in the *Clouds*, which purportedly drove Socrates to inquirying about the noble (*kalon*) from the perfect gentleman Ischomachus. (That Xenophon is jokingly exaggerating the importance of Aristophanes's *Clouds* becomes clear from his *Symposium*, which depicts Socrates as the completely mature political philosopher in the same year in which Aristophanes's *Clouds* was first published.) This goes with Xenophon's witty and allusive rejoinder to Aristophanes's critique of the Socratic way of life—a rejoinder that pervades Xenophon's Socratic writings more than Plato's. Unlike Plato, however, Xenophon does not show Socrates responding to Aristophanes in person, or criticizing tragic poetry led by Homer; nor is there in Xenophon anything comparable to Plato's staging of Socrates's refutational encounter with the young tragedian Agathon at the start of the latter's career, as well as Socrates's encounter with the famous contemporary rhapsode Ion, at the height of the latter's career. On the other hand, Xenophon selects the poet Simonides as a stand in for Socrates—playing the role of the wise man who refutes and attempts to teach the impressive tyrant Hiero.

Plato delineates the Socratic "turn" in manifold aspects and stages—most obviously through the refutation of the young Socrates in the *Parmenides*, and through Socrates's report of Diotima's refutation of his younger self in the *Symposium*, and through the *Apology's* account of the Delphic quest, and (above all) through Socrates's autobiographical account in the *Phaedo*. Only in the opening pages of his *Apology of Socrates* does Plato afford an explicit, if somewhat tantalizing, glimpse of the importance of Aristophanes's comically critical representation of Socrates.

While Xenophon stresses that the *outcome* of Socrates's "turn," or the heart of Socrates's mature philosophizing, was his dialogical pursuit of the "What is . . . ?" questions, Xenophon rarely depicts that pursuit explicitly; and he only allusively reveals that "coming together to deliberate in common so as to separate the affairs of concern according to their species" was a very large aspect of Socrates's "never ceasing to investigate, with (or among) his companions, what each of the beings might be" (*Memorabilia* 1.1.16, 4.5.12–4.6.1). Xenophon does make plain Socrates's continuing study of the cosmos, but Xenophon does so only by showing Socrates repeatedly teaching versions of a quasi-religious cosmic teleotheology that may be said to anticipate, and surely helped to inspire, later Stoic religiosity. Xenophon portrays no encounters of Socrates with other theorists of nature and of mathematics.

By the same token, whereas Plato portrays Socrates frequently interacting with famous political and military and scientific and sophistic and poetic interlocutors, Xenophon provides a fuller, and more or less subtly comical, picture of the much less brilliant and much less memorialized figures who made up the bulk of the circle of rather modest followers among whom Socrates mostly lived, day to day. The lengthier Socratic dialogues in Xenophon (the *Economist* and the *Apology of Socrates to the Jurors*) are with characters—Critobulus, Ischomachus, Hermogenes—who would be more or less unknown to us today were it not for Xenophon's writings depicting Socrates. Many of Socrates's instructive shorter conversations in the *Memorabilia* are with quite minor and in some cases otherwise unknown or even nameless figures, including a beautiful and wealthy courtesan, artists and artisans, farmers, candidates seeking and sometimes acquiring office, and even more mundane acquaintances such as an entrepreneur and a day laborer. A number of these "nobodies" are in various financial or familial straits; in helping them with prudential guidance both spiritual and material, but also in his civic counsels, Xenophon's Socrates appears as sometimes almost ignobly utilitarian and "economic"—especially when compared to the more sublime Platonic portrait of Socrates. In a similar vein, Xenophon brings more clearly to light than does Plato the truth about the rather unelevated economic "infrastructure" making possible Socrates's life of leisure. At the same time, Xenophon makes more vivid than does Plato the rather amazingly wide and affectionate generosity that distinguished Socrates's dealings with his fellow man.

Plato, in sharp contrast to Xenophon, presents numerous encounters between Socrates and theorists of mathematics and of the nature of the cosmos (e.g., Parmenides, Zeno, Theodorus, Theaetetus, the young Socrates, the Eleatic Stranger, Timaeus) and provides vivid examples of Socrates's pursuit of the "What is . . . ?" questions. Plato may even be said to foreground the Socratic study of the whole. *But*, Plato does so in the guise of the quasi-mystical, erotic, metaphysical theory of ideas as transcendent, separate substances, linked to a teaching of the immortality of the human soul—all of which may be said to anticipate, and certainly helped to inspire, later neo-Platonic mysticism and crucial elements of Christian theology.

What is arguably Plato's most brilliant and, down through the ages, most influential dialogue, the *Symposium*, paints a nigh superhumanly continent and militarily courageous Socrates exhanging speeches with illustrious poets and notable friends of poetry and, in that context, elaborating a doctrine of *eros* as a semidivine, all-pervasive, radically transcendent, libidinal dynamo that animates nature and the human soul and conducts the philosophic mind to the vision of and even procreation upon the transcendent ideas of the beautiful and the good; a kindred account is elaborated in the brilliant twin dialogue on *eros*, the *Phaedrus*. (The *Lysis*, to be sure, offers a far more down to earth, if much briefer, teaching on *eros* as love of the kindred rather than of the noble or beautiful and good.)

Xenophon presents Socrates's preoccupation with *eros* in much less exalted and much more humane terms. Xenophon's *Symposium* depicts Socrates being reluctantly drawn with some of his younger friends into the erotic partying of several rather loose, uppercrust members of Athenian society. Socrates is shown transforming the host's planned, conventional, pederastic entertainment in a way that allows Socrates to express something of his unconventional conception of virtue, and thence something of the peculiar character of his loves for, and his being loved by, a diverse array of followers—in illuminating counterpoint to the portraits of several non-Socratic lovers and beloveds of various important sorts. While several of the others are indeed depicted or reported as undergoing profound religious experiences induced by the grip of eros, the evening culminates in a Socratic speech on *eros* that presents the erotic phenomena as mostly human, all too human.

Plato's presentation of a Socrates who has extraordinarily elevated, quasi-religious, erotically metaphysical visions and divinations is counterbalanced by Plato's repeatedly presenting the same Socrates as declaring that his knowledge is of his own ignorance, in general or as regards one or another matter under discussion—and as repeatedly asserting that the sole matter concerning which he is expert is *eros*. Xenophon never feels the need to present Socrates making such counterbalancing, blanket declarations of knowing only that and how he does not know, or that and how he is an expert solely about *eros*. While Xenophon does on a notable occasion (*Economist* chaps. 2–3) present the mature Socrates professing (with tongue planted firmly in cheek) ignorance about important moral matters, the image of the mature Socrates in Xenophon is usually and on the whole that of a resourcefully prudent and down-to-earth sage (anticipating a major aspect of Stoicism). In Xenophon, while personal immortality hovers often and perhaps always in the more or less distant background, immortality of the soul becomes an explicit theme only in the deathbed speech of Cyrus the Great, and in the conclusion of the closing oration by Ischomachus in the *Economist*, and in a brief, explicitly "mythological" portion of Socrates's oration in the *Symposium*.

Both Xenophon and Plato spotlight Socrates's unique *daimonion*. In Xenophon, this occurs mainly in the most apologetic parts of the Socratic writings (the *Apology*, and the beginning and ending of the *Memorabilia*). The *daimonion* is said to give practical advice, both hortative and dehortative, for Socrates's companions as well as for Socrates himself. Socrates is depicted on at least one fraught occasion defying the *daimonion*'s advice until by his own thinking he has made evident to himself the reasonableness of that advice. Xenophon portrays two of Socrates's interlocutors (Aristodemus and Euthydemus) doubting the truthfulness of Socrates's claims to receive guidance from the *daimonion*.

As for Plato, he shows clearly that the claim that he has Socrates make in his public oration in the *Apology* (31c-d), that the *daimonion* "always turns me away from what I am about to do, and never turns me toward," is very misleading. Every "turning away" is also a "turning toward," in some sense: for instance, the *daimonion*'s telling the Platonic Socrates not to depart a room that he was starting to leave turns out to be a way of getting him to encounter and then to engage a beautiful and intelligent youth (*Euthydemus* 272e–273a). More extensively, in what is *the* Platonic dialogue on the *daimonion*—the *Theages*—Plato shows that the *daimonion* is identifiable with Socrates's unique participation in *eros*, especially insofar as that *eros*, by virtue of its quasi-instinctive power of being attracted to the beautiful and good, is also a quasi-instinctive power of being repelled by the less beautiful and good. (This suggests possible reasons why the *daimonion* has no place in Xenophon's *Economist* and need not be mentioned in Xenophon's *Symposium*.)

While Plato in his *Philebus* and elsewhere gives strong hints as to the importance of intellectual pleasures for Socrates's evaluation of the superior goodness of the philosophic life and soul, Plato is considerably less forthcoming in this regard than is Xenophon. The latter's *Apology* highlights how crucial for Socrates's evaluation of the superior goodness of his whole way of life is his continuous enjoyment of intellectual pleasures: specifically, of admiration from competent friends and observers; of self-esteem; and, above all, of awareness of his own constant progress in ever-increasing wisdom. When put together with the teaching on pleasure and the good offered in his *Symposium* and *Hiero* and *Education of Cyrus*, Xenophon affords us a paradoxical insight into the difference between the soul of the political ruler at his best and the soul of the Socratic philosopher: for the political man, loving and being loved is ultimately more important than honoring and being honored or admired, while the opposite is true for the Socratic-philosophic soul.

Plato, who never in his dialogues writes in the first person or makes any direct reference to his role as author, declares in his *Second Letter* (314c): "there are no writings of Plato nor will there be, but those now said to be of him are of Socrates having become beautiful/noble (*kalou*) and new/young (*neou*)." Xenophon, who frequently writes in the first person and foregrounds himself as author, never feels called upon to thus confess that his portrayal of Socrates beautifies and rejuvenates the Master.

# NOTES

## INTRODUCTION

1. Cicero, *Tusculan Disputations* 5.10 and *Brutus* 30–31.

2. All references to texts of Xenophon will be to standard sections, or chapters and subsections, as first divided in the edition of Wells 1690–96.

3. For the translation "the *Economist*," I follow Ruskin 1876.

4. Holden 87–88; Lincke 1890, 12. See similarly Grote 1867, 3.569; Schenkl 1875, 144ff. and 1876, 41ff.; Joël 1893–1901, 1.50; Bruns 1896, 383; Ullrich 2016 [1908], 47; Novo 1968, 3–5. As Pomeroy 216 notes, these scholars stress that each of the three shorter Socratic writings begins with an adversative-connective particle—"and" or "but" (*de, alla*)—on which see also Bäumlein 1861, 13, and Denniston 1954, 21.

5. Taylor 1913, 31: in the *Memorabilia*, Xenophon "carefully suppresses, as far as he can, all mention of the personal peculiarities which distinguish Socrates from the average decent Athenian."

6. A nineteenth- and twentieth-century scholarly tradition simplistically viewed the conventional gentleman Ischomachus as a spokesman or even a stand-in for Xenophon himself, eclipsing Socrates: e.g., Marchant 1923, xxiv; Caster 1937, 49; Luccioni 1953, 114; Riedinger 1995, 11; Bourriot 1995, 294, 299, 305, 316–17, 324; Brickhouse and Smith 2000, 39. As Dorion 2013, 317, critically remarks, Wolff (1985, 106) and Cooper (1998, 8, 10, 19) "ne mentionnent pas *l'Économique* au nombre des *logoi sokratikoi* de Xénophon." Some more recent scholars, understandably reacting against this, now try, with equal but contrary two-dimensionality, to interpret Xenophon as presenting in the figure of Ischomachus "Socrates' 'evil twin'" (Kronenberg 2009, 55, building on Danzig 2003b); contrast Novo 1968, esp. 117–18. I mean to show that the correct interpretation of this Xenophontic character is much more complex and nuanced.

7. Here and the next six chapters, numbered citations without other identification will indicate chapter and section numbers of the *Economist*.

8. "Xenophon is not usually credited with an appreciation of the Socratic irony"—"but surely it is present here in a double measure" (Guthrie 1971a, 17; see also 124 n. 1).

9. In striking contrast to Aristotle in his ethical and political writings, Xenophon in his Socratic writings (contrast *Hellenica* 2.3.19, as well as 3.1.9; see also *Education of*

*Cyrus* 2.2.16, 24) never employs the term "serious" (*spoudaios*) to designate the "gentleman" (but see *Apology* 30 and OT chap. 6, n. 8 and context). The closest Xenophon ever comes in the Socratic writings to designating the "gentleman" as "serious" is when he has Socrates jovially remark that the "seriousness" of the eyebrows of Hermogenes is a mark of the latter's love of "whatever might be gentlemanliness"—*Symposium* 8.3. See also *Memorabilia* 4.2.2 where the term *spoudaios anēr* ("serious man") is used to designate a competent political leader or general, parallel to those who are "serious" in other arts. Compare Bonitz 1870 s.v. *spoudaios* with López and Garciá 1995 s.v.

10. Plato's work may well have been published previously (Higgins 1977, 128 n. 2; Huss 13–18 and 1999, 381; Vander Waerdt 1993, 9–11); but contrast Bowen 1998, 8 as well as Thesleff's complex hypothesis: 1978, 157–68.

## CHAPTER ONE

Portions of this chapter were published in a slightly different form as "The Socratic Founding of Economic Science," *Interpretation: A Journal of Political Philosophy* 45 (2019): 383–402.

1. *autos*; the pronoun thus used "commonly refers to 'the master' ": Pomeroy ad loc., referring to Smyth 1920, 303, para. 1209d. But this usage in this context has decidedly comical overtones: for this is the way Socrates is introduced (by a nameless student) in Aristophanes's *Clouds* (219; see also 1403).

2. *Oikonomikos* is a word that first appears in Plato and in the Socratic writings of Xenophon. Given Aristophanes's ridicule of the distinctive Socratic-philosophic favoring of words with the -kos suffix, the title has some comedic overtones. See Holden ad 12.19 and Peppler 1910, as well as Schwyzer 1939–53, 497ff.; Amman 1953; and Chantraine 1956, 97–171 (whose divergence from Amman has been well rebutted by Szemerényi 1958).

3. XSD 90; see also Galen 1821–33, vol. 18, pt. 1, 301 ("this book of the *Memorabilia of Socrates* is the last"); Levvenklaius 1562 (title); Grote 1867, 3.569; Dindorf 1862, xiv; Schenkl 1875, 147; Holden 87–88; Lincke 1890, 11 ("verba non possunt non coniungi cum iis, quae ad defendenda accusatorum crimina a Xenophonte scripta sunt"); Thompson and Hayes 1895, ad 1.1, and p. 10 (but contrast p. 13b); Persson 1915, 86; Luccioni 1953, 112; Novo 1968, 3–4; Meyer 1975, 92–93; Nickel 1979, 73; Pomeroy 213, 216; and Henderson's revised Marchant (2013), 665. Contrast Caster 1937, 49 and 56: "les liens de *l'Économique* avec les *Mémorables* sont superficiels"—cited in the more balanced judgment of Novo 1968, 117n and context.

4. See XSD, esp. 191–92; Stevens 1994, 227 and Kronenberg 2009, 41, 57. The comedy is also signaled by the frequency, not least in the opening pages, of profane expletives or oaths ("by Zeus!"—see esp. 2.2). In Greek literature prior to the Socratic writings of Xenophon and Plato, profane expletives are characteristic of comedies (Dover 1997, 62); the rare oaths invoking divinities in tragedy are solemn, as for example in Sophocles's *Oedipus the Tyrant* 326, 536, 643–52, 1153, 1432. In Xenophon's non-Socratic writings, profane expletives are frequent only in the dialogue *Hiero*, especially its opening chapter—see López and García 1994 s.v.

5. Gigon 1953, 105: "den Typ des eleganten jungen Herrn, der nichts als Liebe im Kopf hat."

6. Pomeroy 217: "one of the wealthiest men at Athens."

7. Miller 2005 ad 4.12: the *nun* ("now") is "implying that Cleinias is merely the most recent in a series of erotic interests."

8. XSD 107. In the *Memorabilia*, the only occasions when Xenophon explicitly speaks as an eyewitness are 1.4.2 and 4.3.2 (Socrates teaching theology), 1.6.14 (the Socratic reading groups), and 2.4.1–2.5.1 (Socrates teaching about friendship).

9. See XSD as a whole, and esp. 90, 101, 107; Ambler 1996, 104–5; and the insightful remark of Dorion (Bandini and Dorion 2010–11, clxxxv): "one of the principal ways in which the *Memorabilia* is original, in comparison with the dialogues of Plato, is that the principal beneficiaries are often the listeners, and not the interlocutors of Socrates" (see also ibid., cxlvii-cxlviii).

10. Note the concentration of emphatic first-person formulations in these lines (21.10–12)—"I affirm," "I for my part would not admire," "By Zeus! I would not say," "in my opinion," etc.

11. See chaps 4–5 in toto as well as 13.5, together with XSD 87, 113–14, 144, 161, 171, 175, 205, and 207 and OT chap. 2 n.10 and context ("There is ample evidence to show that the *Oeconomicus*, while apparently devoted to the economic art only, actually deals with the royal art as such. 1.23; 4.2–19; 5.13–16; 6.5–10; 8.4–8; 9.13–15; 13.4–5; 14.3–10; 20.6–9; 21.2–12."); see also *Memorabilia* 3.4.12 and 4.2.11; Caster 1937, 51; Pomeroy 1984; Kronenberg 2009, 55; Lu 2015, 212–13, 219–20; Helmer 2011, secs. 7–9, and 2015; Nelsetuen 2017. For the Platonic Socrates's embrace of this view, see *Charmides* 171e, 172d; *Symposium* 209a-b; *Lovers* 138c; *Protagoras* 318c; *Meno* 91a; *Republic* 600c; *Laws* 690a—and similarly the Eleatic Stranger in *Statesman* 258e-259d. For discussion of Aristotle's elaboration throughout book 1 of his *Politics* of a playfully ambiguous critique of this Socratic-Platonic-Xenophontic view, see T. Pangle 2013, chap. 1.

12. *Memorabilia* 4.3.13 (XSD 113), and see similarly Aristotle, *Metaphysics* 1078a13–25; Novo 1968, 93.

13. On the controversial unconventionality of applying the term "science" (*epistēmē*) in this context, see Aristotle, *Politics* 1252a15 and 1253b18; see also Peppler 1910. The fact that Critobulus unhesitatingly answers in the affirmative—though with a hint of awareness that what he is affirming in unusual ("to *me* at least it seems so")—indicates that he has already fallen under the influence of Socrates in this way of thinking. Lincke (1890, 12) suggests that the interrogative particle expression, *ara ge*, may indicate that we are hearing Socrates bring his interlocutor to a conclusion (as at 7.38), but the "tell me" seems to indicate the start of a new topic of conversation.

14. *dokei goun, ephē ho Kritoboulos. . .*; throughout his dialogic writings, Xenophon makes artful use of the insertion "he said" to direct the reader's attention to preceding or sometimes suceeding parts of a sentence (see OT chap. 3b, n. 41).

15. This is the first appearance in the dialogue of the word that stands as the title. As previously noted, this word is distinctively Socratic, and of a sort that is ridiculed by Aristophanes as "Socratic-speak": see Peppler 1910. The word as found in Xenophon would appear to be the original source of our modern term "economics" (Lowry 1987, 247; Ekelund and Hébert 2013, 9).

16. See similarly Aristotle, *N. Ethics* 1180b3–28, and cf. Plato, *Apology of Socrates* 20a-b, 24d–25c.

17. Critobulus's profane expletives here express the impassioned, and somewhat thoughtless, assurance of his self-corrections; but it is also possible that by the flurry here of profanations of Zeus our author means to alert us to a subversive theological dimension that will soon emerge in this part of the dialogue (cf. XSD 123, 170, 194–95).

18. 1.6–7: *ktēmata* connotes possessions or acquisitions in general, while *chrēmata* connotes all properties "whose value can be measured in monetary terms" (Aristotle so defines the latter term in *N. Ethics* 1119b26; see also his definition and discussion of the "art of getting *chrēmata*" in book 1 of the *Politics*). See LSJ s.v.

19. The verb translated "to use" (*chrēsthai*) has the same root as the noun I have translated "riches" (*chrēmata*); for discussion of the connotations, see Redard 1953.

20. Pomeroy 257: "references to the weather are scattered throughout the *Oeconomicus*"; the Attic "climate and amount of rainfall fluctuate widely. Rain can vary from double the normal maximum to one-third of it; four to six dry years may be followed by one to ten rainy ones. Regional variation is enormous. . . . Of course Zeus, as weather-god, was often the recipient of offerings and prayers." Pomeroy refers us also to Aschenbrenner 1986 and Gallant 1991.

21. A conventional translation for *aulos*, a double-reeded wind instrument bearing some similarity to our modern oboe.

22. With Chantraine and Pomeroy ad loc. I follow the attribution discerned by Thalheim 1907, 630ff.; see also Van Groningen 1941.

23. For Xenophon's characteristic indication of the distinct meanings of the two different verbs for market transaction see Cobet 1858, 647 (commenting on *Memorabilia* 2.5.5, where the two verbs also occur): "*pōlein* dicitur qui emtorem quaerit, *apodidosthai* qui reperit"—followed by LSJ s.v. *pōleō*, referring also to *Symposium* 8.21, where again we see the distinction between "offering for sale" (*pōlein*) and "finding a buyer" (*apodidosthai*).

24. Lowry 1997, 828: "Xenophon's discussion of use value and exchange value is worth Xeroxing and circulating to introductory economics students." Amemiya 2007, 118: "a strikingly original theory of values . . . much more profound than what one can learn from a college course on the principles of economics." See also Bragues 2007, 10.

25. Ambler 1996, 106n: "Socrates' concern for what is beneficial to our souls is indicated in 1.13 and 23."

26. For the meaning of this term, in contrast to *pornē* (whore), see the lively portrait of the very wealthy *hetaira* acquaintance of Socrates, Theodotē, in *Memorabilia* 3.11. Cf. Pomeroy 1975, 89–92, and Pomeroy 220: "According to Ps.-Dem. 59.29, the purchase price of a young but experienced slave *hetaira* was 3,000 drachmas." For comparison, from Xenophon's *Ways and Means* 4.23 one can calculate that the average price of a healthy male slave to work the silver mines was 180 drachmas. Evidence from inscriptions suggests that the average price for an average woman slave auctioned in Athens was about the same, 180 drachmas: Pritchett and Pippin 1956, 277.

27. *huoskuamon* = "henbane," or *Hyoscyamus niger*; for the chemical formula and toxicology see Meyer 1975 ad loc., referring us to Lewin 1924, 174ff.

28. I believe that this is one of those rare instances where the word *hōste* does not have the meaning "with the result that," but rather "on the condition that"—as in *Anabasis* 5.6.26: see LSJ s.v., B, I, 4.

29. Ruskin (1876, xxxix) calls this "a faultless definition of Wealth, and explanation of its dependence for efficiency on the merits and faculties of its possessor;—definition which cannot be bettered; and which must be the foundation of all true Political Economy among nations, as Euclid is to all time the basis of Geometry." Lowry 1987, 247 remarks that Xenophon has given us, "in his emphasis upon the human variable, the major clue that helps explain the direction of Greek thought on economic matters." The Greeks' "political economy was the study of the efficient management of personal and political affairs, with emphasis upon the human factor. Modern political economy, on the other hand, concentrates primarily upon the material factors of economic life and only secondarily upon human responses to them. This is why the assumption of scarcity has become so important, even essential, in modern definitions of economics. It could not be otherwise in a discipline focusing on a material-oriented, goods-rationing market process which allocates the wherewithal of economic life to competitive contenders for the gratification of insatiable wants." Ambler 1996, 106: "the first principle of Socratic economics" is "a principle with the potential to reveal the poverty of usual notions of wealth and the folly of ordinary economic activity." See also Dorion 2013, 330. Meikle (1995, 191, 193) observes with regret that "the distinction between use value and exchange value comes to be progressively elided in the nineteenth and twentieth centuries"—citing J. S. Mill, W. S. Jevons, Alfred Marshall, and W. Leontief; "if an independent concept of use value is removed from economics," then "the consequence is that the question of ends cannot be formulated within economics"; yet this "is perhaps the most important question that can be asked in respect of economic matters," and "whatever answer may be favored," it "does not reflect well on a theory if that theory is incapable even of formulating the question."

30. This is a term and a relationship that applies not least to family: see, e.g., *Hiero* 3.7–8; and Millett 1991, 113, 116–18, 127–28.

31. 1.14; see similarly *Memorabilia* 3.11.5; Hartman (1887, 189) is so shocked—"Haeccine in libro Xenophonteo legi et tolerari! Quid enim absurdius est"—that he "suspects" this to be a later marginal note added by some "lectore, cui eiusmodi observatio acuta lepide videretur."

32. Novo 1968, 14n refers us to *Memorabilia* 3.3.6–7.

33. These lines, Plutarch tells us, inspired his essay "How One Might by Enemies Be Benefited" (see 86c-e), an essay which Rousseau refers to as an inspiration for the Fourth Walk of his *Reveries of a Solitary Walker* (his last work) and from which Rousseau derives the frontispiece for his *Discourse on the Arts and Sciences* (his first work).

34. 1.15: *apo tyranniōn*; this is the reading of the manuscripts (for the "hateful" connotation of this rare word *tyranniōn*, see Xenophanes frag. 3, Diels and Kranz 1951). Leading twentieth century editors such as Marchant and Chantraine claim in their apparatuses that the major manuscript Laurentian 55.21 reads "*of those* tyrannizing" = *tyranniōn*, genitive, i.e., *without* the *apo*; but my inspection of a clear photo of that ms. shows this not to be the case. (These editors are correct, however, in reporting that the ms. Paris 1647, whose photo I have also inspected, reads "from tyrants" = *apo tyrannōn*, with an insertion above the line, by a second hand, of a correcting iota to make it read like all the other mss., *apo tyranniōn*.) So provocative is this Socratic observation—that many private persons have enlarged their households "from tyrannizings," as well as from war (Ludwig 2010, 92)—that

editors have insisted that the text we have received must be emended; the most popular such purification has been that of Weiske 1798–1804 ad loc.: he removes the *apo* and, since that leaves a mss. reading that he recognizes as "ineptum," changes "tyrannizings" to "tyrants"—all on the grounds that "opponuntur inter se *idiōtai* et *tyrannoi*"; thus he reconstructs the passage so that it reads as if Socrates says only that many private persons *as well as* tyrants have profited from war.—Xenophontic provocation to thought erased!

35. OT chap. 3a; see also chap. 2, n. 19 and context; XSD 209.

36. 1.23; XSD 96: "Fully stated, the thought suggested by Socrates and imputed by him to Kritoboulos is to the effect that all good things belong to the wise men, and only to them (Cicero, *Republic* I.27; *De Finibus* III.75)." As Ludwig observes (2010, 93–94), this is the first time that the term and concept "gentleman" has appeared in the dialogue.

37. XSD 96; also 127, 202–3 and Ambler 1996, 109–10.

38. For an illuminating comparison of Socrates's refutational education of Critobulus as regards the meaning of property and the Platonic Socrates's refutation of Polemarchus as regards the meaning of justice, in the *Republic*, see Ambler 1996, 105–7.

39. Pomeroy ad loc.: "at Athens Eupatrids were at the top of the social scale, in contrast to the slaves whom Socrates mentioned in the previous sentence."

40. Pomeroy ad loc.: "in his discussion of vices here he may be alluding to Critobulus' predilections."

41. For this meaning of the verbal expression—*pherein kai telein*—see Holden ad loc.

42. See also *Memorabilia* 1.2.19–24 and L. Pangle 2013 and 2014.

43. XSD 99: Socrates's "silence, in the first chapter, on piety as an indispensable ingredient of the management of the household may provisionally be explained as a consequence of the abstraction there practiced by him from justice or legality, for piety depends on law."

44. Ambler 1996, 107n: "Critoboulus' blithe claim to continence is not even complete: he claims to be continent regarding the 'mistresses,' not regarding the 'masters.'"

45. 2.2; Breitenbach 1841 ad loc.: ". . . provocasse videtur Socratem, ut illud *hēmōn* iocose de se etiam acciperet et festivam illam argumentationem subiiceret."

46. Boeckh 1857, 156–57 comments: "according to the price of barley in the time of Socrates, . . . with this he could not have procured even the amount of barley which was requisite for himself and his wife, to say nothing of the other necessaries of life, and of the support of his children."

47. See Pomeroy 229 and Xenophon's *Regime of the Athenians*; Ambler 1996, 107: Socrates "speaks of the Athenians as one might speak of a despotic master."

48. Ambler 1996, 107; Bragues 2007, 12.

49. See Plato's *Republic* 486a, 487a, 490c, 494b, 495d, 503c, 536a; also *Laws* 709e and 710c.

50. *anagruzein*—the word is Aristophanean (*Wealth* 17 and the scholiast; *Thesmophoriazusae* 1095; *Lysistrata* 509; *Wasps* 374); Holden ad loc.; LSJ s.v. In the *Clouds* (945), the word appears when the Unjust Discourse says it will allow the Just Discourse to "grunt" when it has been defeated: Does Xenophon have his Socrates here associate Critobulus with the Unjust Discourse, Socrates himself with the Just?

51. At the same time, by drawing an analogy between a household and a musical instrument, Socrates may be hinting that in his view a knower of the art would not need to "increase" his household in order to maintain and use it beautifully and well.

52. The first mention of justice in this work.

53. Cf. Castiglione 1920, 323: "è pertanto evidente, che il contenuto dei #2.15–18 interrompe la continuazione e diminuisce la speditezza del dialogo."

54. *apethaumasa*—2.17: "vehementur demiratus sum—one of the poetical words used by Xenophon" (Holden ad loc.)

55. Socrates makes no reference to the power in human affairs of chance or luck (*tuchē*)—which is never mentioned in the *Economist* (though see the verbs in 1.4, 2.12, 3.3, 4.19, and 8.3 [*tuchein*], 2.3 and 12.20 [*epituchein*]); contrast esp. *Memorabilia* 1.4 as a whole, as well as 3.9.14 and 3.11.5; also *Skilled Hunting with Dogs* 13.9, as well as 5.29; *Ways and Means* 4.30 and 4.32; *Regime of the Athenians* 2.2. See also OT chap. 7, n. 10 and context. In his *Anabasis* 5.2.24–25 and *Skilled Cavalry Commander* 5.14, Xenophon himself explicitly merges chance or luck with divine providence (see also *Economist* 7.7; and let us not forget that the primary meaning of *tuchē* is "providential act"—see the complex entry in LSJ s.v.).

56. Lord (in Bartlett 1996) in his usually quite accurate translation seems to suggest in a footnote to his rendering at this point that "skilled" (translating the "-kos" ending) is not necessary here, or at 3.3 end: I believe that this is an error that needs to be brought to the reader's attention. For the distinctly Socratic (and Aristophanean-satirical) overtones of the "-kos" ending, see again Peppler 1910.

57. See XS 18; L. Strauss 2016, 60–61. Boeckh 1857, 158: "assuming Xenophon's account is perfectly correct, we must suppose that the mother of [Socrates's] young boys supported herself, and both the children, either by labor or from her dowry, and that Lamprocles supported himself, and that the famed economy of Socrates probably consisted, among other things, in this also, that he kept them at work. . . . And it may boldly be affirmed, without wishing to disparage his exalted genius, that, in respect to his indigence, . . . the representation of Aristophanes was not much exaggerated, but in the essential particulars was delineated from the life." (Aristophanes's *Clouds* depicts Socrates without household servants or slaves—but also, Boeckh fails to note, without a wife or children, and as having to steal to get funds for his and his students' supper.)

58. Pomeroy ad loc.: "In the early fourth century, Rural Dionysia," though "they occurred during the month of Poseidon," were "not held everywhere simultaneously. Critobulus could have attended quite a few festivals in widespread areas of Attica in one month."

59. Cf. 11.15–18. Pomeroy ad 1.8: "Horse-ownership was a mark of great wealth. See e.g. *Hiero* 11.5, *Agesilaus* 9.6, *The Skilled Cavalry Commander* 1.11–12 [to which add 2.1]. . . . In the fourth century the average price of a cavalryman's horse, as listed on tablets found in the agora, was 408 drachmae. But expensive horses might cost 1200 dr. or more: see *Anabasis* 7.8.6, Aristophanes, *Clouds* 21–23, 1224–25. . . . In addition, the cavalryman had to maintain his horse and gear as well as the animal on which his groom rode."

60. Pomeroy ad loc.: "On financial ruin from keeping horses see Strepsiades and his extravagant son Pheidippides ('Horse-sparer') in Aristophanes' *Clouds*." See also Stevens 1994, 226–27. For the full significance of Xenophon's strong allusion here to Aristophanes's *Clouds*, see XSD 112, 127, 163–64, 166. See further L. Strauss 1966, passim.

61. Dorion 2013, 330–31: "La lecture de *l'Économique* laisse en effet l'impression qu'Ischomaque est un personnage à part entière et qu'il participe à l'entretien au même

titre que Socrate et Critobule. Mais c'est là un *effet* du discours de Socrate, car comme il s'agit d'un entretien *rapporté* par Socrate, c'est en fait Socrate qui joue tour à tour son propre rôle, celui d'Ischomaque, et celui de la femme de ce dernier, si bien que Critobule n'entend en realité que le discours de Socrate."

62. By the city: recall 2.6 and see *On Skilled Horsemanship* 2.1.

63. 3.9; I follow all the mss. and editors such as Holden, and do not accept the emendation suggested by Graux 1878 (defended by Schenkl 1876 and 1886) and accepted by most subsequent editors—who replace the word for "beings/properties" (*ontōn*—Sauppe 1865–67 simply excised this word) with the word for "horses" (*hippōn*), thus smoothing out and erasing the provocative Socratic echo of philosophic concerns.

64. Cf. *On Skilled Horsemanship* 2.1–2: "rather than taming young horses, it is far better for a youth to take care concerning his own good character, and to practice horsemanship, if he already knows how to ride; and for an elder to take care concerning his household, friends, affairs of politics and affairs of war—rather than pass time in the company of colt handlers." See also Ludwig 2010, 78.

65. We have here a clue to one solution of the mystery posed by the fact that in Socrates's subsequent report of his education in farming by the gentleman Ischomachus, there is no mention whatsoever of the animal husbandry dimension of farming, despite the stress laid upon the latter in the conversation with Critobulus. Compare chaps. 15–21 with 1.9, 3.11, 5.3, 5.5–6, 5.18 7.20. 10.7; Pomeroy 326–27: "given the attention paid to weaving Ischomachus must own a considerable number of sheep (see vii.6, 22, 36 and ch. 5)." See XSD 117, 123, 172, 196.

66. 3.13 (*paida nean malista*); since in Athens at the time, upperclass girls married at about fourteen years of age, Pomeroy 269 suggests translating as "a mere child." It appears that the modal age for menarche in classical Greece was thirteen or fourteen years, with twelve years a lower limit: Aristotle, *History of Animals* 581a; Amundsen and Diers 1969.

67. "Here the ignorance of Critobulus' wife is seen as a defect in the customary system of women's education"—Pomeroy ad loc.

68. 3.12–14; "may be an example of Xenophon's humour, a teasing and surprising idea"—Pomeroy ad loc. In *Memorabilia* 2.6.36 Socrates tells Critobulus of an important lesson in "matchmaking" that the philosopher heard from the expert Aspasia. Plutarch's *Pericles* 24.3 reports that "there were times when Socrates and his acquaintances visited her, and his associates brought their wives to hear her speak, even though she presided over a business that was neither orderly nor august, but she kept young courtesans."

69. 3.12–14; Ludwig 2010, 94: "Socrates claims Aspasia is more knowledgeable than he"—"even though he had already learned from Ischomachus at this point." Pomeroy ad loc. insightfully observes: "As in 1.3, the conclusion is that even a person like Aspasia can understand *oikonomia* without actually owning an *oikos*"—see similarly the ascription of skill in statesmanship to Aspasia in Plato's *Menexenus*.

## CHAPTER TWO

1. 4.1; Ambler 1996, 110 (see also 113) makes the insightful comment that "it is to Critoboulos that we owe" the focus of the conversation on the noble, and "the remainder of the conversation, including especially the section recounting Socrates' encounter with

Ischomachus, explores the relationship between our need for gain and our attachment to nobility."

2. This is the connotation of the rare Homeric term *alexētēres*: see LSJ s.v. and Pomeroy ad loc.

3. See *Regime of the Lacedaemonians* 1.1 and 7.1–2, as well as the regime of old Persia portrayed in the *Education of Cyrus*; L. Strauss 2016, 57.

4. 4.4; Lincke 1879 expresses the "astonishment" many readers naturally feel at this sudden transition to the praise of the Persian monarch: "diese Worte müssen jeden, der auf den Zusammenhang achtet, in gerechtes Erstaunen verstezen" (58); "so besteht denn in allem was die Form der Darstellung betrifft ein tiefgehender, schroffer Widerspruch zwischen der Erklärung die Socrates in der Einleitung gegeben hat und der hierauf unternommenen Behandlung des Themas" (62). But as Pomeroy says (ad 8.3), "Because Critobulus is an aristocrat he is likely not only to be impressed by the success of the world's most powerful and wealthiest men, but to find it personally relevant to him." In *De Senectute* 59, Cicero presents his chief character, the elderly and completely unironic Cato, as being very favorably impressed by this story in the *Economist*. See also Rahe 2015, 166: "The Great Kings of Persia may have been martial," but "they thought of themselves" also "as defenders of peace and harmonious order, as exponents of prosperity, and as gardeners." In "every land, they and their satraps built elaborate parks and gardens landscaped with care and replete with cultivated trees." See *Anabasis* 1.2.7 and Fauth 1979 along with Tuplin 1996.

5. XSD 118: "many Greeks might have found it difficult that a barbarian should be held up as a model for Greeks."

6. Pomeroy 241n: "the Persian king treated his subjects, even those in positions of authority, as his slaves." This "idea appears" in "e.g., *Anabasis* 2.5.38, 3.2.13; *Hellenica* 6.1.12." XSD 122 points us also to the passage at *Anabasis* 1.9.29, where Xenophon in his own name characterizes Cyrus the Younger as a "slave" under his brother the king.

7. Pomeroy ad 4.6: "The 'eyes' and 'ears' of the Persian kings were well known to the Greeks (see e.g. *Cyrop.* 8.2.1–0–12)"; the "ears were the many spies who relayed to the king information about the Empire, especially the provinces, and who acted independently of the military commanders and civilian governors." Rahe 2015, 71: "the administrative apparatus that Cyrus, Cambyses, and Darius in particular put in place and the system of surveillance that came with it were formidable."

8. The term *paradeisos* is introduced into Greek by Xenophon, here and in other works; he always uses it to refer to the famous parks of the Persian king and nobility; the word is a transliteration of the Persian-Avestan word *pairidaēza*, constructed from "wall" (*daēza*) and "around" (*pairi*): see Pomeroy ad loc.; LSJ s.v.; Hultgard 2000; Rahe 2015, 166.

9. 4.18; obviously a bit of an exaggeration. In *Anabasis* 1.9.29 Xenophon reports that "many" deserted from the king to Cyrus and only a single one did the reverse; but the lexicon *Suda*, in the entry "Xenophon," reports that several thousand troops fled from Cyrus to the king (Münscher 1920, 221–22 and other scholars emend the text of *Suda* to bring it into consistency with what Xenophon and his Socrates say; Lindstam 1926 reasonably protests that *Suda* might well present data in conflict with Xenophon and his Socrates).

10. 4.19; Schäfer 1819, unalive to Socrates's irony (see also Too 1995, 248), deleted this as an insertion that interrupts and contradicts the previous praise of Cyrus. See Kronenberg 2009, 44–45.

11. XSD 118; see the fine brief biography of Lysander in Cartledge 2003, 197–206, and esp. 201–2, reporting on "the paroxysm of personal success and hero-worship that he enjoyed abroad, above all on the island of Samos, where his partisans took a step unprecedented in all Greek history. They paid him divine honors, worshipping a living mortal man as though he were an immortal god. . . . At Delphi, the very epicentre of Greek religion, Lysander went as near as he dared to having that quasi-immortal status enshrined permanently in a public monument."

12. Deity of binding oath and truthfulness. "If Cyrus and his sons really were followers of the prophet whom the Persians called Zarathustra" (as many scholars are inclined to think), then, like Darius later, they recognized Ahura Mazda as the supreme Creator god, under whom Mithra was a subordinate divine creature; but "there are scholars who suspect, with some reason, that Cyrus" gave "allegiance first and foremost to the god Mithra": Rahe 2015, 67–68, referring us esp. to Herrenschmidt 1980, Boyce 1988, Skarjaervø 1999, and Jong 2010.

13. For the somewhat dubious but not altogether unprecedented behavior of this Spartan hero after his defeat of Athens, see, in addition to Plutarch's *Lysander*, Rahe 1977 and Cartledge 2000.

14. L. Strauss 2016, 59: "here even a Spartan gentleman becomes converted to farming, at least in his thought. He cannot do it in practice."

15. Pomeroy ad loc.: "the earliest extensive eulogy of rural life in Greek prose"; the "rhetorical structure is Gorgianic, employed so lavishly as to create a 'purple patch.'" Many of the formulations Xenophon puts in the mouth of Socrates "became topoi in later adaptations of the theme."

16. Consider Ambler 1996, 110. Morris 1880 (177, 179) summarizes the understandable reaction of scholars (such as Lincke 1879, 69—"Alles dies zeigt uns nicht Socrates als Lehrer der Erwerbskunde, sondern ein Wirrkopf, der nicht weis was er seinem Zuhörer schuldig ist"): "Wholly inappropriate and useless is the reference to Cyrus the younger and the account of Lysander's visit to him. Critobulus can derive not the slightest benefit from this"—not to mention the "absurdity of making Socrates pose as an authority on Persian matters."

17. Ambler 1996, 111: "Critoboulos doubts on three occasions that the Persian king was much of a farmer, but he never doubts that he is a proper exemplar of nobility."

18. XSD 119, referring us to *Regime of the Lacedaemonians* 7.1–3 and Plato's *Republic* 547c6-d9. Ambler 1996, 111: Socrates "has made it plain that an aspiring Greek gentleman is attracted by such nobility as inheres in ruling as a great monarch, even a monarch who must seize power by force." See Larsen 1962.

19. For a survey of scholars' struggles, see Pelletier 1944; Pomeroy ad loc. insists that, while the "telescoping of some 150 years of Persian history" is "noteworthy," the "confusion between the two Cyruses is deliberate" because Xenophon *in general* blends the two—but she has been misled by Pelletier (87–88), along with Cousin (1905, xli–xliii) and Hirsch (1985, 76–79), into overlooking crucial distinctions that Xenophon in other contexts subtly draws between the two Cyruses as regards their moral and civic virtues: see Bruell 1987, 112–14, as well as Ruderman 1992; Too 1995, 248; Buzzetti 2014, 69.

20. Not the same as the "*real man* who is free": see XSD 122, "a free man may know of greater pleasures than those connected with farming—cf. *Hiero* 7.3–4." In the latter

passage, Simonides speaks of "those believed to be no longer human beings (*anthropoi*) merely, but real men (*andres*)."

21. Stobaeus, but not our mss., reads: "adorn *gods and* altars and sacred statues."

22. 5.2; in the sole possible mention of divinity (earth), at 4.13, Socrates spoke of Cyrus caring for "whatever things that are noble-and-good/gentlemanly that the earth wishes/is willing (*thelei*) to grow"; Critobulus replied by saying that Cyrus's care was for "trees and all the other noble/beautiful things that the earth grows."

23. 5.1, 2, 3, 8, 9, 10, 11; this aspect of the speech is redolent of Aristophanes and his rural heroes or antiheroes; Xenophon's Socrates here signals a certain kinship with that poet.

24. The rather emphatic mention of "the skilled herding art" (*hē probateutikē technē*) circumscribes the fact that Socrates has made no mention of "the skilled farming art" (*hē geōrgikē technē*), or "the art of farming" (*hē technē tēs geōrgias*). We will hear of the former only as the report of Ischomachus's instruction of Socrates culminates, with the words that "the skilled farming art is the most well-bred because it is the easiest to learn" (18.10, Ischomachus speaking; see also 19.1 and 21.1, where Socrates speaks); we will not hear of the latter until, at 15.3–4, Ischomachus introduces the education in "the art of farming." In speaking directly to Critobulus, Socrates has not even spoken of "*skilled* farming" (*geōrgikē*—5.18 [Critobulus], 21.2 [Ischomachus]), nor even—in contrast to Critobulus (4.12) and to Cyrus (4.24)—of "the *works* of *skilled* farming" (*tōn geōrgikōn ergōn*). Only at the end of the present speech, and in reference to placating the gods, will Socrates speak of "the skilled farming *actions*" (*tōn geōrgikōn praxeōn*—5.20); Socrates will speak once of the "skilled farming *tools*" (*tois geōrgikois organois*—5.13). Most striking is Socrates failure to speak of the farming art at 5.8. Could Socrates have concluded, from subsequent reflection on Ischomachus's case for farming, as being so very easy to learn, that it is therefore questionable if the activity (as pursued and taught by the gentleman) fully deserves to be called an art? See infra our study of the chapters on education in farming.

25. Holden ad loc. cites the parallel deification of Nature and Her tough love in Milton's *Comus* 764, but Holden overlooks the contrast: Xenophon never has Socrates refer to *nature* in this context of his deification of Earth.

26. The mss. have "Earth" in the dative case, making farming the subject, helping the Earth—though the word order is a bit problematic; like other editors, starting with Sauppe 1865–67 ad loc., I follow Stobaeus and Stephanus, but I do so with less confidence than the editors. Holden ad loc. comments: "Schaefer Ind. graec. to Gregorius Corinthius p. 1040 reads the dative," which "he translates: ut venationibus operam demus, (agricultura) una cum regionis natura nos aliquantum (*ti*) pellicit."

27. The verb, *sumparatrephō*, occurs nowhere else: for the parasitical connotation of the word (which LSJ s.v. fail to recognize) and of *paratrepho* from which it is derived, see Holden and Chantraine ad loc. Socrates is expressing the perspective of the yeoman small farmer: the wild animals cause trouble and "are not worth their keep" (Holden ad loc.). By contrast, in the famous parks of the Persian nobility, wild animals (rather than domestic) are prized and cultivated for hunting.

28. With Chantraine ad loc. I follow the reading in Stobaeus (*theos ousa*); some major manuscripts have "willingly" (*thelousa*), some other manuscripts *theousa*, which Cobet 1858, 579 and Schenkl 1876, 106–7 suggest is likely to have arisen from a slip in copying

the reading as we find it in Stobaeus. Holden ad loc. adopts the reading *thelousa*, but notes in favor of the Stobaeus reading: "observe the propriety in the use of *therapeuontas* [in the next phrase], which means both 'worshipping' and 'cultivating.'"

29. Thompson and Hayes 1895 ad loc. and ad 1.4: "*ara*—this particle is used in drawing an inference which may be startling but is true." See also Hogenmüller 2007, 235, ad *Apology* 27.

30. 5.14: *sumpaideuei*; the word occurs only here in Xenophon; pace LSJ s.v. and most translators, I see no reason to give the word a meaning different from what it has when used by other contemporary authors such as Isocrates.

31. Note Socrates's silence on civic participatory freedom, in his proof in the *Apology* (16) that he is the most free of human beings.

32. As for the difference between the piety of free Greek farmers and the piety of the Persian despot as model farmer and warrior, we note that in his first oration to his Persian followers, Xenophon's Cyrus reminds them that they can have "a great deal of confidence" since they know that he has himself, in person, already taken care of all their necessary relations with the gods; then we hear from Cyrus's father (a quasi-Socratic figure) that he taught his son knowledge of divine matters that made the young ruler entirely independent of prophets; and in response Cyrus assures his father that "I am disposed to the gods as though they were my friends" (*Education of Cyrus* 1.5.14, 1.6.2–4). In the range of dependence on divine guidance, Cyrus stands somewhere between Socrates and the independent Greek citizenries.

33. After 4.18, there are no more profane oaths in the dialogue between Critobulus and Socrates; in the long narration to Critobulus of his encounter with Ischomachus, Socrates utters no profane oaths in his narrative voice (though he quotes himself as having voiced nineteen profane expletives in conversing with Ischomachus, who is quoted as having voiced twenty).

34. Conventional scholars are bewildered; the consensus is summed up by Chantraine ad loc.: "It faut supposer, ou que les #6 et 7 sont interpolés (par qui?), ou qu'ils ont été transferés ici du ch. iv (par quel accident?), ou qu'ils se réfèrent à une partie de iv, aujourd'hui perdue. Autre hypothèse chez Castiglione 1920"—who speaks of "una strana strontura."

35. "Up to the present not a word has been said about its being a science easy to acquire."—Holden ad loc.; XSD 127.

36. XSD 128–29: "Socrates thus brings about a shift from 'household management' to 'perfect gentlemanship'; the question is no longer what the work of household management is but what the work of the perfect gentleman is. It is an important shift, although it was prepared by Kritoboulos' desire to hear of the lucrative science which is reputed to be most noble or beautiful." Recall 4.1 and ff. See also Ambler 1996, 113b. Ischomachus is in an important sense *the* outstanding civic-republican alternative to Cyrus. Socrates proceeds to relate that he met and conversed with Ischomachus in the colonnade of "Zeus the Deliverer"—"the deliverer of the Greeks in particular from the Persian danger" (XSD 131, who refers us to Simonides frag. 169 Edmonds = Simonides Epigram XV Loeb: "Then there was a time when the Greeks, by strength of Victory, by deed of Ares, / having driven out the Persians, for free Greece in common / set up the altar to Zeus the Deliverer"). See also Meyer 1975 ad loc., referring to Pausanias 1.3.1–2 and the scholiast there; also Pomeroy ad 7.1, Ambler 1996, 115b, and Kronenberg 2009, 54.

37. This is the first mention of *eros*, or the first use of a term with the same root as *eros*; for references to human sexual desire in the previous sections see 1.13, 1.22, 2.7, 3.14.

38. Consider again *Symposium* 8.3: "as for Hermogenes, who among us doesn't know that, whatever gentlemanliness [*kalok'agathia*] may be, he is melting away with erotic love of it?"—and see our discussion of the character of Hermogenes in our chapter on the *Apology*.

## CHAPTER THREE

1. 6.13: *epi tēn skepsin autou*; the pronoun, *autou*, seems deliberately ambiguous: Marchant 1923 and Pomeroy translate "him"; Dindorf 1824 as "illum hominem"; Holden (explicitly criticizing Dindorf) as "it," followed by Lord (in Bartlett 1996) and Chantraine (as "en examiner le sens").

2. Socrates presents himself as having been, previous to this, unacquainted with any beauties! We are reminded of Aristophanes's repeated claims that the associates of Socrates are notorious for all looking pale, emaciated, like starved prisoners, or even bats or corpses: *Clouds* 103, 186, 1112; *Birds* 186, 1296, 1555–64; *Wasps* 1414.

3. *idōn*—Socrates's first word in his account of his encounter with Ischomachus.

4. This stoa is also the setting of Plato's *Theages*, where Socrates converses with Demodocus and the latter's son Theages; the brief exchanges with Demodocus constitute one of the very few intimate Socratic dialogues with a statesman and/or a gentleman in the Platonic corpus. For what has been discovered about this stoa as an important site, see Thompson and Wycherley 1972. See also Pomeroy ad 7.1 and Kronenberg 2009, 54.

5. No extended dialogue between Socrates and a gentleman (or a statesman) is ever depicted by Plato; the closest may be the conversation in *Laches*, but precisely there (187e–188b) Nicias refers to previous, fraught conversations he has had with Socrates that are never portrayed by Plato. See Rabieh 2006, 41.

6. This is stressed even more strongly at 12.2 (see Pomeroy ad 7.2 and 12.2).

7. 7.2; see also 7.9: Does this not signal that the inquiry that follows has major theological implications for Socrates? As Zeune 1782 points out ad loc., Cicero in his translation made this profane expletive even stronger: "proh deum immortalium!"

8. It is to the credit of Ischomachus that he genially tolerates "questions which it might be supposed a long acquaintance only could justify," exhibiting "that republican freedom of speech which overleaps the fences of modern politeness and reserve" (the words of a nineteenth century English—i.e., monarchic—gentleman): Mitchell 1819, 175.

9. As depicted by Aristophanes in the *Clouds*, Socrates prior to his turn to political philosophy spent his time indoors with his pale, spindly students, in the *phrontisterion* or "think tank."

10. The fact that the crucial first long theme of the dialogue—the gentleman's education of his wife—is thus entered into not by the design of Socrates would seem to indicate how at this point in his life Socrates was not the expert dialectician or conversationalist that he later became, always fully controlling his interrogations. See *Memorabilia* 1.2.14: Socrates "in speeches dealt as he wished with all who conversed (*tois de dialegomenois autōi pasi*) with him."

11. Socrates's lack of success as a husband may therefore be taken as a Xenophon's comedic presentation of the philosopher's limitations as a *practitioner* of the political science or art—of which he had so complete a *theoretical* understanding: XSD 132–33, 195; XS 178 as well as 41–42, 147.

12. XSD 154; Ambler 1996, 117t; Kronenberg 2009, 56.

13. *Politics*, 1259a37-b6, 1259b30–60b23; *N. Ethics*, 1160b33–61a3.

14. 7.12; this is especially remarkable given that "the reconstruction of the life of Chrysilla"—the notorious wife of the historical Ischomachus (Davies 1971, 265–68; supplemented by Stevens 1994, 217–20)—"requires that she gave birth to her daughter soon after her marriage to Ischomachus" (Pomeroy 269). The silence about children as part of the gentleman's household is made conspicuous by the facts that children of farmers are mentioned at 5.10, and children are repeatedly mentioned in the long initial instructional speech by Ischomachus to his wife (7.11, 19, 21, 24, 30, 34).

15. Mitchell 1819, 175 commits an illuminating error when he characterizes Ischomachus as beginning "his labours by a sacrifice to the gods, and a prayer for assistance; arguing, like a wise and pious man, as he was, that no better means existed for *ascertaining what was fittest for the preceptor to teach* and the pupil to learn": as a matter of fact, Ischomachus gave no indication of having asked the gods for *advice* as to the *content* of his education of his wife. He in effect followed a teaching about what it is right to pray for that Xenophon attributes to the mature Socrates (was that teaching then inspired by listening to Ischomachus?): *Memorabilia* 1.1.8–9.

16. 7.10: Mitchell 1819, 176: "he speaks of his wife as we should speak of a young colt." Mahaffy 1902, 276n: "this is the prose side to the fine writing of the poets about Hymenaeus, and about the joys of the nuptial state." See also Pomeroy ad loc.

17. And perhaps inadvertently ironic, given the later infamous sexual escapade of Chrysilla, the historical wife of Ischomachus, during her rather young widowhood: Davies 1971, 265–68. Breitenbach 1841 ad loc. speaks of "de conditione paulo liberiore, qua Ischomachi uxor utitur."

18. 7.11; with this and what follows, contrast Kant's account of the rightful meaning of marriage: *Metaphysics of Morals, Doctrine of Right*, part 1, chap. 2, "On the Right of Domestic Society," title 1: "Marriage Right."

19. Holden ad loc.: "the expression is a poetical one, see Soph. Oed. R. 314, Oed. Col. 247, Philoct. 950, Eur. Med. 228." We soon learn that the young lady is literate—9.10. Pomeroy comments ad 8.4: "she may have seen artistic representations or heard descriptions of them" and "certainly will have had personal experience of synchronized choruses."

20. Thompson and Hayes 1895 ad loc.: "the wife of Ischomachus uses this word in its narrower sense of a woman guarding her honour." Mahaffy 1902, 277 translates "chaste," and refers to Euripides, *Heracles* 476–77.

21. Pomeroy 59 comments that Xenophon "is the first Greek author to give full recognition to the use-value of women's work, and to understand that domestic labour has economic value even if it lacks exchange-value. This idea was radical in the formal literature of classical Greece, and has yet to gain acceptance in modern times." Yet Xenophon has his Socrates put this idea in the mouth of a superior but not untypical upperclass Greek gentleman, which suggests that it was *not* radical among such gentlemen.

22. 7.16; consider the last two paragraphs of OT.

23. The gentleman's strong statement of the moral limits on acquisitiveness (7.15; see also 11.8 and 14.9–10) shows how incorrectly debasing of Ischomachus it is to say, as does Kronenberg commenting on this passage (2009, 56), that "according to Ischomachus, the goal of a moral quality like *sōphrosunē* [sensible moderation] is *to make as much material profit as possible.*" Contrast Breitenbach 1841 ad loc.: "Ischomachus hoc verbum accipit sensu ampliori et graviori, in philosophica Socratis doctrina perquam usitato."

24. *hēgemōn*; Ischomachus uses the feminine direct article here (7.17) and at 7.32 (as does his wife), and at 7.38, and also the feminine demonstrative at 7.33; his wife switches to the masculine direct article at 7.40. The word can take either the masculine or the feminine: LSJ s.v. The sex of the leader of the beehive (and whether the "leader" was "the mother" of the hive) was a matter of uncertainty or controversy among the Greeks: Aristotle, *History of Animals* 553a26-b1; Hudson-Williams 1935, 2–4.

25. Ischomachus characterizes his theology as "my opinion" no less than four times: 7.18, 22, 23, 32.

26. See similarly Hermogenes's theology: *Symposium* 4.46–49, 8.3. Contrast the outlook of the tyrant Hiero, as depicted by Xenophon: see OT chap. 7.

27. See esp. *Memorabilia* 1.4 and 4.3; characteristically, the gentleman, "in contradistinction to Socrates, is silent about *eros* in marriage and in particular about the gods' particular kindness to men in not limiting their sexual pleasures to special seasons of the year—*Mem.* I.4.7, I.4.12" (XSD 137). More generally (Ambler 1996, 117b): "it is only at the end of the chapter, after the discussion of divine and natural duties is complete, that pleasure is mentioned (7.41–42)"; his wife's "life will be pleasant," the gentleman "insists, but he is careful not to feature pleasure too prominently in" her life's "justification. It is not for such reasons that one does what is divinely ordained."

28. 7.22–23: since the edition of Stephanus (1561) editors dumbfounded by Ischomachus's silence on the god's having distinctly ordained anything for male human nature have inserted here, without any manuscript warrant, a phrase: "and the *nature* of the man for outdoor works and concerns" (Stephanus) or "and the *nature* of the man for matters outside" (other editors). The editors have thus inadvertently spotlighted what is a strikingly revealing omission in Xenophon's Socratic report of the theology of Ischomachus.

29. Ischomachus indicates that he is not giving to Socrates a verbatim report of what he said to his wife—*pōs* at 7.10, and see 7.43, 8.23; cf. XSD 133, 136–37.

30. 7.32; Mitchell 1819, 177 archly comments: "the young lady, however, was not much versed in apiaries."

31. Sommerstein 2009, 18: "the great majority" of "oaths were used exclusively by men or exclusively by women. Over time, too, there seems to have been a tendency for this sexual segregation of oaths to become more complete." See, e.g., Aristophanes, *Assembly of Women* 155–58; see also Austin and Olson 2004, 224 as well as 129, 136, 176, 207–8, 211. The gentlemanly English commentator Mitchell (1819, 177) feels a need to excuse the young lady's profanity: she "exclaims with a pardonable vivacity."

32. Pomeroy ad loc.; given that "broken pots were not uncommon," drawing water, "carrying it, and then discovering it had leaked out must have been a frequent occurrence producing intense despair and vexation."

33. Mahaffy (1902, 278–79): "he develops, too, as we should expect a Greek gentleman to do, the satisfaction arising from the exercise of power."

34. Thompson and Hayes 1895 ad loc. draw attention to the force of the middle voice of the verb here ("*poiēsē*: middle, 'make *for yourself.*' ").

35. 7.16; fans of Aristophanes will not be able to resist wondering if the missing item might have been a jug of wine (see, e.g., Praxagora's opening speech in *Assemblywomen*). Wine is a major product of Ischomachus's farming: 19.1–12, 18–19; 20.3–4, 20–21; see also 9.3, 11.

36. The stress on "human beings" (*anthrōpoi*) reminds us that the chorus is engaged in worship of divinity—conceived and experienced as a living presence among the worshippers. As we soon learn, Ischomachus seems to have had in mind especially a circular, therefore Dionysian-dithyrambic chorus (of fifty members): 8.20; Chantraine and Pomeroy ad loc.; LSJ s.v. *kuklios* II (who cite Aristophanes *Clouds* 333 and *Frogs* 366); Webster 1970, 68, 91. Dionysus is not a god noted for his orderliness; is not the choreographed, dithyrambic ritual a way in which human beings bring order to the unruly god and his influence?

37. This despite the fact that "order *in battle*" is a or the primary meaning of the term that Ischomachus used for "order"; see LSJ s.v. *taxis* and *tassō*. Only near the end of his teaching on order (8.20) did Ischomachus employ the more adorning and cosmological (though still also military) term *kosmos*: by the singularity of this employment, Socrates in his narration spotlights the stress on the less lovely, harsher term in Ischomachus's teaching on order and disorder. (For usage of the term *kosmos*, see Rahe 2016, 144 n. 18.)

38. 8.8; Pomeroy ad loc.: "the ecphasis of the trireme contains a liberal sample of obvious rhetorical devices"; "the present passage is fulsome"; "at the same time, balance and repetition of words and rhetorical figures serve to emphasize the importance of order."

39. Weiske 1798–1804 ad loc.: "plane repugnans et ridiculum." Schneider 1812 ad loc. is not quite so astonished. XSD 141 drily characterizes the examples as "not altogether inept." Pomeroy ad loc.: while "she certainly will have had personal experience of synchronized choruses," it is "unlikely that Ischomachus' wife will have been familiar with the sight of a real army."

40. The very need for this lecture of the gentleman on order arose from the fact that his house had not yet been ordered by him together with his wife and was thus in disorder; Pomeroy ad loc., referring also to what we can gather from the continuation of the teaching on order in 9.6ff., comments: "evidently Ischomachus has been without a woman to run the house for quite some time: his possessions are a mess." Recognizing a certain degree of overstatement in this last, Pomeroy adds: "however, the disorder may be a didactic device" (see also Meyer 1975 ad loc.; contrast XSD 140).

41. This is the sole example that the gentleman gives here of an ordering that is a separation of natural species.

42. Ischomachus's lecture on order at this point (8.10) falls into syntactical disorder. If we assume (as all sober scholars must) that this is not an intentional, impish joke on Xenophon's Socrates's part, and assume that our manuscripts have been corrupted, I opt to go with Zeune 1782 ad loc., who reports, with the help of notes from Johann August Bach, a leading disciple of "the celebrated" Johann August Ernesti, that the latter suggested trying to restore the presumed original, orderly text by inserting an "if" at this point (perhaps following, Zeune suggests, the somewhat loose Latin translation of Strebaeo 1543 ad loc.—"Ut in eam rerum perturbationem cadas non erit necesse, cara

coniunx, *si* cognoscere velis. . . ."). Earlier editors ad loc.—Stephanus et al. 1561, Levvenklaius 1562, Camerarius 1564—tried to restore the presumed original order by inserting a *hina* ("so that") immediately after "wife." More recent editors have followed Schneider 1812 ad loc., who inserted an "if" immediately after "wife" (the editors wrongly ascribe this to Ernesti—see the erroneous apparatus in Pomeroy, Marchant 1921, and Chantraine; as Schneider 1812 ad loc. writes, "particulam *ei* omittunt libri omnes, eam addidit Ernesti; sed ante *bouloio* insertam voluit."). Especially if one follows the recent editors, however, a new disorder creeps in: as Holden remarks ad loc. (writing in 1884), "it is strange that none of the commentators have called attention to the irregularity of the use of *ei* [if] with the optative and the imperative in the apodosis, instead of *ei* with the indic. or *ean* anticipatory with the subj." Subsequently, Thompson and Hayes 1895, ad loc., also remark this new disorder. Chantraine in his translation seems to interpret the irregular use of the optative as Ischomachus suddenly adopting a bantering tone with his wife—"wife, if you should *by any chance* desire to avoid such confusion. . . ." ("si tu désires *par hasard* éviter une telle confusion. . . ."). An irreverent wit might suggest that our manuscripts have been corrupted by some imp who possessed a knowledge of Greek that allowed him to baffle our editors.

43. 8.10: *onta* plural of *on*, the participle form of the verb "to be," means primarily one's belongings (or "substance"), and came derivatively to be the philosophic term for being(s) or "things-that-are"—see *Memorabilia* 2.1.27 and 4.6.7.

44. *mē on* (literally, "not being") is both a homely word for something absent or gone, and a philosophic term for nonbeing.

45. Schneider 1812 ad loc.: "Exemplum navis Phoeniceae, ut ineptum colloquio cum uxore Ischomachi, taxavit Weiske [1798–1804 ad loc.]; sed non animadvertit, Ischomachum hic Socratem alloqui, nex uxorem." See also Ruderman 2015, 207–8.

46. Holden (see also Pomeroy; Breitenbach 1841) ad loc.: "probably a well-known vessel performing a regular service between Athens and some foreign port or ports."

47. XSD 143, comparing the theologies of the boatswain and Ischomachus: "The boatswain is more certain than Ischomachus about the gods punishing (and therefore noticing) the slack. On the other hand, he is as doubtful as Ischomachus about evil befalling only the bad, i.e., about whether one can speak in strict parlance of divine punishment."

48. Chantraine in his apparatus ad 8.11 notes that Nitsche 1879 ad loc. responded to the puzzling fact that Ischomachus tells his wife only about "small" ships, after having made clear to Socrates that his revelatory experience was with a "large" ship, by suggesting that the text of the description of the Phoenician ship should be emended—substituting "a certain not big ship" (*ou mega ploion ti*) for the manuscript reading "the big ship" (*to mega ploion to*). This inadvertently underlines Xenophon's provocation to thought.

49. Ruskin 1876 ad loc.: "*eurythmos*. A remarkable word as significative of the complete rhythm (*ruthymos*) whether of sound or motion, that was so great a characteristic of the Greek ideal (cf. xi.16, *metarruthymizō*). The statement here that even pots and pans may look fair and graceful when arranged in order, finds certain verification in one of the bas-reliefs at the base of Giotto's Tower."

50. *to kompson* is a characteristic of "all the speeches of Socrates" according to Aristotle (*Politics* 1265a12). Unlike Critobulus (recall 3.7–8), Ischomachus does not suspect Socrates of laughing at him.

51. The English gentleman Mitchell (1819, 178) salutes Ischomachus's "discourse on order, his details of the various causes, by which a kind of beau ideal of the beauty of arrangement had been gradually fostered in his own mind, and the ingenuity, with which a sort of dignity is thrown over the meanest branches of household economy." See also Holden xix. Pomeroy, in contrast, says ad loc. that "the rhapsodic and hyperbolic quality of the entire passage might make it seem funny to the reader." Chantraine ad loc. is convinced that Xenophon is echoing Plato's presentation of the jesting exchange between Socrates and Hippias in the *Hippias Major* 288.

52. 9.1, accepting Stephanus's (1561 ad loc.) correction of the accent on *pōs* in the mss.

53. Breitenbach 1841 ad loc. points out the repetition, in both texts, of the term *poikilmata* for "decorations."

54. *Hiero* 4.3–4 and 10.4: "indeed, many are the masters who have died by violence from slaves." Consider the context.

55. Sextus Empiricus, *Adversus Mathematicos* IX 92ff.; Diogenes Laertius 2.45; Fouillée 1874, vol. 1 passim; Gigon 1953 ad loc.; Theiler 1965; Long 1988, 162–63; DeFilippo and Mitsis 1994, 255–61; Gray 1989, 183; Brisson and Dorion 2004; Sedley 2008; Powers 2009; Bandini and Dorion 2010–11, ad 1.4.1, 1.4.8, 4.3.18.

56. XSD 147–50, referring to *Memorabilia* 4.5.12 and 4.6.1 as well as 1.1.16 and 4.6.13–15.

57. As reported by Columella, *On Agricultural Matters* 12.1.3.

58. Consider OT chap. 7 in conjunction with XSD 170 n. 5.

59. Recall in sharp contrast especially what we heard recently at 7.7–8, as well as at 6.1, and what we will hear at 11.8; contrast too the teachings of Socrates in *Memorabilia* 1.1.8–9 and 2.6.8 on the need to consult the gods in making such choices—and the teaching of Xenophon himself in *Ways and Means* 6.2–3.

60. In the previous dialogue with Critobulus, the virtue of justice was mentioned only at 5.12. For previous mentions of "the just," see 2.15, 3.13, 4.16, 4.25, 6.12, 7.15. It of course did not occur to the gentleman that he and his wife needed to raise and to pursue the Socratic question, "*what is* just/justice?" A gentleman is absolutely certain that he knows what is the just and what is the virtue of justice.

61. So, e.g., Lord, in Bartlett 1996; Pomeroy; Marchant 2013; Holden references an analogue—a slave in his place—in *Anabasis* 5.6.13.

62. "Atque eam ipsam quoque in numero proborum justorum collocabamus"—Camerarius 1564 ad loc. "Ea in conditione ut posset splendide et liberaliter, ut homines honestiores, vivere"—Breitenbach 1841 ad loc. following Weiske 1798–1804 ad loc. "D'une manière digne d'un homme libre"—Chantraine ad loc. See also Holden ad loc. and Pomeroy ad 13.9. On manumission of slaves in ancient Greece, see Amemiya 2007, 28.

63. Holden ad loc. paraphrases: "I warned my wife, added Ischomachus, that she must not allow any undue confidence in our housekeeper."

64. An institution found historically in Sparta and in older aristocratic regimes (Aristotle, *Politics* 1287a21, 1298b29, 1322b39, 1323a8), and holding decisive power in the mixed aristocratic regime envisaged in Plato's *Laws*.

65. XSD 152: "In the chapters on order it is only Ischomachos' wife who ever speaks of nature or the natural; she never speaks of order. Her husband, the teacher of order, on the other hand, speaks of law."

66. 10.1; in the *Oeconomicus* "the wife is presented as the ruler of the husband rather than the husband as the ruler of the wife"—XSD 177.

67. See again Sommerstein 2009, 18 on the gendered "segregation" of oaths in classical Greece, as well as Austin and Olson 2004, 224. Bonnette 1994, ad *Memorabilia* 1.5.5, refers us to Aristophanes's *Assembly of Women* 155–56 and 189–90, "where women attempting to disguise themselves as men are chastised for continuing to use" the oath "by Hera!" For the use of this oath "by Hera!" in Plato (Socrates in *Apology* 24e, *Theaetetus* 154d, *Phaedrus* 230b, *Gorgias* 449d, *Hippias Major* 287a and 291e; Lysimachus in *Laches* 181a), see Rabieh 2006, 31 and 176 nn 13 and 14 and Calder 1983, as well as Wilamowitz-Moellendorff 1920, 416 and Huss ad *Symposium* 4.45.

68. XSD 153: "In his report to Kritoboulos and the other friends, he underlines the fact that he uses a woman's oath, that he behaves like a woman, in contrast to the masculine character of Iscomachos' wife, whose reply revealed that virile concern with one's own which makes human beings good defenders of their own. We recall again that manliness is not mentioned by Xenophon among Socrates' virtues."

69. Contrast "the *Hiero*, the parallel work, in which the wise man conversing with a ruler is a poet" and "in which 'philosophy' is not mentioned at all" (XSD 185): there we see the worry of the tyrant Hiero about his inscrutable but indubitably wise interlocutor, the *poet* Simonides—who refers to the sangfroid he has displayed in his extensive military experience (*Hiero* 6.7–9): see OT chap. 3a.

70. Xenophon gives no explicit indication of it, but the stoa of Zeus in which the conversation took place was "probably" designed "from the beginning" to be "a picture gallery" and certainly later had famous paintings of Euphranor in it: Thompson and Wycherley 1972, 96–103 and esp. 101–2; Pausanias 1.3.1–4 and 9.15.5; Pliny 35.128–29; Kronenberg 2009, 54.

71. 11.1; XSD 156–57; Thompson and Hayes 1895 ad loc. paraphrase: "enough as a first installment"; Pomeroy ad 10.3 inadvertently heightens the comedy, by attributing Socrates's motive to fastidiousness: "Socrates, not wanting to hear further confidences about this intimate subject, abruptly terminates the discussion of marriage here."

72. Contrast Xenophon's romances of Panthea and Abradatas, and of Tigranes and his wife, in the *Education of Cyrus*.

73. "One can safely say that what Xenophon's Socrates reports about Ischomachos and his wife is perfectly compatible with the possibility that that woman proved in later years to be less good than her pedagogic husband expected her to become and that this disappointing truth was known to Socrates and his friends when he gave them his report."—XSD 158 and see context, as well as Ambler 1996, 118n. Strauss may seem to go a bit overboard in calling Chrysilla "that most impudent hag," but he is only quoting Andocides. It is certainly the case that respectable Athenian wives remained anonymous (see Thucydides 2.46) and that we only know Chrysilla's name because of the scandalous account of her in Andocides 1.118ff.

## CHAPTER FOUR

1. According to a note on Virgil's *Georgics* 1.43 by the fourth century grammarian Marus Servius Horatus (1881), Cicero made this the beginning of a second of three books of his translation of the *Economist*: the third book translated the conversation through

which Ischomachus educated Socrates in farming (this might be taken to imply that Cicero did not translate the conversation with Critobulus, but in *De Senectute* 59 Cicero has his character Cato praise especially the Lysander-Cyrus incident reported in the Socrates-Critobulus conversation, which Cicero proceeds to quote in his own translation).

2. *adoleschein*; in Aristophanes's *Clouds* 1480, and also in a play about Socrates by the comic poet Eupolis (frags. 386 and 388 in Kassel and Austin 1983–2001), this derogatory term (see Aristotle, *N. Ethics* 1117b35) is applied to the didactic talk of Socrates; the term is sardonically echoed by Plato's Eleatic Stranger (*Statesman* 299b).

3. *aerometrein*: this word appears nowhere else, and Socrates would seem to be making it up, echoing the natural scientist Meton as he is mockingly presented in Aristophanes's *Birds* 995 and ff., and echoing also Aristophanes's *Clouds* 225, where Socrates himself is depicted as asserting that he "treads the air" (*aerobatein*), a statement eventually repeated by Strepsiades in a quotation mocking Socrates (*Clouds* 1503). In Plato's *Apology* (19c) Socrates quotes the latter word *aerobatein*, as he reports the "older accusations." One late manuscript, Vaticanus Graecus 128, reads *aerobatein* here, instead of *aerometrein*. Breitenbach 1841 ad loc. refers us also to Plato's *Apology* 18b.

4. XSD 162: "Ischomachus acts then on the view stated by the Phoenician boatswain; but he states that view in a somewhat less shocking or savage manner than the Phoenician."

5. XSD 162: "to this extent the pupil Socrates has become convinced by Ischomachos' defense of the perfect gentleman's way of life." It is certainly incorrect to say that Ischomachus is presented as if he "conceives of his benefit in a purely material way" (Kronenberg 2009, 58); contrast Novo 1968, 7, 67–68, 96–99.

6. 11.9–11; also 11.13; contrast Aristotle, *N. Ethics* 1122a18-b33, esp. 1122b20.

7. #3; see also #16 and 18 as well as XSD 165–66.

8. Plato, *Laws* 730d: "He who does not do injustice is indeed honorable; but he who does not allow unjust men to work their injustice is more than twice as honorable. The former has a value of one, but the latter, by reporting the injustice of the others to the magistrates, is equal in value to many others. Yet the great man in the city, the man who is to be proclaimed perfect and the bearer of victory in virtue, is the one who does what he can to assist the magistrates in inflicting punishment." See also 731b-c: "Every real man should be of the spirited type, but yet also as gentle as possible [etc.]." XSD 166 refers us to *Gorgias* 480b7–481b1. See also Ambler 1996, 123m.

9. Pomeroy ad loc.: "Rhetoric was fundamental to Athenian education. . . . xi 23 implies that Ischomachus' slaves (like his wife, xi 25) had some understanding of rhetoric. According to *Cyr.* 1.2.6–7, a substantial part of the Persian boys' curriculum consisted of bringing one another to court on criminal charges. Their officers spent most of the day judging these charges."

10. Pomeroy ad loc.: "Here Ischomachus relates that he endowed his wife with judicial powers in the *oikos* just as in ix 15 he told her to consider herself a *nomophulax* [guardian of the laws]."

11. Holden ad loc.: "as Socrates was often accused of doing—Aristoph. *Clouds* 114ff., Plato *Apology* 23D," and "Aulus Gellius, Noct. Att. v 3." See also Breitenbach 1841 ad loc.; Graux 1878, 103; and Pomeroy ad loc., who refers also to Plato, *Apology* 18b and 19b.

12. See especially Plato's *Theages*, together with L. Strauss 1983, 46–47, and T. Pangle 1987.

13. Holden as well as Pomeroy ad loc.; LSJ s.v. *agora* IV.

## CHAPTER FIVE

1. Meyer 1975, 104: "der zentrale Begriff im ganzen Oikonomikos."

2. See Ambler 1996, 126–27 on the skeptical, retrospective implications regarding the earlier claim of the gentleman to have succeeded in educating his wife in diligence (7.7, 8.1, 9.1, 9.14, 9.17–18).

3. See *Education of Cyrus* 5.1.12 and the subsequent story of Araspas; Pomeroy ad loc. directs us also to *Agesilaus* 5.4–6. Contrast *Hiero* 1.26–38: the successful tyrant is unabashedly erotic; for the full implications, consider OT chap. 5, n. 60. In sharp contrast to Cyrus the Great, Cyrus the Younger was erotically self-indulgent (*Anabasis of Cyrus* 1.10.2–3, 2.12; Bruell 1987, 112).

4. *erōtikōs echousi tou kerdainein*—Holden ad loc. suggests translating as "are in love with lucre"; similarly XSD 169, 199.

5. Holden ad loc. notes that this word is "not found elsewhere in Xenophon."

6. *philokerdeis*: Socrates substituted the less passionate *philia* for eros and tacitly pointed to the question of how severely "measured" the fondness for money must be, in the case of slave overseers.

7. As Holden indicates ad 12.19, the use of words with the -kos ending here is redolent of Aristophanean comedy; see also again Peppler 1910.

8. Holden ad loc. suggests translating, "put it into his head," and refers us also to the use of the term in Plato's *Republic* 600c.

9. Cf. the Athenian Stranger's extreme dismissal of any claim to wisdom on the part of farming: "for not by art, but by nature, in accord with god, do we all manifestly work earth" (the Platonic *Epinomis* 975b).

10. Holden ad loc.: the somewhat unusual definite article is "used to give special prominence to the notion."

11. See *Memorabilia* 2.1 and 3.2–7 and *Education of Cyrus*, beg.

12. 13.5; Socrates presents himself as having expressed a version of the perspective on rule that Aristotle opens his *Politics* attacking as "ignoble" (for a discussion, see T. Pangle 2013, chap. 1). See similarly *Memorabilia* 3.4 and Plato's *Statesman* 258e–59d, as well as *Charmides* 171e and 172d, *Symposium* 209a-b, and *Lovers* 138c; see also XSD 171.

13. 13.6–8; Hartman 1887, 205–6 is so unfavorably astonished that he suggests this is some sort of interpolation. Here again the scholar is deaf to Xenophon's wry wit.

14. This may help explain why Ischomachus was silent on self-restraint as regards food, or "the stomach," as a needed qualification in potential overseers, when he had so stressed its importance when speaking of his wife's upbringing and of the qualifications of the housekeeper—contrast 12.11–14 with 7.6 and 9.11; see XSD 169–70, 172–73 and Pomeroy ad 13.9. Note that Ischomachus did not exclude the overseers from the set of slaves who can be taught obedience by the beastly education.

15. Courage or manliness in a field overseer or slave might even be tantamount to a vice—consider again *Hiero* 4.3 and 10.3–4. Ischomachus of course does not include

military exercise or weapons training in his education of his overseers: recall 5.14–16 and our commentary thereupon; contrast *Hiero* 9.6–7 and 11.3, 11.12. "One may say that the gentlemanship of the stewards is akin to the gentlemanship of which subjects of tyrants are capable": XSD 176, referring us to OT chap. 4—in which, see esp. n. 11 and context, referring us also to *Hellenica* 2.3.41.

16. See OT chap. 4 and also chap. 3, sec. c and sec. b, n. 37 (pointing out that remarks of the tyrant Hiero at *Hiero* 4.4 and esp. 6.10 disclose the essential lawlessness of tyranny).

17. *Memorabilia* 4.6.12; see OT chap. 4, n. 5, referring us also to *Education of Cyrus* 1.3.18 and *Hellenica* 7.1.44–46.

18. Consider the observation on republics and republican citizenries, as well as monarchies and their subjects, with which Xenophon opens his *Education of Cyrus*: "Human beings unite against none more than against those whom they perceive attempting to rule them."

19. XSD 174–75; on the "despotic" and "tyrannical" elements at the heart of all republican rule of law, see Plato, *Laws* 712e–713a, 715d, 719e–720e, 722b–723b, 757d.

20. Presumably through gifts and profit sharing rather than through wages or property holdings; cf. Chantraine ad loc.: "L'esclave qui en principe n'a pas de personalité ne peut pas avoir de patrimoine. Mais des dons ou de menus profits lui permettent de se faire un pécule qui aidera à son affranchissement."

21. We note again that Xenophon never includes manliness or courage among his various lists of the virtues of Socrates, and in his *Education of Cyrus* Xenophon portrays what seems to be an avatar of Socrates living at the court of the Armenian king. It is true that the Armenian king did eventually execute the Socratic philosopher; that sad event occurred when the king became aware that the philosopher had led the king's son to care more for the philosopher than for his royal father; but might not this be an avoidable danger?

22. Editors and commentators such as Hartman 1887, 206, and Marchant 1921 ad loc. are so astonished at this formulation that they declare the text corrupt and propose various emendations. The earnest defenses of the mss. text by Breitenbach 1841, Holden, and Chantraine ad loc. invoke parallels in Xenophon that are not quite apt. All of these scholars are unalive to Xenophontic-Socratic irony.

23. "it would not be reasonable to expect the master to be just in this lofty sense toward his slaves"—XSD 178.

## CHAPTER SIX

1. As a matter of fact, Ischomachus had *not* said at 13.2 that knowledge was "the greatest thing"—which would contradict the long and vivid oration he was to give at the end of his education in farming, insisting that diligence rather than knowledge is what is decisive in farming (20.2ff.).

2. Curiously, Socrates thus reports himself as having omitted mention of what had been the central of three things that have to be learned, according to Ischomachus: *the time when* things need to be done; Xenophon thus subtly draws our attention to this aspect—which will soon prove to be the part of the art of farming that involves theology: 17.1–6.

3. *isōs*—the word can just as well mean the weaker "perhaps."

4. Recall 2.18, 5.19–20, 6.1, 7.7–8, 11.8–9; cf. 1.16–22; *Memorabilia* 1.1.9; XSD 197.

5. Socrates quoted Ischomachus uttering ten profane expletives in his account of his moral education of his stewards, but he quotes the gentleman uttering only a single such expletive (at 17.11) in the course of teaching the art of farming. This reminds us of the complete absence of profanity in Socrates's rather pious praise of Greek farming in chaps. 5–6.

6. Cf. Breitenbach 1841 ad loc.: "facile intelligitur Socratem, ut tandem aliquando de ipsa agicultura audiat urgentum, quum iterum declinet Ischomachus (nimirum ad *philanthropia tēs technēs*), iam simulata indignatione interrumpere disserentem."

7. XSD 181: "One wonders whether Ischomachus can see Socrates more easily as a teacher of farming than as an actually farming man."

8. According to Diogenes Laertius 9.48 and Varro, *On Agricultual Matters* 1.1.7–8, Democritus wrote a (now lost) treatise on farming (for what is known about it, see Wellmann 1921 and 1928). In Theophrastus's two botanical works, *Enquiry into Plants* and *On Causes of Plants*, we find a rich compendium of previous Greek natural science's understanding of soils as well as of the other aspects of farming. As Rostovtzeff (1941, 1182–83; see also Jardé 1925, 62–64) stresses, we see from these writings of Theophrastus that the scientific-philosophic study of the nature of plant life-forms was combined with and dependent upon the scientific study of farming (insofar, that is, as farming is plant, rather than animal, husbandry). See esp. *On Causes of Plants* bk. 3 beg.: "theorizing about plants comprises two inquiries and is in two ranges: one about the coming into being of the spontaneous, of which the principle is nature, the other about the coming into being from thought and preparation, which we declare indeed to work with nature toward the end."

9. XSD 195–96: "One must also wonder why the *Oeconomicus* is so severely limited to agriculture and does not at all teach cattle-raising." Strauss adds: "this failure is particularly striking in light of Mem. IV.3.10. Cf. especially Oec. V.3." Then Strauss observes: "*Phyta* ('plants') has the same root as *physis*: by being concerned with farming, Socrates continues, in a properly qualified and subdued way, his early interest in *physiologia*."

10. Ischomachus's language of "knowing" here is curiously strained. Thompson and Hayes 1895 remark ad loc. that "this construction"—"accusative of the thing learnt and the genitive of the source"—is "common with 'to hear' and 'to enquire'" but "is found nowhere else in Attic prose with 'to know.'"

11. XSD 183: "if Ischomachus were right, no innovation, no improvement in this particular province, would be possible."

12. We recall that when Socrates praised, for Critobulus, the Greek practice of farming he spoke of "the Earth, being god" (5.12).

13. After he has completed his teaching on farming, Ischomachus will take a big step back, incidentally admitting that "some one may be entirely ignorant as to what the earth will bear, and unable to see either its crop or planting, nor be able to hear the truth about it from another" (20.13; XSD 198).

14. Holden's felicitous translation.

15. Pomeroy ad loc. inadvertently underlines the comedy when, in trying to make Socrates sound more serious, she suggests that by fishermen who "can recognize the qualities of soil at a glance," Socrates must have meant "probably only part-time, seasonal fishermen. The rest of their livelihood would have been derived from farming." But Socrates explicitly spoke of fishermen whose work was at sea, without qualification! See Hobden 2017, 167.

16. As various commentators have noted, Xenophon here starts having his Socrates playfully hint or suggest that he was led by his conversation with the gentleman Ischomachus to his famous doctrine of learning as "recollection": Holden ad loc.; XSD 184; Guthrie 1971a, 17; Meyer 1975 ad ch. 19; Pomeroy ad 18.1 and 19.15.

17. Holden ad loc. remarks that we have here an instance of "the use of *andros* with nouns implying a man's profession"—so Socrates is not referring to the philosophic man as "manly."

18. Nightingale 1995, 16–17; Moore 2018.

19. 16.9; Thompson and Hayes ad loc. note that the plural forms here signify multiple crops. Chantraine ad loc. is understandably taken aback by this characterization of the philosopher: "le propre du philosophe est de rechercher la vérité: ici encore cette notion socratique est un peu inattendue." See similarly, ad loc., Weiske 1798–1804 and Breitenbach 1841.

20. Theophrastus, *Enquiry into Plants* 8.8.1: "each of the seed types harmonizes with the nature of the land, and in general, kind with kind as well as within those of the same kind—and they [the experts in botany] try to distinguish these." Socrates is the chief originator of natural science based on distinction among "kinds"; indeed, Xenophon writes that Socrates "never ceased examining amidst his companions what each of the beings is," in the sense of what *kind* each is: see *Memorabilia* 4.5.11–4.6.1. It would follow that throughout the *Economist* Socrates is ceaselessly if subtly examining what each kind of the beings is, and would presumably be doing the same while he farmed, and/or taught farming, if he ever were to do so.

21. Consider Plato, *Republic* 499b-c; and the son of the Armenian king in Xenophon's *Education of Cyrus*.

22. *hupergazesthai*: see LSJ s.v. and Theophrastus, *Enquiry into Plants* 3.1.6 beg.

23. This peculiar spelling of the word for "fallow" is repeated at 16.13, 16.15, 17.1, and 20.3, always by Ischomachus, never by Socrates. See LSJ s.v. *neios*; the spelling used here by Xenophon is found in one later fourth century inscription (at Amorgos) and in the mss. of Theophrastus, *On the Causes of Plants* 3.20.7—a passage which Einarson and Link 1990 emend so as to insert the Xenophontic-type spelling, but I think this is a highly dubious alteration. If anything, I would suggest instead, or on the contrary, an emendation of the odd usage *neous*, changing it to the usual spelling, *neious*.

24. An anticipation of the wordplay is found in, and may be derived from, Antiphon the sophist (referred to prominently in Xenophon's *Memorabilia*): see frag. #60 (Diels and Kranz 1951): "for even as, from the sort of seed that one sows in the earth ought one to expect the harvest to be, so when one ploughs a wellborn education in the young/fallow body (*en néōi sōmati*), this lives and flourishes through the whole of life, and neither rain nor drought can remove it." Guthrie 1971a, 18n observes that the "analogy between education and farming" was a "common fifth-century" one, and was "used by [the Platonic] Socrates at *Phaedrus* 276b and e" and by the Platonic Protagoras at *Theaetetus* 167b-c. See also Guthrie 1971b, 168–69, quoting the Hippocratic work *Law*, chap. 3. What Guthrie fails to note is that the analogy is not with farming as a whole, but *only* with *plant* husbandry—*animal* husbandry is left out (animal husbandry is a common analogy, not least in Xenophon, for *political* rule); here we have yet another reason for the curious (and playful) silence on animal husbandry in the *Economist*'s presentation of the farming art.

25. Pomeroy assumes (ad 16.13; see also ad 16.11), following Guiraud 1893, 472 (see also Meyer 1975 ad loc.), that this implies that Ischomachus "can afford to leave some land fallow in alternate years"—a "system" that was "traditional" when it could be afforded. The use of the verb "begin" would then have an important agricultural meaning, in that the fallow would have been left unstirred for an entire year, and the plowing in question would be a kind of new commencement of cultivation of that piece of land. For this "system," see also Dickson 1788, 1.444; Gallant 1991, 56; *Iliad* 10.353, 13.703, 18.541; and *Odyssey* 13.31–34 (see Ridgeway 1885, 338); also Pindar's *Nemean Odes* 6.9–11; and the many surviving records of land leases cited by Pomeroy. But: it is most curious that Socrates presents Ischomachus as utterly failing to remind Socrates of this crucial fact about the source of the fallow, and about the agricultural meaning of "beginning." Furthermore, Socrates has Ischomachus leave out an allied, common and more complex practice: crop rotation in which legumes were planted in the off year, or off season, to replenish the soil for cereal crops (Dickson 1788, vol. 1, ch. 6; Guiraud 1893, 473–74; Jardé 1925, chap. 2; see also Theophrastus, *On the Causes of Plants* 3.20.7). In the third place, Ischomachus is also presented as failing to refer to the normal third plowing in the autumn before sowing, and to the fourth plowing in the winter: Guiraud 1893, 475; Jardé exclaims in wonder (1925, 23–24): "Xénophon ne souffle mot du labour d'automne. Est-ce intentionellement?"; Pomeroy ad 16.11 refers us to the phrase "thrice-ploughed field" in *Iliad* 18.542 and *Odyssey* 5.127, as well as Hesiod, *Works and Days* 463–64 and *Theogony* 971; see also the four plowings recommended by Theophrastus, *On the Causes of Plants* 3.20.8. Given these remarkable omissions, Ischomachus is presented by Socrates as teaching about working the fallow, the major first step in cereral farming, in a strangely "un-farmer-like" way. This all goes with the wordplay regarding the *neos*.

26. Contra Theophrastus, *On the Causes of Plants* 3.20.6–7: "the working of the fallow is in both seasons, summer and winter"—"as was said in regard to planting" (3.4.1); see similarly *Enquiry into Plants* 8.6.3.

27. 16.11–12; as regards fertilizer, once again we note the silence on the animal husbandry dimension of farming, needed to supply the dung manure which was—as Jardé (1925, 25–30) stresses—crucial for Greek farmers (see also 17.10, 18.2, 20.3, and 20.10). Pomeroy draws attention to the silence with her excuse (ad 16.12): "the use of animal waste will have been so obvious to readers of the *Oeconomicus* as not to require discussion"—and she refers us to Theophrastus, who stresses, however, the need to distinguish the powers of various kinds of dung as suitably complementary for various kinds of soil; indeed, the philosophic botanist links the scientific analysis of the kinds of dung and their powers to the scientific analysis of the kinds of soil and their powers: *On the Causes of Plants* 3.6.1–2 and 3.9.4–5; see also *Enquiry into Plants* 2.7.4.

28. Pomeroy ad loc., following Theophrastus, *On the Causes of Plants* 3.20.8, comments that the herbal fertilizing was generally understood to be *the* reason/cause for plowing the fallow in spring.

29. *optēn*: the verbal form *optaō* is used metaphorically for the seductions of erotic love in Aristophanes (*Lysistrata* 839) and elsewhere (see LSJ s.v.).

30. Theophrastus, *On the Causes of Plants* 3.20.8 says those who best understand farming "praise rather the working with the mattock; that from the plow is held to omit many things." See also Jardé 1925, 20.

31. 17.1; XSD 187; Holden ad loc.: "'yes, indeed, we are of the same opinion,' not 'yes, it seems so.' . . . The *oun* has a restrictive, not a consecutive, force." Lord's translation (in Bartlett 1996) accordingly needs to be corrected.

32. 17.2; Breitenbach 1841 ad loc. notes that this verb *keleuein* is used for oracular pronouncements at *Hellenica* 3.3.3 and 7.2.20.

33. XSD: "the Socratic statements just discussed are the only ones occurring in the Ischomachus section that set forth the Socratic theology" (188)—"the most serious of all arts or sciences" (192).

34. Holden ad loc.: "*ti gar*: a lively way of passing to a new point for consideration, 'what do you say to this?'"

35. The *cithara* was a harp-like instrument normally played by professionals, unlike the lyre, which was played by amateurs. Meyer 1975 ad loc. comments critically: "Der Vergleich (Auswerfen des Samens—Schlagen der Kithara) ist ohne Zweifel überzogen." But with this (playful) exaggeration (see 20.3 and XSD 197) Socrates is highlighting the long practice required for *truly* knowing *how to* sow.

36. Holden ad loc. has a long comment on the importance of this practice, referring us to Theophrastus, *Enquiry into Plants* 8.9.1; Pliny's *Natural History* 18.12 and 18.20; Varro, *Agricultural Matters* 1.23.3; Columella, *Agricultural Matters* 11.2.44; Palladius, *Work of Agriculture* 6.4; Dickson 1788, chap. 11; and (without specific page ref.) Harte 1770. See also Meyer 1975 ad loc. It appears that if Socrates had not expressed his perplexity about the contrary analogies, Ischomachus would not have mentioned this very important complexity in sowing. See also 18.2.

37. *haliskei ep'autophōrō*: "caught red-handed"—Pomeroy ad loc.

38. *N. Ethics* 1108a19–22, 1127b23–33; the *eirōn*, a character defined by habitual deceptive self-deprecation, and the *alazōn*, a character defined by habitual boasting, were stock figures in Attic comedy.

39. Socrates asked about the planting of *trees* (*dendrōn*); Ischomachus immediately initiated a discussion that applied to planting *grapevines* (*ampelōn*), as he made explicit at 19.12 (Holden ad loc.: "It is evident that Ischomachus has all along been speaking of the culture of the vine"). XSD 193n: "Socrates mentions the vine and its fruits altogether less frequently than Ischomachus" (see especially 19.18–19, 20.3–4, 20.20): Strauss refers us to Aristophanes's *Clouds* 417, where the Clouds say the potential student of Socrates must stay away from wine. See also the "menu" of Socratic dinners as described in the *Memorabilia* 3.14: wine is notably absent. The gentleman loves his wine; the philosopher does not, to say the least (but see *Symposium* 8.24).

40. See Theophrastus, *On the Causes of Plants* bk. 3 for a compendium of the Greek scientific understanding of *planting*. The keynote is struck at 3.2.3: "About each matter there is a rational account giving the cause; he who acts without this and by custom and coincidences perhaps does correctly, but without knowing—just as in medicine. Completion comes from both."

41. 19.2; we note that in what followed Ischomachus did not say a word about the various *kinds* of earth suitable for the various *kinds* of tree or vine (he spoke only of the important difference between wet and dry soils, and the implications for rooting). Contrast Theophrastus, *Enquiry into Plants* 2.5.7: "the most important thing, so to speak, is to assign to each [kind of tree planted] the appropriate soil. . . . and it is necessary also

not to be ignorant of the various soils that belong to the varieties of the same species. . . . For some say that as many kinds of earth as there are, so many are the kinds also of grape vines; when planted in accord with nature they become good and when against nature, fruitless—now these remarks apply pretty much in common to all plantings." See similarly *Causes of Plants* 3.11.1. Recall our discussion of the revealing dispute that occurred at 16.1–6 (which was about planting as well as sowing), and especially Socrates's declaration at 16.2, "he who does not know what the earth is capable of bearing, would also not know what to sow, I think, *nor what he ought to plant*." As previously noted, Socrates eventually has Ischomachus incidentally disclose the fact that it is disastrous to plant vines in the wrong kind of soil (20.3). Meyer 1975 ad loc. notices the discrepancy between the aspects of planting that Socrates here said he was ignorant of and the aspects that Ischomachus proceeded to show Socrates to be in fact knowledgeable about.

42. 19.13; Holden ad loc.: "temptas interrogando."

43. Socrates reports Ischomachus uttering not a single profane expletive in this part of the conversation: Ischomachus is depicted as especially earnest in his teaching of planting—in marked contrast to Socrates's mood as student, especially at this point in his education by the gentleman.

44. When Socrates asked Ischomachus how they would plant an olive tree (19.13), the gentleman exclaimed that this is what Socrates "knows best of all" (*malista pantōn epistamenos*), but as the scholarly commentary shows, Ischomachus's elaboration of the technique he claimed Socrates knew is lacking in clarity: see Meyer 1975 ad loc.; Pomeroy ad loc. suggests that he is "probably referring to grafting shoots onto rooting stocks" and refers to accounts in Theophrastus (*Enquiry into Plants* 2.1.4, *Cause of Plants* 3.5.1ff.) as well as Leontinus (*Geoponica* 9.11.1) describing "the method of propagating olives from truncheons of old olive-trunks"; Chantraine refers to *Geoponica* 9.5, 9.6, and 9.11. As to what the point might be of putting a "shell" over the mud (19.14—Ischomachus does not explain), Holden ad loc. refers to Bradley 1727 ad loc., who writes: "it is, I suppose, put there to keep out the wet and ill weather." Pomeroy confidently says it is to prevent the wood from rotting (but wouldn't the shell inhibit the evaporation of moisture?). In contrast, Jacob suggests, in Graux and Jacob 1897 ad loc., that the point is to prevent drying out; Meyer 1975 ad loc. agrees with the latter and adds, as another possible aim, prevention of root branching.—Nobody can figure out for sure what in the world Ischomachus is talking about!

45. XSD 194; Jacob in Graux and Jacob 1897 ad loc.; Meyer 1975 ad loc.; Pomeroy ad loc. goes so far as to assert that "implicit in the elenctic process enacted here is the theory that the soul is immortal."

46. Consider esp. *Memorabilia* 1.1.16, 1.2.9, 1.2.39–46, 3.4, 4.2, 4.4.9, and 4.6 (esp. 4.6.13–14), as well as *Symposium* 4.1 and Plato's *Apology* 21b–23d.

47. *Memorabilia* 4.5.12–4.6.1, 4.6.13–15; XS 122–23.

48. A playful adumbration of the testing, to distinguish true from false entities, that is central to Socratic refutational dialogues and thus to Socratic political philosophizing: see *Memorabilia* 1.1.16.

49. 19.17; Pomeroy ad loc.: "here, as in v. 4, 5, 6, *geōrgia* is personified as a beneficent female who teaches human beings how to use her gifts." See also Meyer 1975 ad 20.11 and 20.13.

50. Jacob, in Graux and Jacob 1897, 110 proposes emending the text by inserting "nature" (*hē phusis*) after "She," thus making the personified subject of Ischomachus's first sentence in 19.18 "Nature Herself" (*autē hē phusis*); subsequent editors are impressed enough with the suggestion to note it—see the apparatus in Chantraine, Pomeroy, and Marchant 1921 (but not in Marchant 1923, or 2013, both of which follow Sauppe 1865–67).

51. See again Theophrastus, *Causes of Plants* 3.1 beg. The closing comments by Ischomachus on what is revealed by the natural growth of the vines point to the most amazing omission from his account of plant husbandry and thus farming: the total silence about the delicate and complex art of *pruning* that must be applied to all vines and trees: see Meyer 1975 ad chap. 19. Theophrastus devotes much more space to pruning and thinning than to planting—*Causes of Plants* 3.7–8, 3.13–15; see also Cicero, *De Senectute* 52–54 (not only pruning but grafting as well). One suspects that pruning may be a practical art whose acquisition is even more difficult than acquisition of the art of sowing; consider the metaphorical application to Socratic teaching.

52. Consider again Theophrastus, *Causes of Plants* 3.2.3.

53. Recall again 2.18, 5.19–20, 6.1, 7.7–8, 11.8–9; cf. 1.16–22; *Memorabilia* 1.1.9; XSD 197.

54. For the role of prophecy and revelation in Theophrastus's botany, see *Enquiry into Plants* 2.3, as well as 1.9.5.

55. Unlike Bonnette 1994 and Pomeroy ad loc., I do not follow the emendation by Marchant (1921 ad loc., whose apparatus does not indicate that an emendation has been made), who replaces "good" (*agathous*) with "lazy" (*argous*). Marchant himself does not follow this in his 1923 Loeb text (which is taken from Sauppe 1865–67), but only notes "the text is corrupt here." In the 2013 revision of Marchant's Loeb by Henderson, however, the emendation is inserted (again without any indication that it is an emendation). The manuscript text is certainly irregular (*kakous te k'agathous*), and thus invites emendations (see esp., ad loc., Jacob in Graux and Jacob 1897, and Thalheim's revision of Dindorf 1910). But with Chantraine I follow all the manuscripts. Breitenbach 1841 ad loc. reports that the ms. Guelferbytanus [Wolfenbüttel] 71, 19 (labelled "G" by Breitenbach, "N" by Marchant and Chantraine) has the reading *kalous te k'agathous*: but inspection of a clear photo supplied to me by the Wolfenbüttel library shows that this is not the case (folio p. 20 bottom).

56. See esp. 20.14–15; this passage so baffled Schenkl 1876, 134–35 that he was sure there were two gaps, and a line or more dropped.

57. 20.6–9; in Xenophon's *Skilled Cavalry Commander*, stress on diligence is pervasive, and esp. prominent at 4.5, 6.2–3, and 9.2—"understanding things correctly does not bear fruit in *farming*, shipbuilding, or ruling unless one also takes care to bring into effect what one knows." As this quotation shows, however, along with esp. ibid. 6.1, 6.6, and 7.1 as well as 9.1, Xenophon simultaneously places equal or greater stress on the importance of knowledge and prudence (and not least, cleverness in deceiving and in trickery; see 5.9–12). Most remarkable and important for our purposes is the fact that, in contrast to Xenophon in his treatise on the skilled commander (see esp. the beginning and ending; see similarly Machiavelli, *Discourses on Livy* 1.11–14), the gentleman as presented here by Xenophon's Socrates does not say a word about the importance for a general (or for a farmer) of diligence in piety, praying, and sacrificing (including, for a commander, praying to the gods to give one capacity as a good deceiver—*Skilled Cavalry Commander* 5.11).

58. See again *Memorabilia* 1.2.19–24 and L. Pangle 2013 and 2014.

59. Pomeroy ad loc.: Ischomachus's sentiments are "consistent with the idea expressed earlier that material success is evidence of virtue."

60. 20.25–26; Socrates reveals in the *Apology* (#5–6) and *Memorabilia* (4.8.6–11) that the greatest human pleasure is consciousness of one's own self-improvement through continuing progress in beloved wisdom (*philosophia*), together with consciousness of one's own completed wisdom concerning justice and piety. See XSD 199n, which refers us to the revelatory final paragraph of OT chap. 6.

61. A word sometimes used pejoratively for philosophic thinking by Aristophanes (e.g., *Clouds* 101) and by others, including Xenophon himself (*Memorabilia* 1.1.14, 4.7.6): see LSJ s.v.

62. Holden ad loc.: "a word that does not occur elsewhere."

63. But as noted in XSD 200, we see from his formulation that "Ischomachus does not expect Socrates himself to gain money through acting on this lesson; he is not even certain whether Socrates wishes to teach the lesson to others." In other words, Socrates presents Ischomachus as having had some awareness that the philosopher does not share the gentleman's attraction to "progress" in his (monetary) sense.

64. Meyer 1975 ad loc.: "Die Ironie der sokratischen Einlassung ist unverkennbar, und es erhebt sich die Frage, auf wessen Seite denn nur der Autor steht."

65. See also *Memorabilia* 2.6.22–23; Aristotle, *Politics* 1256a–59a (on which, see T. Pangle 2013, 51–62); Karl Marx, *Capital*, chap. 4, and esp. Marx's long footnote on Aristotle; Meyer 1975, 176; XSD 200–204, and esp. 203: "one may say" that Socrates "goes further than Ischomachos or his father," inasmuch as at the start of his teaching of Critobulus (recall chap. 1), i.e., "a considerable time after his conversation with" Ischomachus, he "defines that art of managing the household as the art of increasing one's wealth, without saying anything about" any "limitations imposed by justice"—"this is no doubt connected with the fact that" the "individual's enriching himself by war, if not by tyranny, was not yet excluded."

66. Many recent editors, following a suggestion attributed to Johann Heinrich Bremi, have excised this word, without any warrant in the major mss. and with obtuseness to Xenophon's irony.

67. 21.2; recall 13.5 and see XSD 205: "Socrates had indeed spoken very highly of rulership in the central chapter of the section devoted to the stewards, yet he had not mentioned its intellectual ingredient." Recall 11.25: Could this be another instance of Ischomachus knowing something important about Socrates from Aristophanes's *Clouds* or from reports he has received of that comedy?

68. Chantraine 114n: "Ischomaque si simple ailleurs se laisse aller à l'éloquence." Pomeroy 345: "the tone of this last speech of Ischomachus is unexpectedly lofty. Thus the *Oeconomicus* ends like a sermon."

69. Ischomachus in fact went on to speak about only two of the four spheres of rule that he had mentioned—conduct of war and of farming, which are the two essentially subordinate spheres that acquire and defend what is put to fulfilling use in the two higher spheres—of political and of household rule; do the subordinate spheres not tend in practice to eclipse the higher, even or precisely in the mind of the statesman and of the household manager? Recall the puzzle concerning the distinction between outdoor-manly and indoor-feminine household activities in chap. 7.

70. "In the *Oeconomicus* the pupil is as silent about the concluding speech of the teacher as in the *Hiero*"—"the parallel work" (XSD 185, 205). OT chap. 5 n. 32: "Ruling over willing subjects is called an almost divine good, not by Socrates but by Ischomachus (*Oeconomicus* 21.11–12)." As is so often the case, conventional scholars unalive to Xenophon's comic art complain—e.g., Meyer 1975, 177: "Die Vermutung liegt nahe, daß lediglich eine abschließende Überarbeitung fehlt, die durch einen dialogisierten Anhang den Rahmen geschlossen hätte."

71. Ischomachus passed over in silence the heavy armed phalanx, the core of the Greek military, which was what Greek generals actually led into battle—exercising a leadership of free citizen-soldiers that demanded conspicuous individual superiority in a general who served as a stalwart infantry fighter and anchor of the front line. Accordingly, Greek generals not infrequently suffered wounds or died in battle, and in defeats, indeed, they *normally* perished (Hanson 1996, 603).

72. *megalognōmonas*: a rare and distinctively Xenophontic word: see LSJ s.v. and López and García 1994 and 1995 s.v.; *Agesilaus* 8.3 and 9.6; Chantraine ad loc.—"un composé rare et expressif qui exprime la maîtrise à la fois dans le jugement et la décision"; Holden ad loc.—"men of powerful minds."

73. Recall yet again the puzzle in chap. 7 concerning the relative ranking of outdoor-manly and indoor-feminine household activities.

74. Pomeroy ad loc.: "*Menos* is principally a poetic word, used frequently in Homer"; "Xenophon uses it of dogs (*On Hunting* 6.15) as well as people."

75. 21.10; Ischomachus does not go quite as far as Socrates did at 13.5 (XSD 207t), but he does now stress "the profound difference between the steward and the master" (XSD 207m).

76. Note the concentration of emphatic first-person formulations in these last lines: "I for my part would not admire," "I affirm," "By Zeus! I would not say," "in my opinion," etc.

77. With Jacob, in Graux and Jacob 1897 ad loc. ("chose que [les dieux] épargnent, c'est-à-dire réservent pour, etc. Le nominatif *hoi theoi* est contenu implicitement dans *theion*"), and with Dindorf 1824 ad loc., I stick more closely to almost all the manuscripts and do not accept the verb found in two closely associated secondary manuscripts (Ambrosianus E-119 and Venetus Marcianus 513), which is preferred by most editors and translators: *didotai* (= "it is given to"). This latter ms. reading, confirming in part a suggested emendation by Stephanus, was brought to the attention of scholars by Bolla 1892, 130 and then Vitelli 1897, 328—the latter of whom remarked, however: "Le lezioni caratteristiche del codice certamente non rappresentano una tradizione diverse, ma sono dovute a congetture (qualcuna non infelice) di dotti."

78. That the chief intellectual component, or knowledge, requisite for rule in farm and household management comes from divine revelation or inspiration goes with the fact that Ischomachus does not speak of any mental effort on his own part by which he acquired this knowledge. See also Ambler 1996, 122n.

79. Ischomachus was referring to the myths according to which Tantalus was condemned to lie forever under a boulder that appeared about to fall upon him. For the many literary sources—above all Pindar's first Olympian ode, which tells the story of Tantalus in the context of praising the virtues and the (not entirely secure) divinely alloted blessedness of the tyrant Hiero—see Pomeroy ad loc. and Grimal 1986 s.v. Tantalus. XSD

208: Xenophon's "tyrant Hiero asserts that the tyrant spends night and day as if he were condemned by all human beings to die for his injustice—*Hiero* 7.10."

80. Contrast *Hiero* 11.14: Simonides proclaims to the tyrant: "if you do all these things [that I teach], know well, that of all the things among humans, you will acquire the noblest and most blessed possession—for, being happy, you will not be envied!"

## CHAPTER SEVEN

1. On the abrupt opening expression—"All' emoi dokei . . ."—see Bäumlein 1861, 13; Denniston 1954, 21; and Huss ad loc. See Eunapius's earnest counterargumentative response to this opening sentence at the start of his *Lives of the Philosophers and Sophists*.

2. Consider the way in which Socrates appears in the *Hellenica* (1.7.15), the work in which Xenophon treats the serious deeds of gentlemen (XS 143; Bartlett 1996, 174).

3. Xenophon indicates at 4.10 (in this chapter, numbered citiations without other identification will indicate chapter and section numbers of the *Symposium*) that he has not always written exactly what was said or done at the banquet: "*houtō pōs*—'etwa so'. Eine absichtliche Unschärfe, die dem 'Bericht' des Erzählers die Aura eines authentisch erinnerten Ereignisses verleihen soll" (Huss ad loc.).

4. For a response to this provocation, see XS 143–44, together with XSD 86: the deeds of his own that Xenophon wrote about were not playful, but very serious—grappling successfully with grave dangers and challenges. See *Anabasis* as a whole and Buzzetti 2014.

5. Ollier 1972 ad loc.: "Callias exprime ici avec affectation son dédain d'homme qui s'est tenu jusqu'alors à l'écart de la vie publique."

6. About fifteen years of age, Huss surmises ad loc.; "about eighteen"—Danzig 2017, 132, who puts the age of the lover Callias at "about twenty-eight."

7. Bowen 1998 ad loc.: "Kallias uses the verb proper for a sophist's performance, an *epideixis*." See similarly 3.3, and Socrates's playful counter, *apodeiknunai* at 4.1.

8. 1.7; for this meaning of *epainein*, see LSJ s.v. III and Sturz 1801–4 s.v.

9. Moorhouse 1959, 126: "Notice the tenses . . . the imperfect of *hupischnounto*, of the continued refusal." See also Huss ad loc.

10. Bowen 1998 ad 1.7: "*ei mē epsointo*—use of the future optative shows that the original clause was" indicative rather than subjunctive and thus marks "an element of threat."

11. Ollier 1972 ad loc.: Callias "les agace par sa vanité prétentieuse, et ils ne tiennent guère à demeurer en sa compagnie."

12. Because of his youthful age, convention demanded that the boy remain seated upright and silent while all the mature men reclined (and usually talked): Catoni 2010, 72; Wecowski 2014, 34, 36.

13. *Philippos* = "Lover of Horses": this was the name of both Aristophanes's father and his eldest son, and recalls the comical name "Pheidippides" (= "Thrifty with Horses") in the *Clouds*, which was first produced a year or so before the date at which this symposium is dramatically set—August of 422 BC (known from the date of the famous victory of Autolycus in the *pancratium*: Athenaeus 5.216c-d). The *Clouds* may have been produced a second time, and was probably published in the revised version that we now

have, in the same year as this symposium is supposedly set (Edmonds 1957–61, 1.996). Jazdzewska remarks (2018, 190): "the verb *gelōtopoieō* creates a clear link between Plato's Aristophanes and Xenophon's *gelōtopoios* Philip."

14. Cursing by Zeus, the jester declared that he could no more be serious than he could be immortal. "As this passing remark suggests (unwittingly to be sure), seriousness and immortality seem to belong together"—Bartlett 1996, 184; and see the context. We may add that Aristophanes, that most profound comedian, seems to seek to create some immunity to preoccupation with mortality and immortality (consider *Birds* 586–610); Socrates in his moderate mingling of the serious and the comic ought perhaps to be understood as the self-conscious mean, as regards the human concern with mortality, between "pure" (Aristophanean) comedy and "pure" (tragic) seriousness.

15. 2.1; the expression is somewhat contemptuous—"etwas abwertende" (Huss, referring to LSJ s.v., I 5; see also Fehr 1994, 185).

16. 2.2; Huss ad loc.: "diese *urbanitas* ist für Sokrates in X. *Symp.* charakteristisch." This is in sharp contrast to the presentation of Socrates by Aristophanes, as Athenaeus (5.188c) stresses in his critical comments, blaming Xenophon for presenting Socrates in a manner inconsistent with the philosopher's "austerity."

17. Bowen 1998 ad loc.: "Sokrates' recourse to the authority of Theognis is particularly apt in context. . . . Sokrates' quotation of him is a relic of what would have been the main occupation of symposia in an earlier generation, the exchange of verses. . . . The couplet contains Homeric words and forms."

18. 2.3–5: as Bartlett 1996, 177 comments, "Socrates here seems to imply that Autolycus has yet to pay sufficient attention to virtue (see also 8.38) and that his father, who should be consulted in choosing a teacher of virtue, is presumably not adequate as a teacher of virtue himself"—but these implications are urbanely muted.

19. Huss ad loc. cites the ancient testimonials (Giannantoni 1990, V A 77, 99, 134) to Antisthenes's stress on the importance and teachability—through practice in deeds rather than through reasoning or learning—of courage or manliness.

20. 2.9–14; as Bartlett 1996, 178 remarks, "the Syracusan here seems to be a better teacher of virtue so understood than is Socrates." The most prominent named Syracusan character who figures in Xenophon's work is the intelligent tyrant Hiero, in the dialogue of that name. There Xenophon depicts the Syracusan tyrant receiving instruction from the wise poet Simonides on how he might transform his Syracusan tyranny into a regime that cultivates civic virtue in his subjects (see OT chap. 4, together with especially *Hiero* 10.3). Recall also what the perfect gentleman Ischomachus taught Socrates about the education of slaves in gentlemanliness: *Economist* 12.4–15.5 (with highpoints at 13.5 and 14.9), compared with chap. 21 as a whole (see esp. 21.9); see also 1.23 (the first mention of "gentlemen" in the *Economist*), together with 1.15 end. For helpful discussions of various aspects of Xenophon's Socratic teaching on education in civic virtue, see Newell 1983, 904; Ruderman 1992; Nadon 1996, 364–69; see also Lutz 1997.

21. Athenaeus 188d; contrast the present banquet with the quasi-Stalinesque (Gera 1993, 151—"puritanical and subdued") "symposium" that takes place under the aegis of the model prince and civic educator Cyrus: *Education of Cyrus* 8.4; and consider the attitude toward jovial common meals expressed by the last upholder of old Persian republican virtue, Aglaitadas, at ibid. 2.2.11–16.

22. Jazdzewska (2018, 197) comments ad loc.: "the word *gastēr* is not a frequent occurrence in Plato's and Xenophon's dialogues, but is at home in comedy."

23. For a concrete example of the private spiritual recreation allegorized by Socratic "dancing," one might consider the fact that in the immediately preceding lines, Xenophon has Socrates stress that the wisdom of Homer becomes known only to those who study the epics in order to discover their author's esoteric or "hidden" thoughts (*hyponoias*—3.6). May not this high, but perhaps strictly speaking subphilosophic, study of Homer's esoteric teaching be one major example of Socrates's solitary spiritual "dancing"?

24. See Barlett 1996, 190 (referring us also to Plutarch, *De Gloria Atheniensium* and Maclaren 1934). We presently learn (4.55) that what the "Syracusan" prides himself on is hoodwinking his audience—or the "unthinking" part that makes up most of it; see Strauss 1939, 536, on Xenophon: "such a man was he that he preferred to go through the centuries in the disguise of a beggar rather than to sell the precious secrets of Socrates' quiet and sober wisdom to a multitude which let him escape to immortality only after he had intoxicated it by his artful stories of the swift and dazzling actions of an Agesilaus or a Cyrus, or a Xenophon."

25. 2.21–23; XS 149: "as Kallias said, they had become thirsty because they had laughed so much about" Philip. "He did not say that they *all* laughed: did Socrates laugh?"

26. In Aristophanes's *Wasps* (1301), produced about a year before the time at which this symposium is set, Lycon is satirized as a notoriously heavy drinker at symposia.

27. 3.1–3; Danzig 2017, 137; Bowen 1998 ad loc.: "Kharmides replaces Sokrates' 'thoughts of friendliness' (II 24) with Aphrodite, who can represent sexual intercourse as Bakkhos can wine. Sokrates intervenes too quickly for anyone to follow Kharmides' line, substituting *terpein*, 'to cause enjoyment,' and then shifting the ground further with *ōphelein kai euphrainein*, 'to cause benefit and pleasure.' Symposia could end in sexual intercourse, as vase-paintings show; the topic returns in VIII and IX." For further evidence see Fabian et al. 1991, esp. 182. Twentieth century editors insufficiently alive to Xenophon's erotic playfulness have entertained Mosche's (1799 ad loc.) suggested emendation of what is found in all manuscripts so as to remove the reference to sex: see the apparatus ad loc. in Thalheim 1910 and Marchant 1921.

28. *apodeiknunai*; wordplay countering Calllias's repeated claim to make a sophistic "display" (*epideixō*—1.6, 3.3).

29. See 6.5 and Classen 1984, 160; Brancacci 1990, esp. 165 n. 36.

30. The son of Nicias, the famous and very wealthy Athenian general: see Plato's *Laches* and Thucydides, as well as Plutarch's life of Nicias. Niceratus was put to death during the reign of the Thirty Tyrants, 404–403 BC.

31. Bowen 1998 ad loc.: "he turns his knowledge into a joke against himself."

32. For an indication of the piety that can be descried overlain by Critobulus's playboy exterior, see *Economist* 5.18–6.1, 6.4–11, together with 7.7.

33. Huss ad 4.17: "Genau dieser Einwand wird abert von Sokrates in 8, 14 gemacht werden, wenn er die körperliche Liebe gegenüber der seelischen abwertet."

34. Huss ad 4.28: "Ziemlich genau in der Mitte des Werkes bringt X. das Grundmotiv von *Symp.* wieder zum Klingen: die Mischung von *spoudē* and *paidia*."

35. *Hellenica* 2.4.19 and 2.3.39 (where we learn that Niceratus was also executed by the Thirty). According to Diodorus Siculus 14.5.5–7, the restored democratic regime of

Athens erected in the Prytaneum a statue commemorating Autolycus and his defiance. See also Plutarch, *Lysander* 15.5; Pausanias 1.18.3, 9.32.8; Pliny, *Natural History* 34.79; Higgins 1977, 17; XS 157.

36. As Socrates will later say, rather mischievously, Antisthenes loves not Socrates's soul but only his body (8.6). Bowen 1998 ad loc.: "Sokrates' indifference to physical comfort" was "for him incidental. In Antisthenes we see that indifference turned into an enabling principal" (sic).

37. 4.46; could it have been Xenophon? See Huss ad 1.1, 3.12, and 4.46.

38. See 8.5: Antisthenes evidently believes that Socrates lies when he alleges that he is guided or prohibited by his *daimonion*.

39. The expression *ta onta*, in its literal meaning "the things that are," is used just twice in the *Symposium*: by Xenophon as narrator at 4.45, describing the reaction to a joke by Niceratus; and by Hermogenes at 4.47, describing what is known to the gods. It is used by Antisthenes in its primary colloquial meaning, to refer to his material possessions (4.40).

40. I cannot agree with Konstan's claim (1997, 168 and context—followed by Huss ad loc.) that *philoi* here and later at 8.3 does not mean "friends" but instead "favored by the gods," on the grounds that gods as "friends" would not conform to Greek religious conventions. Konstan and Huss fail to recognize and to reckon with the radical unconventionality of Xenophon as poetic portrayer of Hermogenes.

41. 4.53–54; compare the fate, and the reason for the fate, of the Armenian "Socrates" in *Education of Cyrus* 3.1.38–40.

42. 4.55; Miller 2005 ad loc. references "P. T. Barnum's 'There's a sucker born every minute.'"

43. 4.56–61. Bowen 1998 ad loc.: "there is parody of Plato, especially in the repeated 'Absolutely' (*panu men oun*); there is surely parody of Socrates too in the repetitions of *oukoun* (therefore), *men* without *de*, and *ti de* (what then?). This is a fine example of the fun which X. set out to show." In a similar spirit Miller 2005 ad loc. refers us to Denniston 1954, 434 (*oukoun*) and 466 (*panu men oun*). But as Jazdzewska remarks (2018, 197–98), Xenophon most obviously here has the Xenophontic Socrates engaging in self-parody ("in Xenophon's *Memorabilia*, the expression *panu men oun* occurs twenty-five times").

44. 4.61; it is relevant to note here that Antisthenes became famous as the originator of the line of thinkers known as the "Cynics," out of which grew what became known as "Stoicism"—a form of Socratic political philosophizing that has rivaled or outdone even Platonism in its wide and lasting popularity. See Diogenes Laertius 6.1–2, 14, 19, 85, 104; 7.1–3,19; Giannantoni 1990, 3.223–33 and 3.512–27.

45. This sentence of Antisthenes is unfortunately mistranslated by Bartlett 1996 (along with some other translators like Ollier 1972), inserting a "your" before "art," without warrant in the Greek.

46. In the comedy *Connus*, by Ameipsias, which was produced at the same time as the *Clouds* (and was victorious in the competition for the prize), Socrates also appeared as the butt, and, in a fragment which has come down to us, was addressed in the following words: "Here's Socrates! Best when among a few men, and most useless when among many. . . ."—Edmonds 1957–61, 1.481 (frag. 9).

47. Miller 2005 ad loc.: "*psēphos* literally means 'pebble,' since voting was carried out by placing pebbles in urns." Bowen 1998 ad loc.: "some process involving jars and

mimicking the Athenian process of voting was being used, such as Aristophanes makes play with at *Wasps* 987–94."

48. "Die offizielle, persönliche und sachliche Strafe unterscheidende Formel für die Bestimmung des Strafmasses durch die Richter in einem attischen öffentlichen Prozess"—Huss ad loc.

49. 5.8–10; Winans 1883 ad loc.: "Socrates in *dikastas* keeps up to the last the illusion of a court-trial."

50. 6.1; Brown 1816, 36: "nam significat *etiam ibi silebat* scil. ubi omnes loquebantur et jocabantur."

51. 4.49; see Radt 1990, 27 ("daher auch Hermogenes' Schweigsamkeit—6.2!")—plausibly correcting the reading of this passage in LSJ s.v. *euphemeō* II 2.

52. The Syracusan invoked *Clouds* 94, 101, 154, 215, 266, 414 (Socrates as "the Thinker"), then 144–52 (Socrates measuring flea distances) and 201–5 (Socrates's students engaged in "land surveying," *geometrein*—see Bowen 1998 ad loc.). The Syracusan seems to be intimately familiar with Aristophanes's play.

53. 7.1–2; drinking songs (*skolia*) sung by one after another of the guests were a major feature of conventional gentlemanly symposia, a feature which has been otherwise notably absent from this unique party dominated by Socrates: cf. Plato, *Protagoras* 347c-d with Aristophanes, *Wasps* 1222–49; Gera 1993, 142–48 (and the literature she collects and summarizes); the vase evidence is collected in Vierneisel and Kaeser 1990, 238–46.

54. The licentiousness (*aselgeia*) of Callias was a target of the comic poets: see Edmonds 1957–61, 1.27 (frag. 12), 371, 729 (frag. 572), 845 (frag. 14). See also Andocides, *On the Mysteries* 115ff. A year or two after the time at which Xenophon has the *Symposium* set (421 BC), Eupolis presented his comedy *Autolycus* (presented again in 411): in this play Autolycus, along with his father, in association with Callias, was apparently satirized in erotically unsavory terms: Edmonds, 1957–61, 1.331 (frag. 56); Davies 1971, 331; Athenaeus 216d.

55. "Lycon's tribute is important for X.'s apologetic purpose"—Bowen 1998 ad 9.1.

56. Bowen 1998 ad loc.: "having used *erōs*, 'passion,' and its verb *eran* as the right words for the feelings of Kallias for Autolykos, Sokrates replaces them almost entirely in the next six sections with softer terms: *philia*, 'friendship' (used nine times in this chapter and only once outside it) and its verb *philein*. . . . At the end of section 18 he brings *eran* and *philein* together in the phrase *erōntes tēs philias*, 'being passionate about their friendship.'"

57. The verb, *stergō*, connotes love of kindred, seldom sexual love: Huss ad loc. and LSJ s.v. I 3, as well as Sturz 1801–4 s.v.

58. *tōn paidikōn*—standard Greek for the beloved boy in a conventional pederastic relationship, but a term Socrates had not used previously for the relationship he had been praising.

59. 8.17—*tis misein dunait'*—Miller 2005 ad loc.: "The elliptical construction continues (who could hate a person . . . who could hate a person)."

60. Miller 2005 ad loc.: "there seems to be a hint of deliberate paradox in the phrase."

61. In the particular example Socrates gave, he spoke of a single student (Achilles) with two older teachers: one a human (Phoenix), the other a centaur (Chiron).

62. As Bowen 1998 and Huss ad loc. and Miller 2005 ad loc. point out (see also Schmidt 1876, 241), the LSJ definition of this word—"caressing" (followed by most

translators)—fails to convey the core meaning and the licentious connotation, going along with the sexually carnal term that I have translated "excitedly reaching for" (*oregomenos*); the fact that the language Socrates employs here is a bit obscene is made evident by his apologizing for it.

63. "Sokrates' attempt to reinterpret the story here is almost perverse"—Bowen 1998 ad loc.

64. XS 175: "the superiority of love of the soul to love of the body cannot be established on the plane of manliness and even of political life as a whole."

65. Barlett 1996, 180–81: "this exhortation" to "tend to the affairs of the city is greeted enthusiastically by Callias, and he indeed became a statesman and military commander, as Xenophon tells us in the *Hellenica* (4.5.13, 14; 5.4.22; 6.3.2ff.; cf. Symp. 1.4, end). Unfortunately, Callias was incompetent (*Hellenica* 6.3.2ff.)." This "instance of Socrates' pimping is therefore a failure. This accords with the fact that it is one of the 'playful deeds' presented in the *Symposium*."

66. At Cyrus's "symposium," the model political ruler and educator proclaims himself an expert at finding suitable spouses for his subordinate friends: *Education of Cyrus* 8.4.13–26 (Gera 1993, 187–88).

## CHAPTER EIGHT

1. In this chapter, numbers with hashtags will indicate section numbers of Xenophon's *Apology*.

2. Burnet 1924, 66: "it should be observed that *megalēgoria* is generally used in a bad sense, and that the Socrates of Hermogenes and Xenophon really is insufferably arrogant." Guthrie 1971a, 28: "producing an impression of intolerable smugness and complacency." Ollier 1972, 97: "On s'est étonné du ton rude et orgueilleux de Socrate s'addressant à ses juges dans *l'Apologie* de Xénophon, et sa *megalēgoria* a paru vraiment excessive. Il faut bien avouer que par moments elle nous choque." See also Danzig 2003a, 286–87. Richards 1898, 193 notes: "the very word is distinctly Xenophontic, for Xenophon uses the verb three times: *Anabasis* 6.3.18; *Cyropaedeia* 4.4.2–3; 7.1.17 [in the last cited passage, Xenophon writes: "Cyrus employed *megalēgoria* when a battle was imminent; otherwise he hardly used *megalēgoria* at all"]; and the adjective once (*Cyropaedeia* 7.1.17), while elsewhere [in extant Greek literature] it hardly occurs (Aeschylus, *Seven Against Thebes* 565 [ascribed to "impious men"]; Euripides, *Heracleidae* 356)." To which we would add that Xenophon also employs the verb in a key passage in *Agesilaus* (8.2–3), where he makes it an opposite of "gracefulness" (*to euchari*): "But his gracefulness also merits not being passed by in silence. . . . He was the least given to *megalēgoria*, but he did not take ill hearing others praise themselves, holding that they did no harm to anyone and thus gave indication that they might become good men." Translations such as "lofty speech," employed by Dakyns (1890–97) and by Todd (Marchant 1923), as well as by Navia (1984, 52) and even Guthrie (1971a, 18), looking back to Aretino's "magniloquentia" (Stephanus 1581), are so softening as to be very misleading. Still further off is Gray's rendering (1989, 136–40), "high-mindedness"; while Gray admits that "Socrates talks very big in the *Defence*," she attributes to Dionysius of Halicarnassus (*On Thucydides* 43–45) a judgment that Pericles employed similar "high-mindedness" (as she puts it)—but in

fact, in the passage she cites, Dionysius makes no mention of or reference to *megalēgoria*. Henderson's recent (Marchant 2013) correction of Todd—using the rather colloquial and petty-sounding word "cockiness"—obscures the oratorical dimension as well as the altiloquence of Socrates's boasting.

3. So Burnet 1924, 65–66: Xenophon "excogitated the theory that Socrates deliberately provoked his condemnation in order to escape the troubles of old age"; the "*megalēgoria* of Socrates was something Xenophon felt bound to accept as a fact, though the justification of it was beyond the reach of his understanding." And Ollier, 96–97: "La raison pour laquelle Socrate, dans notre *Apologie*, accepte facilement de mourir a paru à certains déconcertante et peu digne du philosophe, puisqu'il s'agirait *uniquement* pour lui d'éviter les inconvénients et les misères de la vieillese. . . . [this is] le motif *essentiel* de l'attitude du philosophe devant ses juges" (my italics). See similarly Taylor 1926, 166; Cornford 1964, 31; Guthrie 1971a, 18; Lacey 1971, 34; Allen 1981, 35; Brickhouse and Smith 1989, 60–62; Vlastos 1991, 291–92; Reeve 2002, vii and 177. Notable exceptions are Shero 1927, Gray 1989, Vander Waerdt 1993, and Pucci ad loc.

4. #9; cf. XS 138 and Ollier 1972, 86; Dorion 2005, 134. See Shero (1927, 109)—who goes a bit too far, however, when he asserts that "there is *no suggestion* of deliberate provocation of the jury."

5. As Pucci observes, ad #14: in contrast to Plato's *Apology*, "no favorable group of judges is recorded in this *Apology*." This is in line with Xenophon's comically boastful presentation: so successfully arrogant was Socrates in his boastfulness that he secured a practically unanimous guilty verdict!

6. B. Strauss 1986, 95: "Anytus probably expected Socrates to accept banishment, not martyrdom."

7. I follow Ollier's plausible suggestion (in his apparatus 1972 ad loc.) of *tote to*, which incorporates the reading *to* of the first printed edition (in 1520, which had access to a manuscript that we lack—Schmoll 1990—and whose reading is adopted by Marchant 1921).

8. *peri pantos epoieito*: Marchant 1923 goes so far as to translate, "Socrates' *whole* concern was."

9. For the meaning of the word, *liparēteon*, which is uncommon, see Richards 1898, 193, and *Economist* 2.16 as well as *Education of Cyrus* 1.4.6.

10. XS 138–39: "Xenophon replaces *megalegoria* by the overriding concern with not appearing to be impious or unjust; *megalegoria* and what replaces it are interchangeable." Xenophon's courtroom speech by Socrates is then very much a "defense"—aimed not at fending off conviction and execution, but rather at defending the philosopher's reputation, as being neither impious to gods nor unjust to humans. Failing to follow the subtlety of the work, scholars have complained that its title is a misnomer, on the grounds that there is no "defense" or "apology" portrayed in it! See Wilamowitz-Moellendorff 1897, 99; Edelstein 1935, 150 n. 25; Gigon 1946, 219; Breitenbach 1967, col. 1888; see the kindred misunderstanding by Dorion 2005, 130–31.

11. Callias was reputed to be *the* wealthiest man in all of Greece: Davies 1971, 260, relying in part on Xenophon's *Ways and Means* 4.15.

12. Plato, *Cratylus* 383b (Cratylus teasing Hermogenes about his poverty) and 391c; Cobet 1836, 64; Davies 1971, 269–70 suggests that Hermogenes was illegitimate, but concedes that if he is the same Hermogenes whom Xenophon reports (*Hellenica* 4.8.13)

as one of a committee of ambassadors under Conon sent to the Persian general Tiribazus in 394 BC (so Sealey 1956, 183), he must have been legitimate, or have been legitimated previous to the embassy; in the *Memorabilia* (2. 10) Socrates tells a story of how, when Hermogenes was in dire financial straits, Socrates saved him by discreetly bringing his plight, and his talents, to the attention of a wealthy acquaintance. There is no hint in the story that Hermogenes might be helped by his brother Callias (who did suffer enormous financial losses from his profligacy and from the effects of the Peloponnesian War, but who was not penniless: Lysias 19.48; Davies 1971, 260ff.; B. Strauss 1986, 56). Cobet (1836, 64) plausibly suggests that the remark of Antisthenes, in the presence of Hermogenes and Callias, in the *Symposium* (4.35) is a glancing blow struck at Callias: "I also know of brothers who had equal inheritances, one of whom now has sufficient, and excess, for his expenses, the other of whom is in need of everything."

13. As Cobet (1836, 64) notes, in Plato's *Cratylus* 386d Hermogenes expostulates to Socrates, "By Zeus! Often I have had experience that leads me to opine that some humans are very wicked, and indeed this is true of very many!"

14. Cicero, *Tusculan Disputations* 1.71: "Socrates sought no advocate at his capital trial and was not a supplicant to the jurors but displayed a liberal contumacy arising from greatness of soul, not from pride" (adhibuitque liberam contumaciam a magnitudine animi ductam, non a superbia). Consider here the final paragraphs of Spinoza's *Theologico-political Treatise*.

15. There is a further play on words here, as the verb for lodging a civic prosecution is *eisangelō*: *exangelō* counters *eisangelō*.

16. In Plato's writings, Hermogenes makes an appearance twice: once as a member of the group that was present at Socrates's death (*Phaedo*) and, more importantly, as the chief interlocutor of one of the longer dialogues, *Cratylus*. The portrait of Hermogenes in the *Cratylus* confirms and complements Xenophon's depiction. The *Cratylus* is the dialogue devoted to the theme of language, especially names and nouns, and more precisely Greek names and nouns. In it Socrates leads Hermogenes back from an overly enthusiastic attachment to nature, and overly scornful attitude toward convention (derived, perhaps, in part from a study of Anaxagoras), to a new respect for Greek tradition, especially the names of the Greek gods and heroes (cf. Cobet 1836, 65). Socrates accomplishes this partly by appealing to the teachings of Euthyphro (cf. the *Euthyphro*). The opinions of a Euthyphro are a kind of antidote or counterweight to the bent of a Hermogenes: Plato shows Hermogenes to be the opposite, in the subphilosophic sense, of a fanatic traditionalist or "bible-belt preacher" like Euthyphro.

17. Cf. Pucci 3: "this *Apology* is a disguised form of a sensational encomium of Socrates:. . . . the jury and the trial are the fictional public frame Xenophon uses in order to emphasize Socrates' awareness of his own worth. . . . As a consequence Socrates' speech . . . has simply loftiness of language (another meaning of *megalēgoria*) for its readers, the only *real audience* this speech has ever had." (Original emphasis; in this last sentence the otherwise insightful Pucci shows that he fails—in my judgment—to appreciate Xenophon's comic vein.) Pucci continues: "this revaluation of Xenophon's *Apology* is consonant with a series of critical stances that have recently emerged with regard to Socrates and his sources. . . . Is then the 'simple' and 'garrulous' Xenophon in reality a

sort of perverse writer?" And again (ibid., 15): the reader "must keep in mind this double register with their several shades, and the double audience involved."

18. See Aristotle, *N. Ethics* 1127a12-b33 and Cicero, *Brutus* 292 (Atticus speaking): "I do consider, he said, that irony (*ironiam*) that Socrates is shown using, in the books of Plato and Xenophon and Aeschines, to be humorous and elegant." Many conventional scholarly interpreters of Xenophon fail to detect the irony in Xenophon's portrait of Socrates: see, e.g., Taylor 1932, 21; Vogel 1962; Burnet 1964, 103 n. 12; Vlastos 1980, 1 (partially self-corrected in 1991, 30–31); Long 1988, 152; Canto-Sperber 1996, 814; Bandini and Dorion 2010–11, vol. 1, lxvi, cxvii, and 102–3, 170, but contrast civ n. 1; Hobden 2017, 162–63.

19. The somewhat ponderous discussion in Dorion 2005 is characteristically unalive to Xenophon's comic and even Aristophanean proclivities; see also Gray 1989 and Vander Waerdt 1993

20. The same expression is used in *Memorabilia* 4.8.4. In the *Apology* this is the only participation in the noble (*kalon*) that is attributed to Socrates; most remarkably, his mode of undergoing death is never said to be noble (contrast *Memorabilia* 4.8.2–3). "The *Apology* speaks only of the *easy* character of Socrates's death; the *Memorabilia* speaks only of its *noble* character" (XS 138, my italics).

21. Conventional scholars, unalive to Xenophon's subtlety, have ascribed to Xenophon a "blunder" in writing: Arnim 1923, 34; Dorion 2005, 128n. Pucci, with characteristic independence of mind, repeatedly remarks (25 and 63–64) that "some of the old editors could not believe that Socrates would twice defy the order of the god, and corrected the text in #8 so that it was not Socrates, but his friends that 'decided that the arguments for acquittal should by all means be found' (see Thurot 1806, 143)"—and Pucci refers also to Weiske 1798–1804 ad loc. In addition, Pucci (62) persuasively questions the commonly accepted reading (against our mss.) of the first printed edition (Reuchlin 1520): *mou* inserted for the *men* in the mss.

22. In the *Memorabilia* (4.4.4), Xenophon says that Socrates could have "easily secured release by the jurors" if he had "gratified them and flattered them and begged them, *contrary to the laws.*"

23. See OT, chap. 5, para. 20 and chap. 6, esp. para. 17.

24. XS 137: "One does not do full justice to this difference by saying that according to the *Memorabilia* his life was a progress, while according to the *Apology* it was not a progress."

25. The *kalon* is mentioned fourteen times in Plato's *Apology*: see Brandwood 1976, s.v.

26. *Symposium* 6.6–8; *Economist* 11.3; cf. *Memorabilia* 1.1.11–16 and XS 130; also Plato, *Apology* 19c.

27. Vander Waerdt 1993, 33–34; as Pucci 13 puts it: "In his *Apology*, Xenophon evacuates all political matters. He accomplishes a radical surgical operation."

28. *Memorabilia* 2.2.4; *Symposium* 2.10; *Economist* 3.11.

29. Vander Waerdt 1993, 34–35, 37–38.

30. The Clouds, like Hermogenes, loved Socrates for his proud swagger and manifest sense of his own superiority: Aristophanes, *Clouds* 360–65.

31. Compare 1.1.20 with 1.2.1 (see XS 10 and 133–34).

32. LSJ s.v. *nomizō*; Fahr 1969, esp. 96–97, 113–20, 160–62; Burkert 1985, 275; Parker 1996, 201 n. 8; Pucci 26.

33. XS 18; cf. 1.2.64 and also *Apology* 24; Burkert 1985, 317 and Hadot 1995, 123—"all that mattered was one's inner attitude; therefore the sage conformed to 'life,' i.e. to the opinions of non-philosophers"; "but he did so with" an "inner freedom" (and ibid., 103–4).

34. "An unrestrained piece of self praise"—Gray 1989, 137.

35. #14; the word *eleutheria* means primarily "liberty," and designates the virtue that marks a free human being in antithesis to one who is slavish or vulgar; and since noble generosity with money and property is an especially distinguishing characteristic of the free gentleman, *eleutheria* also designates, in particular, "liberality" in this sense. See *Symposium* 4.14–15 and 8.16; *Memorabilia* 2.1.22, 2.8.4, and 3.10.5; see also Aristotle, *N. Ethics* 1119b22ff. on *eleutheriotēs*.

36. #15; Pucci ad loc. comments: "The Narrator seems to enjoy the effects of Socrates' provoking *megalēgoria*."

37. Following Reuchlin 1520, who used ms. Vaticanus gr. 1950 and also worked with a manuscript that we no longer possess. The mss. Vaticanus gr. 1335 and Britannicus Harleianus 5724 have "superior to many humans," which sounds insufficiently boastful for this context (Hogenmüller 2007, 212, ad loc.).

38. Consider *Hiero* 1.16, 5.1; OT chap. 3a, para. 14 and chap. 4, para. 7.

39. XS 131, referring us to *Memorabilia* 4.4 and 4.8.11.

40. Arnim (1923, 87) is so shocked that he suggests emending the text. See XS 131: "the god had been silent on Socrates' wisdom. . . . [i]n his examination of the oracle Socrates is silent about his moderation: moderation is the opposite of *hybris* (*Apol. Socr.* 19) and out of place in the context of his *megalegoria*."

41. Ollier 1972 ad loc.: "Xénophon semble perdre de vue la réponse à l'acte d'accusation."

42. Pucci ad loc.: "the perfect implies that Socrates' dangerous persuasion still conserves its effects; it has become the state of affairs. Those whom he has corrupted are incurable." See also Hogenmüller 2007, 220 ad loc.

43. Pucci ad loc.: "Already in Aristophanes' *Clouds* (424 B. C.) Socrates' teaching subverts paternal authority. . . . it is left to the readers to assume that Meletus argues on the ground of what Anytus, another prosecutor, must have experienced when his own son became for some time an associate of Socrates." For the full gravity, in Xenophon's eyes, of this confession by his Socrates, consider *Education of Cyrus* 3.1.38–39.

44. Ollier 1972 ad loc.: "C'est toujours le même ton de hauteur et de dédain."

45. In effect, Socrates declared the entire proceeding "a corrupt trial"—Pucci ad loc.

46. The best manuscript—Vaticanus gr. 1335—has "wicked" (*kakois*), corrected in a second hand, two centuries later, to "strange/novel" (*kainois*).

47. This has caused such consternation among commentators that the text has been emended, without warrant in any manuscript, replacing "naming" with the participle form of the word that means "believing" (*nomizōn*): see Schäfer 1818, followed by Marchant 1921 but not Marchant 1923 (which follows Sauppe 1865–67).

48. Danzig 2003a, 287: "failure in the Greek *polis* of the fourth century, as today, was perhaps the most powerful source of humiliation"; see also ibid., 289 and Adkins 1960, 259–61.

49. Palamedes is never mentioned in Homer. Philostratus (*Heroicos* 19.5–6) tells a wonderfully amusing tale about a conversation in which Odysseus contrived, from Hades, to relate to Homer everything that he needed to know about the Trojan War, for his poems, in return for Homer promising to exalt Odysseus in them, while ignoring Palamedes—thereby lessening the punishment that Odysseus was suffering in Hades for committing the murder: in this tale, as Homer departs, the shade of Odysseus says to him, "Other poets will no doubt talk about Palamedes; but what they say will be regarded as inexact and unlikely, since you will say nothing about him!" See also Vellay (1956), "Le silence d'Homère."

50. The word (*parepomenoi*) is never used elsewhere in Xenophon for the adherents or companions of Socrates (Pucci ad loc.).

51. For notable examples, see *Education of Cyrus* 2.1, *Anabasis* 2.6.29 end, *Regime of the Lacedaemonians* 10.8; see the list of occurrences in López and García 1995, esp. *Memorabilia* 2.7.14, 3.5.11, 3.6.12, 4.2.33; *Apology* #15; *Symposium* 4.5, 8.29; *Economist* 4.16, 4.18, 4.20, 12.20, 21.12, and also 7.40. This doubting connotation of "*legetai*" goes far back in Greek literature: see, for example, Aeschylus, *Eumenides* 229 and Sommerstein 1989 ad loc.—"more a matter of reputation than of reality." See also Pucci ad loc and Hogenmüller 2007 ad loc., as well as Buzzetti's discussion in 2014, 13–15.

52. Pucci ad loc.: "This poetical word is used by Homer always in the feminine . . . : for a man it is used here probably with irony (Gautier 1911, 89)."

53. Pucci ad loc.: "Notice that the *daimonion* is here silent."

54. Pucci ad loc.: "It is remarkable that Xenophon does not mention here Socrates' piety and justice (see #22)."

55. Pucci ad loc., after noting that the penultimate word, *axiomakaristotaton*, occurs nowhere else in written Greek, comments: "Socrates' uniqueness is in some way challenged. And who could be this most blessed man, who would have the chance to find a more useful adviser than Socrates?"

# WORKS CITED

Citations from primary sources are by standard pagination, or section and subsection, of critical editions. Specific editions of primary sources are listed for cases where references have made peculiarities or page numbers of the editions significant. Translations are my own unless otherwise noted.

Photos of some of the original manuscripts whose variant readings are discussed in the notes may be accessed through the portal of the Princeton University Library at: http://library.princeton.edu/byzantine/search/site/xenophon.

## ABBREVIATIONS FOR WORKS FREQUENTLY CITED

Chantraine — Pierre Chantraine, ed. and trans., *Xénophon Économique*. Paris: Budé, 1971.

Holden — Hubert Ashton Holden, ed. and trans., *The Oeconomicus of Xenophon*, with introduction, explanatory notes, critical appendix, and lexicon. London: Macmillan, 1884.

Huss — Bernhard Huss, *Xenophons Symposium: Ein Kommentar*. Stuttgart: B. G. Teubner, 1999.

LSJ — Henry George Liddell and Robert Scott, *A Greek-English Lexicon*. Revised by Henry Stuart Jones with the assistance of Roderick McKenzie et al. 9th ed. Oxford: Clarendon Press, 1940.

OT — Leo Strauss, *On Tyranny*. Corrected and expanded edition, including the Strauss-Kojève correspondence. Chicago: University of Chicago, 2013.

Pomeroy — Sarah B. Pomeroy, *Xenophon, Oeconomicus: A Social and Historical Commentary*. Oxford: Clarendon Press, 1994.

Pucci — Pietro Pucci, *Xenophon, Socrates' Defense. Introduction and Commentary*. Amsterdam: Adolf M. Hakkert, 2002.

XS — Leo Strauss, *Xenophon's Socrates*. Ithaca, NY: Cornell University Press, 1972.

XSD — Leo Strauss, *Xenophon's Socratic Discourse*. Ithaca, NY: Cornell University Press, 1970.

Adkins, Arthur W. H. 1960. *Merit and Responsibility: A Study in Greek Values*. Oxford: Oxford University Press.

Allen, Reginald E. 1981. *Socrates and Legal Obligation*. Minneapolis: University of Minnesota.

Ambler, Wayne. 1996. "On the *Oeconomicus*." In Bartlett 1996.

Amemiya, Takeshi. 2007. *Economy and Economics of Ancient Greece*. London: Routledge.

Ammann, Adolf. 1953. *-IKOS bei Platon*. Freiburg: Paulus.

Amundsen, Darrel W., and Carol Jean Diers. 1969. "The Age of Menarche in Classical Greece and Rome." *Human Biology* 41: 125–32.

Arnim, Hans Friedrich August von. 1923. *Xenophon's Memorabilien und Apologie des Sokrates*. Copenhagen: Ost.

Aschenbrenner, Stanley. 1986. *Life in a Changing Greek Village: Karpofora and Its Reluctant Farmers*. Dubuque, IA: Kendall Hunt.

Austin, Colin, and S. Douglas Olson. 2004. *Aristophanes: Thesmophoriazusae*. Oxford: Oxford University Press.

Bandini, Michele, and Louis-André Dorion. 2010–11. *Xénophon Mémorables*. 3 vols. Text established by Bandini; translation, textual essays, introduction, commentary, and notes by Dorion. Paris: Budé.

Bartlett, Robert, ed. 1996. *Xenophon: The Shorter Socratic Writings: "Apology of Socrates to the Jury," "Oeconomicus," and "Symposium."* Ithaca, NY: Cornell University Press. [The most accurate English translations.]

Bäumlein, Wilhelm Friedrich Ludwig von. 1861. *Untersuchungen über griechische Partikeln*. Stuttgart: Metzler.

Boeckh, Augustus. 1857. *The Public Economy of the Athenians*. Trans. Anthony Lamb. Boston: Little, Brown.

Bolla, Ermenegildo. 1892. "I manuscritti ambrosiani dell' 'Economico' di Senofonte." *Memorie del reale istituto lombardo di scienze e lettere* 19: 121–30.

Bonitz, Hermann. 1870. *Index Aristotelicus*. In *Aristotelis Opera*, vol. 5. Berlin: Reimer.

Bonnette, Amy L., trans. 1994. *Xenophon, Memorabilia*. Ithaca: Cornell University Press. [The most accurate English translation.]

Bornemann, Friedrich August, ed. 1824. *Xenophontis Convivium et Socratis Apologia*. Leipzig: Hartmann.

Bourriot, Félix. 1995. *Kalos Kagathos—Kalokagathia: D'un terme de propagande de sophistes à une notion sociale et philosophique*. Hildesheim: Olms.

Bowen, Anthony J., ed. and trans. 1998. *Xenophon, Symposium*. Warminister: Aris and Phillips.

Boyce, Nora Elizabeth Mary. 1988. "The Religion of Cyrus the Great." In A. Kuhrt and H. Sancisi-Weerdenburg, eds., *Achaemenid History III: Method and Theory*. Leiden: Brill.

Bradley, Robert. 1727. *The Science of Good Husbandry, or, The Oeconomics of Xenophon: Shewing the Method of Ruling and Ordering a Family and of Managing a Farm to Best Advantage*. London: Corbet.

Bragues, George. 2007. "Socrates on Management: An Analysis of Xenophon's *Oeconomicus*." *Social Science Research Network Electronic Journal*. Available online at https://papers.ssrn.com/sol3/papers.cfm?abstract_id=997057.

Brancacci, Aldo. 1990. *Oikeios logos: La filosofia del languaggio di Antistene*. Naples: Bibliopolis.

Brandwood, Leonard. 1976. *A Word Index to Plato*. Leeds: Maney.

Breitenbach, Hans-Rudolph. 1967. "Xenophon von Athen." *Paulys Real-Encyclopädie*.

Breitenbach, Ludwig Phillipp. 1841. *Xenophontis Oeconomicum*. Gotha: Hennings.

Brickhouse, Thomas C., and Nicholas D. Smith. 1989. *Socrates on Trial*. Oxford: Oxford University Press.

———. 2000. *The Philosophy of Socrates*. Boulder, CO: Westview.

Brisson, Luc, and Louis-André Dorion. 2004. "Pour une relecture des écrits socratiques de Xénophon." *Les Etudes philosophiques* 69: 137–40.

Brown, Johannes. 1816. *Specimen literarium inaugurale, exhibens observationes in Xenophontis Symposium et Cyropaediam*. Leyden: Hazenberg.

Bruell, Christopher. 1987. "Xenophon." In L. Strauss and J. Cropsey, eds., *History of Political Philosophy*. Chicago: University of Chicago Press.

Bruns, Ivo. 1896. *Das literarische Porträt der Griechen im fünften und vierten Jahrhundret vor Christi Geburt*. Berlin: Salzwasser.

Burkert, Walter. 1985. *Greek Religion*. Cambridge: Harvard University Press.

Burnet, John, ed. 1924. *Plato: Euthyphro, Apology, Crito*. Oxford: Clarendon Press.

———. 1964. *Greek Philosophy, Thales to Plato*. London: Macmillan.

Busse, Adolf. 1930. "Xenophons Schutzschrift und Apologie des Sokrates." *Rheinisches Museum für Philologie* 79: 215–29.

Buzzetti, Eric. 2008. "The Political Life and the Socratic Education." Introduction to *Xenophon's Anabasis of Cyrus*. Trans. Wayne Ambler. Ithaca, NY: Cornell University Press.

———. 2014. *Xenophon the Socratic Prince: The Argument of the Anabasis of Cyrus*. New York: Palgrave Macmillan.

Calder, William M. III. 1983. "The Oath by Hera in Plato." In *Mélanges Edouard Delebecque*. Aix en Provence: Publications de l'Université de Provence.

Camerarius, Joachim [the elder]. 1564. *Oeconomica scripta quae extant titulo Aristotelis adiunctque eis interpretatio Oeconomici libri Xenophontis*. Leipzig: Voegelin.

Canto-Sperber, Monique. 1996. "Socrates." In J. Brunschwig and G. E. R. Lloyd, eds., *Le savoir grec: Dictionnaire critique*. Paris: Flammarion.

Cartledge, Paul. 2000. *Agesilaos and the Crisis of Sparta*. London: Duckworth.

———. 2003. *The Spartans: The World of the Warrior-Heroes of Ancient Greece, from Utopia to Crisis and Collapse*. New York: Overlook.

Caster, Marcel. 1937. "Sur 'l'Économique' de Xénophon." In *Mélanges offerts à A. M. Desrousseaux par ses amis et ses élèves*. Paris: Hachette.

Castiglione, Luigi. 1920. "Studi Senofontei IV: Intorno all' 'Economico.'" *Rivista di filologia e di istruzione classica* 48: 321–42.

Catoni, Maria Luisa. 2010. *Bere vino puro: Immagini del Simposio*. Milan: Feltrinelli.

Chantraine, Pierre. 1956. *Etudes sur le vocabulaire grec*. Paris: Klincksieck.

Classen, Carl Joachim. 1984. "Xenophons Darstellung der Sophistik und der Sophisten." *Hermes* 112: 154–67.

Cobet, Carel Gabriel. 1836. *Commentatio, qua continentur Prosopographia Xenophontea*. Leiden: Luchtmans.

———. 1858. *Novae lectiones quibus continentur observationes criticae in scriptores graecos*. Lugduni-Batavorum: Brill.

Cooper, John M. 1998. "Socrates." In E. Craig, ed., *Routledge Encyclopedia of Philosophy*, vol. 9. New York: Routledge.

Cornford, Frances Macdonald. 1964. *Before and After Socrates*. Cambridge: Cambridge University Press.

Cousin, Georges. 1905. *Kyros le jeune en Asie mineure (Printemps 408–Juillet 401 avant Jésus-Christ)*. Paris: Berger-Levrault.

Dakyns, Henry G., trans. 1890–97. *The Works of Xenophon*. 4 vols. New York: Macmillan.

Danzig, Gabriel. 2003a. "Apologizing for Socrates: Plato and Xenophon on Socrates' Behavior in Court." *Transactions of the American Philological Association* 133: 281–321.

———. 2003b. "Why Socrates Was Not a Farmer: Xenophon's *Oeconomicus* as a Philosophical Dialogue." *Greece and Rome* 50: 57–76.

———. 2017. "Xenophon's *Symposium*." In Flower 2017.

Davies, John Kenyon. 1971. *Athenian Propertied Families 600–300 BC*. Oxford: Oxford University Press.

DeFilippo, Joseph G., and Phillip T. Mitsis. 1994. "Socrates and Stoic Natural Law." In Vander Waerdt 1994.

Denniston, John D. 1954. *Greek Particles*. 2nd ed. Oxford: Clarendon Press.

Dickson, Adam. 1788. *The Husbandry of the Ancients*. 2 vols. Edinburgh: Dickson and Creech.

Diels, Hermann, and Walther Kranz. 1951. *Die Fragmente der Vorsokratiker*. 6th ed. Zurich: Hildesheim.

Dindorf, Ludwig. 1824. *Xenophontis Scripta Minora*. Leipzig: B. G. Teubner.

———. 1910. [The same as previous, revised by Theodor Thalheim.]

———. 1862. *Xenophontis Memorabilia Socratis*. Oxford: Oxford University Press.

Dorion, Louis-André. 2005. "The *Daimonion* and the *Megalēgoria* of Socrates in Xenophon's *Apology*." *Apeiron* 38: 127–42.

———. 2013. *L'Autre Socrate: Études sur les écrits socratiques de Xénophon*. Paris: Les Belles Lettres.

Dover, Kenneth. 1997. *The Evolution of Greek Prose Style*. Oxford: Oxford University Press.

Edelstein, Emma. 1935. *Xenophontisches und platonisches Bild des Sokrates*. Berlin: Ebering.

Edmonds, John M. 1957–61. 3 vols. *The Fragments of Attic Comedy*. Leiden: Brill.

Einarson, Benedict, and George K. K. Link, eds. and trans. 1990. *Theophrastus: De causis plantarum*. Vol. 2, *Books III–IV*. Loeb Classical Library. Cambridge: Harvard University Press.

Ekelund, Robert B., and Robert F. Hébert. 2013. *A History of Economic Theory and Method*. 6th ed. Longrove, IL: Waveland.

Fabian, Klaus, Ezio Pellizer, and G. Tedeschi. 1991. *Oinēra teuchē*. Studi Triestini di Poesia Conviviale. Alessandria: D'elle Orso.

Fahr, Wilhelm. 1969. *Theous nomizein: Zum Problem der Anfänge des Atheismus bei den Griechen*. Berlin: Olms.

Fauth, Wolfgang. 1979. "Der königliche Gärtner und Jäger in Paradeisos: Beobactungen zur Rolle des Herrschers in der vorderasiatischen Hortikultur." *Persica* 8: 1–53.

Fehr, Burkhard. 1994. "Entertainers at the *Symposion*: The *Akletoi* in the Archaic Period." In Murray 1994.

Finley, Moses I. 1973. *The Ancient Economy*. Berkeley: University of California Press.

Flower, Michael A., ed. 2017. *The Cambridge Companion to Xenophon*. Cambridge: Cambridge University Press.

Fouillée, Alfred. 1874. *La Philosophie de Socrate*. 2 vols. Paris: Ladrange.

Galen, Claudius. 1821–33. *Opera omnia*. Leipzig: Cnobloch.

Gallant, Thomas. 1991. *Risk and Survival in Ancient Greece: Reconstructing the Rural Domestic Economy*. Stanford: Stanford University Press.

Gautier, Léopold. 1911. *La langue de Xénophon*. Geneva: Georg.

Gera, Deborah Levine. 1993. *Xenophon's Cyropaedia: Style, Genre, and Literary Technique*. Oxford: Clarendon Press.

Giannantoni, Gabriele. 1990. *Socratis et socraticorum reliquiae*. 3 vols. Naples: Bibliopolis.

Gigon, Olof. 1946. "Xenophons Apologie des Sokrates." *Museum Helveticum* 3: 210–45.

———. 1953. *Kommentar zum ersten Buch von Xenophons "Memorabilien."* Schweizerische Beiträge zur Altertumswissenschaft 5. Basel: F. Reinhardt.

Graux, Charles Henri. 1878. *Xénophon: Economique, chapitres I à XI*. Paris: Hachette.

———. 1886. *Les textes grecs*. Paris: Vieweg.

———, and Alfred Jacob. 1897. *Économique: Texte grec accompagné d'une introduction et d'une analyse de l'ouvrage complet et de notes en français*. 2nd ed. Paris: Hachette.

Gray, Vivienne. 1989. "Xenophon's Defence of Socrates: The Rhetorical Background to the Socratic Problem." *Classical Quarterly*, n.s., 39: 136–40.

Grimal, Pierre. 1986. *The Dictionary of Classical Mythology*. Trans. A. R. Maxwell-Hyslop. Oxford: Blackwell.

Grote, George. 1867. *Plato and the Other Companions of Socrates*. 3 vols. London: Murray.

Guiraud, Paul. 1893. *La propriété foncière en Grèce jusqu'à la conquête romaine*. Paris: Hachette.

Guthrie, William Keith Chambers. 1971a. *Socrates*. Cambridge: Cambridge University Press.

———. 1971b. *The Sophists*. Cambridge: Cambridge University Press.

Hadot, Pierre. 1995. *Philosophy as a Way of Life: Spiritual Exercises from Socrates to Foucault*. Oxford: Blackwell.

Halliwell, Stephen. 2008. *Greek Laughter: A Study of Cultural Psychology from Homer to Early Christianity*. Cambridge: Cambridge University Press.

Hanson, Victor Davis. 1996. "Appendix F: Land Warfare in Thucydides." In Robert Strassler, ed., *The Landmark Thucydides*. New York: Simon & Schuster.

Harte, Walter. 1770. *Essays on Husbandry*. Bath: Frederick.

Hartman, Jacobus Johannes. 1887. *Analecta Xenophontea*. Lugduni-Batavorum: Van Doesburgh.

Helmer, Étienne. 2011. "Le remodelage politique de l'*oikos* dans la *République*." *Plato: Le journal internet de la Société Platonicienne Internationale* 11. https://impactum.uc.pt/pt-pt/node/116659.

———. 2015. "Le lieu controversé de l'économie antique entre 'oikos' et 'polis.'" *Philosophie antique* 15: 179–204.

Herrenschmidt, Clarisse. 1980. "La religion des achéménides: État de la question." *Studia iranica* 9: 325–39.

Higgins, William Edward. 1977. *Xenophon the Athenian: The Problem of the Individual and the Society of the Polis*. Albany, NY: SUNY Press.

Hirsch, Steven W. 1985. "1001 Iranian Nights: History and Fiction in Xenophon's *Cyropaedia*." In M. Jameson, ed., *The Greek Historians, Literature, and History: Paper Presented to A. E. Raubitschek*. Stanford: Stanford University Press.

Hobden, Fiona. 2017. "Xenophon's *Oeconomicus*." In Flower 2017.

Hoepfner, Wolfram, and Ernst-Ludwig Schwandner. 1994. *Haus und Stadt im klassischen Griechenland*. Munich: Deutscher Kunstverlag.

Hogenmüller, Boris. 2007. "Xenophon, Apologie des Sokrates: Ein Kommentar." PhD dissertation, Julius Maximilians Universität, Würzburg.

Horatus, Maurus Servius. 1881. *In Vergilii carmina commentarii*. Ed. Georgius Thilo and Hermannus Hagen. Leipzig: B. G. Teubner.

Hudson-Williams, T. 1935. "King Bees and Queen Bees." *Classical Review* 49: 2–4.

Hultgard, Anders. 2000. "Das Paradies: Vom Park des Perserkönigs zum Ort der Seligen." In Martin Hengel et al., eds., *La cité de dieu / Die Stadt Gottes*. Tübingen: Mohr Siebeck.

Huss, Bernhard. 1999. "The Dancing Socrates and the Laughing Xenophon, or the Other Symposium." *American Journal of Philology* 120: 381–409.

Jackson, Henry. 1874. "The *diamonion sēmeion* of Socrates." *Journal of Philology* 5: 232–47.

Jardé, Auguste. 1925. *Les céréales dans l'antiquité grecque: La production*. Paris: Boccard.

Jazdzewska, Katarzyna. 2018. "Laughter in Plato's and Xenophon's Symposia." In G. Danzig, D. Johnson, and D. Morrison, eds., *Plato and Xenophon: Comparative Studies*. Leiden: Brill.

Joël, Karl. 1893–1901. *Der echte und der xenophontische Sokrates*. 3 vols. Berlin: Gaertner.

Jong, Albert de. 2010. "Religion at the Achaemenid Court." In Bruno Jacobs and Robert Rollinger, eds., *Der Achämenidenhof / The Achaemenid Court*. Wiesbaden: Harrassowitz.

Kassel, Rudolfo, and Colin Austin. 1983–2001. *Poetae comici graeci*. 8 vols. Berlin: De Gruyter.

Konstan, David. 1997. *Friendship in the Classical World*. Cambridge: Cambridge University Press.

Kronenberg, Leah. 2009. *Allegories of Farming from Greece and Rome: Philosophical Satire in Xenophon, Varro, and Virgil*. Cambridge: Cambridge University Press.

Lacey, A. R. 1971. "Our Knowledge of Socrates." In Gregory Vlastos, ed., *The Philosophy of Socrates. A Collection of Critical Essays*. Notre Dame: University of Notre Dame.

Larsen, Jakob Aall Ottesen. 1962. "Freedom and its Obstacles in Ancient Greece." *Classical Philology* 58: 230–34.

Levvenklaius [a. k. a. Leuunklavius, Leunclavius, Lenklau, Lwenklaü], Johannes, trans. 1562 [also 1569, 1572, 1594]. *Xenophontis Opera*. 2 vols. Basel: Guarinum.

Lewin, Louis. 1924. *Phantastica: Die betäubenden und erregenden Genussmittel: Für Ärzte und Nichtärzte*. Berlin: Stilke.

Lincke, Karl F. A. 1879. *Xenophons Dialog peri oikonomias in seiner ursprünglichen Gestalt*. Jena: Neuenhahn.

———. 1890. *De Xenophontis libris Socraticis*. Jena: Neuenhahn.

Lindstam, Sigfrid. 1926. "Xenofoncitaten hos Lakapenos." *Eranos* 24: 121–22.

Long, Anthony Arthur. 1988. "Socrates in Hellenistic Philosophy." *Classical Quarterly*, n.s., 38: 150–71.

López, Alfredo Róspide, and Francisco Martín García. 1994. *Index Xenophontis Opusculorum*. Hildesheim: Olms-Weidmann.

———. 1995. *Index Socraticorum Xenophontis Operum*. Hildesheim: Olms-Weidmann.

Lowry, Stanley Todd. 1987. *The Archaeology of Economic Ideas: The Classical Greek Tradition*. Durham, NC: Duke University Press.

———. 1997. Review of Sarah B. Pomeroy, *Xenophon, Oeconomicus*. *Southern Economic Journal* 63: 828–29.

Lu, Houliang. 2015. *Xenophon's Theory of Moral Education*. Newcastle upon Tyne: Cambridge Scholars.

Luccioni, Jean. 1953. *Xénophon et le socratisme*. Paris: Presses universitaires.

Ludwig, Paul W. 2010. "Educating the Perfect Wife: Piety and Rational Control in the *Oeconomicus*." In Andrea Radasanu, ed., *The Pious Sex: Essays on Women and Religion in the History of Political Thought*. Lanham, MD: Lexington Books.

Lutz, Mark J. 1994. "The Problem of the Noble and the Practicality of Platonic Political Philosophy." *Journal of Politics* 56: 95–114.

———. 1997. "Civic Virtue and Socratic Virtue." *Polity* 29: 565–92.

Maclaren, Malcolm, Jr. 1934. "Xenophon and Themistogenes." *Transactions and Proceedings of the Philological Association of America* 65: 240–47.

Macleod, Matthew Donald. 2008. *Xenophon Apology and Memorabilia I*. Oxford: Oxbow.

Mahaffy, John Pentland. 1902. *Social Life in Greece From Homer to Menander*. London: Macmillan.

Marchant, Edgar Cardew. 1921. *Xenophontis Opera Omnia*. 5 vols. 2nd and revised ed. Oxford: Oxford University Press.

———. 1923. *Xenophon in Seven Volumes*. Vol. 4, *Symposium* and *Apology*, translated by O. J. Todd. Cambridge: Harvard; Loeb Library. [Oddly, Marchant indicates on p. xxix that he does not follow his own text—see previous—but the text of Sauppe 1865–67.]

———. 2013. [The same as previous, revised by Jeffrey Henderson with a new introduction.]

Meikle, Scott. 1995. *Aristotle's Economic Thought*. Oxford: Clarendon Press.
Meyer, Klaus. 1975. *Xenophons "Oikonomikos" Übersetzung und Kommentar*. Marburg: Kaesberger.
Miller, Andrew M. 2005. *Xenophon's Symposium*. Bryn Mawr, PA: Thomas Library.
Millett, Paul. 1991. *Lending and Borrowing in Ancient Athens*. Cambridge: Cambridge University Press.
Mitchell, Thomas. 1819. "On the State of Female Society in Greece." [Review essay occasioned by Henry David Hill, *Essays on the Institutions, Government, and Manners of the States of Ancient Greece*.] *Quarterly Review* 22 (43): 163–203.
Moore, Christopher. 2018. "Xenophon on 'Philosophy' and Socrates." In G. Danzig, D. Johnson, and D Morrison, eds., *Plato and Xenophon: Comparative Studies*. Leiden: Brill.
Moorhouse, Alfred Charles. 1959. *Studies in the Greek Negatives*. Cardiff: University of Wales Press.
Morris, C. D. 1880. "Xenophon's Oeconomicus." *American Journal of Philology* 1: 169–86.
Morrison, Donald R. 1994. "Xenophon's Socrates as Teacher." See Vander Waerdt 1994.
Mosche, C. J. W. 1799. *Xenophons Oekonomikus Apologie des Sokrates Symposium und Hiero*. Frankfurt a. M.: Osterrieth.
Münscher, Karl. 1920. *Xenophon in der griechisch-römischen Literatur*. Leipzig: Dieterich'sche.
Murray, Oswyn. Ed. 1994. *Sympotica: A Symposium on the Symposion*. Oxford: Clarendon Press.
Nadon, Christopher. 1996. "From Republic to Empire: Political Revolution and the Common Good in Xenophon's *Education of Cyrus*." *American Political Science Review* 90: 361–74.
———. 2001. *Xenophon's Prince: Republic and Empire in the "Cyropaedia."* Berkeley: University of California Press.
Navia, Luis E. 1984. "A Reappraisal of Xenophon's Apology." In Eugene Kelly, ed., *New Essays on Socrates*. Lanham, MD: University Press of America.
Nelsetuen, Grant A. 2017. "*Oikonomia* as a Theory of Empire in the Political Thought of Xenophon and Aristotle." *Greek, Roman, and Byzantine Studies* 57: 74–104.
Newell, Waller R. 1983. "Tyranny and the Science of Ruling in Xenophon's 'Education of Cyrus.'" *Journal of Politics* 45: 889–906.
Nickel, Rainer. 1979. *Xenophon*. Darmstadt: Wissenschaftliche Buchgesellschaft.
Nightingale, Andrea Wilson. 1995. *Genres in Dialogue: Plato and the Construct of Philosophy*. Cambridge: Cambridge University Press.
Nitsche, Wilhelm. 1879. "Bericht über die 1874–1877 veröffentlichten auf Xenophon bezüglichen Arbeiten." *Jahresbericht über die Fortschritte der klassischen Altertumswissenschaft* 9: 14–80.
Novo, Sandra Taragna. 1968. *Economia ed ethica nell'Economico di Senofonte*. Turin: Giappichelli.
Ollier, François. 1972. *Xénophon: Banquet—Apologie de Socrate*. 2nd ed. Paris: Budé.
Pangle, Lorraine Smith. 2013. "Virtue and Self-Control in Xenophon's Socratic Thought." In Ann Ward and Lee Ward, eds., *Natural Right and Political Philosophy*. Notre Dame: University of Notre Dame Press.

———. 2014. *Virtue is Knowledge: The Moral Foundations of Socratic Political Philosophy*. Chicago: University of Chicago Press.

———. 2017. "Xenophon on the Psychology of Supreme Political Ambition." *American Political Science Review* 111: 308–21.

Pangle, Thomas L. 1987. "On the *Theages*." In T. Pangle, *The Roots of Political Philosophy: Ten Forgotten Socratic Dialogues*. Ithaca: Cornell U.

———. 1996. "On the *Apology of Socrates to the Jury*." In Bartlett 1996.

———. 2010. "Socratic Political Philosophy in Xenophon's *Symposium*." *American Journal of Political Science* 54: 140–52.

———. 2013. *Aristotle's Teaching in the "Politics."* Chicago: University of Chicago Press.

———. 2018. *The Socratic Way of Life: Xenophon's "Memorabilia."* Chicago: University of Chicago Press.

Parker, Robert. 1996. *Athenian Religion: A History*. Oxford: Clarendon Press.

Pelletier, A. 1944. "Les deux Cyrus dans l'Economique de Xénophon." *Revue de Philologie* 18: 84–93.

Pellizer, Ezio. 1994. "The *Symposion* as Entertainment." In Murray 1994.

Peppler, Charles W. 1910. "The Termination *-kos*, as Used by Aristophanes for Comic Effect." *American Journal of Philology* 31: 428–44.

Persson, Axel W. 1915. *Zur Textgeschichte Xenophons*. Lund: Lunds Universitets Arsskrift, Bd. 10, 2.

Pomeroy, Sarah B. 1975. *Goddesses, Whores, Wives, and Slaves*. New York: Schocken.

———. 1984. "The Persian King and the Queen Bee." *American Journal of Ancient History* 9: 98–108.

Powers, Nathan. 2009. "The Natural Theology of Xenophon's Socrates." *Ancient Philosophy* 29: 249–66.

Pritchett, William Kendrick, and Anne Pippin. 1956. "The Attic Stelai: Part II." *Hesperia* 25: 178–328.

Rabieh, Linda R. 2006. *Plato and the Virtue of Courage*. Baltimore: Johns Hopkins University Press.

Radt, Stefan Lorentz. 1990. "Zu Xenophons Symposion." *Mnemosyne* 43: 22–32.

Rahe, Paul A. 1977. "Lysander and the Spartan Settlement, 407–3 BC." PhD dissertation, Yale University.

———. 2015. *The Grand Strategy of Classical Sparta: The Persian Challenge*. New Haven: Yale University Press.

———. 2016. *The Spartan Regime: Its Character, Origins, and Grand Strategy*. New Haven: Yale University Press.

Redard, Georges. 1953. *Recherches sur chrē, chrēsthai: Etude sémantique*. Paris: Champion.

Reeve, Charles David Chanel, trans. 2002. *The Trials of Socrates: Six Classic Texts*. Indianapolis: Hackett.

Reuchlin, Johannes, ed., with Johan Secerius. 1520. *Xenophontos: Apologia Socratous pros tous dikastas. Agesilaus. Hieron ē Tyrannikos*. Hagenau, France: Anschelm. [The editio princeps, or first printed edition, of Xenophon's *Apology*—with a translation into Latin that was done in 1473–74 and apparently based on a manuscript that we no longer possess; see Schmoll 1990 below.]

Richards, Herbert. 1898. "The Minor Works of Xenophon: *Apologia Socratis*." *Classical Review* 12: 193–95.

Ridgeway, William. 1885. "The Homeric Land System." *Journal of Hellenic Studies* 6: 319–39.

Riedinger, Jean-Claude. 1995. "Introduction." *Xénophon: l'Économique*. Paris: Rivages.

Robinson, David Moore. 1946. *Excavations at Olynthus, xii: Domestic and Public Architecture*. Baltimore: Johns Hopkins University Press.

Rostovtzeff, Michael. 1941. *Social and Economic History of the Hellenistic World*. Oxford: Clarendon Press.

Ruderman, Richard. 1992. "The Rule of a Philosopher-King: Xenophon's *Anabasis*." In Leslie G. Rubin, ed., *Politikos II: Selected Papers of the North American Chapter of the Society for Greek Political Thought*. Pittsburgh: Duquesne University Press.

———. 2015. "On Leo Strauss's Presentation of Xenophon's Political Philosophy in 'The Problem of Socrates.'" In Timothy W. Burns, ed., *Brill's Companion to Leo Strauss' Writings on Classical Political Thought*. Leiden: Brill.

Ruskin, John. 1876. *Bibliotheca Pastorum*. Vol. 1, *The Economist of Xenophon*. Translated by Alexander D. O. Wedderburn and W. Gershom Collingwood, with preface and annotations by Ruskin. London: Ellis and White.

Sauppe, Gustav Albert. 1865–67. *Xenophontis Opera*. Leipzig: Tauchnitz.

Schäfer, Gottfried Heinrich. 1819. *Xenophontis Opera*. Vol. 5, *Oeconomicus, Apologia Socratis, Convivium, Hiero, Agesilaus*. Leipzig: Tauchnitz.

Schenkl, M. Karl. 1875. "Xenophontische Studien, 2: Beiträge zur Kritik der Apomnemoneumata." *Sitzungsberichte der Kaiserlichen Akademie der Wissenschaften Philosophisch-Historische Classe* 80: 87–182. Vienna: Gerold's Son.

———. 1876. "Xenophontische Studien, 3: Beiträge zur Kritik des Oikonomikos, des Symposion und der Apologie." *Sitzungsberichte der Kaiserlichen Akademie der Wissenschaften Philosophisch-Historische Classe* 83: 103–78. Vienna: Gerold's Son.

———. 1886. "Extrait de La Zeitschrift für die Österreichischen Gymnasien 31 (1880) 745–48." In Graux 1886, 295–98.

Schmidt, Johann Hermann Heinrich. 1876. *Synonymik der griechischen Sprache*. Vol. 1. Leipzig: Teubner.

Schmoll, Edward A. 1990. "The Manuscript Tradition of Xenophon's *Apologia Socratis*." *Greek, Roman, and Byzantine Studies* 31: 313–21.

Schneider, Johann Gottlob. 1812. *Xenophontis quae extant ex librorum scriptorum fide et virorum doctorum conjecturis recensuit et interpretatus est*. 6 vols. Oxford: Clarendon Press.

Schwyzer, Eduard. 1939–53. *Griechische Grammatik auf der Grundlage von Karl Brugmannsgriechischer Grammatik*. 4 vols. Munich: Beck.

Sealey, Raphael. 1956. "Callistratos of Aphidna and His Contemporaries." *Historia: Zeitschrift für Alte Geschichte* 5: 178–203.

Sedley, David. 2008. "Socrates' Place in the History of Teleology." *Elenchos* 29: 317–34.

Shaftesbury, Anthony Ashley Cooper, Third Earl of. 2001 [orig. publ. 1711]. *Characteristicks of Men, Manners, Opinions, Times*. 3 vols. Ed. Douglas den Uyl. Indianapolis: Liberty Fund.

Shero, L. R. 1927. "Plato's *Apology* and Xenophon's *Apology*." *Classical Weekly* 20: 107–11.

Skarjaervø, Prods Oktor. 1999. "Avestan Quotations in Old Persian? Literary Sources of the Old Persian Inscriptions." *Irano-Judaica* 4: 1–64.

Smyth, Herbert Weir. 1920. *Greek Grammar*. Cambridge: Harvard University Press.

Sommerstein, Alan H. 1989. *Aeschylus: Eumenides*. Cambridge: Cambridge University Press.

———. 2009. *Talking About Laughter; and Other Studies in Greek Comedy*. Oxford: Oxford University Press.

Stephanus, Henricus [a.k.a. Henri Estienne], et al. 1561. *Xenophontis, quae extant opera*. Geneva: Stephanus. [Contains the Greek text with a revised version of the translation of Xenophon's *Apology* by Leonardus Brunus Aretinus/Leonardo Bruni—which was in manuscript maybe as early as 1407 and printed in Venice without the Greek text ca. 1471 and then in Milan ca. 1501–2, Bologna 1502, and Lyons 1504.]

Stevens, John A. 1994. "Friendship and Profit in Xenophon's *Oeconomicus*." In Vander Waerdt 1994.

Strauss, Barry. 1986. *Athens after the Peloponnesian War: Class, Faction, and Policy 403–386 BC*. Ithaca, NY: Cornell University Press.

Strauss, Leo. 1939. "The Spirit of Sparta Or the Taste of Xenophon." *Social Research* 6:502–36.

———. 1966. *Socrates and Aristophanes*. New York: Basic Books.

———. 1983. *Studies in Platonic Political Philosophy*. Chicago: University of Chicago Press.

———. 2016. "Lectures on Xenophon: A course offered in the winter quarter, 1963, Department of Political Science, University of Chicago." https://leostrausscenter.uchicago.edu/course/xenophon-winter-quarter-1963.

Strebaeo, Jacobo Ludoico [a.k.a. Strebaeus; Iacobi Lodoici Strebaei; Jacques-Louis d'Estrebay]. 1543. *Aristotelis et Xenophontis oeconomica, ab Jacobo-Lodoico Strebaeo é greco in latinum conversa*. Paris: Vascosan.

Sturz, Friedrich Wilhelm. 1801–4. *Lexicon Xenophonteum*. 4 vols. Leipzig: Gleditschia.

Szemerényi, Oswald. 1958. Review of Pierre Chantraine, *Etudes sur le vocabulaire grec*. *Journal of Hellenic Studies* 78: 147–48.

Taylor, Alfred E. 1913. *Varia Socratica*. Oxford: Parker.

———. 1926. *Plato: The Man and His Work*. London: Methuen.

———. 1932. *Socrates: The Man and His Thought*. London: Davies.

Thalheim, Theodor. 1907. "Zu Xenophons Oikonomikos." *Hermes* 42: 630–42.

———. 1910. *Xenophontis Scripta Minora*. Leipzig: Teubner.

Theiler, Willy. 1965. *Zur Geschichte der teleologischen Naturbetrachtung bis auf Aristoteles*. Berlin: De Gruyter.

Thesleff, Holger R. 1978. "Interrelation and Date of the Symposia of Plato and Xenophon." *Bulletin of the Institute for Classical Studies of the University of London* 25: 157–70.

Thompson, Homer A., and Richard E. Wycherley. 1972. *The Agora of Athens: The History, Shape, and Uses of an Ancient City Center*. The Athenian Agora 14. Princeton: American School of Classical Studies at Athens.

Thompson, John, ed., and Bernard John Hayes, trans. 1895. *Xenophon: Oeconomicus*. London: Clive.

Thurot, Jean-François. 1806. *Apologie de Socrate d'après Platon et Xénophon*. Paris: Didot.

Too, Yun Lee. 1995. Review of Sarah B. Pomeroy, *Xenophon, Oeconomicus. Classical Review* 45: 246–48.

Tuplin, Christopher J. 1996. "The Parks and Gardens of the Achaemenid Empire." In *Achaemenid Studies*. Stuttgart: Steiner.

Ullrich, Friedrich. 2016 [orig. publ. 1908]. *Entstehung und Entwicklung der Literarturgattung des Symposion: Das Literarische Gastmahl bis Xenophon*. South Yara, Australia: Leopold.

Vander Waerdt, Paul A. 1993. "Socratic Justice and Self-sufficiency. The Story of the Delphic Oracle in Xenophon's *Apology of Socrates*." *Oxford Studies in Ancient Philosophy* 11: 1–48.

———, ed. 1994. *The Socratic Movement*. Ithaca, NY: Cornell University Press.

Van Groningen, Bernard Abraham. 1941. "Xenoph. Oecon. I 10–11." *Mnemosyne* 9: 257.

Vierneisel, Klaus, and Bert Kaeser. 1990. *Kunst der Schale—Kultur des Trinkens*. Munich: Staatliche Antikensammlungen und Glyptothek.

Vellay, Charles. 1956. "La Palamédie." *Bulletin de l'Association Guillaume Budé* 2: 55–67.

Vitelli, Girolamo. 1897. "L'Economico di Senofonte nel cod. Marc. Ven. 513." *Studi italiani di filologia classica* 5: 328.

Vlastos, Gregory. 1980. "The Paradox of Socrates." In Vlastos, ed., *The Philosophy of Socrates. A Collection of Critical Essays*. Notre Dame: University of Notre Dame.

———. 1991. *Socrates: Ironist and Moral Philosopher*. Ithaca, NY: Cornell University Press.

Vogel, Cornelia Johanna de. 1962. "Who Was Socrates?" *Journal of the History of Philosophy* 1: 143–61.

Waterfield, Robin, trans. 1992. *Xenophon: Conversations of Socrates (Socrates' Defence, Memoirs of Socrates, The Dinner-Party, The Estate-Manager)*, with introduction and notes. London: Penguin.

Webster, Thomas Bertram Lonsdale. 1970. *The Greek Chorus*. London: Methuen.

Wecowski, Marek. 2014. *The Rise of the Greek Aristocratic Banquet*. Oxford: Oxford University Press.

Weiske, Benjamin. 1798–1804. *Xenophontis Atheniensis Scripta*. 6 vols. Leipzig: Fritsch.

Wellmann, Max. 1921. *Die Georgika des Demokritos*. Berlin: Akademie der Wissenschaften.

———. 1928. *Die Phusika des Bolos Demokritos und der Magier Anaxilaos*. Berlin: Akademie der Wissenschaften.

Wells, Edward. 1690–96. *Xenophontis Opera Graece et Latine*. 8 vols. With the translation by Levvenclaius (see above). Oxford: Oxford University Press. [Orig. publ. 1671; this is the edition from which derive our divisions of Xenophon's works into numbered sections, or chapters and subsections.]

Wilamowitz-Moellendorff, Ulrich von. 1897. "Die Xenophontische Apologie." *Hermes* 32: 99–106.

———. 1920. *Platon*. Vol. 2. Berlin: Weidmann.

Winans, Samuel Ross. 1883. *Xenophon's Symposium*. Boston: Allyn.

Wolff, Francis. 1985. *Socrate*. Paris: Presses universitaires.

Zeune, Johann Carl. 1782 [with notes also by Johann August Bach]. *Xenophontis Oeconomicus; Apologia Socratis; Symposium; Hiero; Agisilaus; epistolarum fragmenta Recensuit et Bachii suisque notis explicavit*. Leipzig: Fritsch.

# INDEX OF NAMES

The following names have not been indexed because they are referred to pervasively: Callias, Critobulus, Hermogenes, Hubert Ashton Holden, Ischomachus, Sarah B. Pomeroy, Leo Strauss, Socrates, Xenophon (except for the non-Socratic works), and Zeus.